SOCIAL APPEARANCES

Columbia Themes in Philosophy, Social Criticism, and the Arts

Columbia Themes in Philosophy, Social Criticism, and the Arts

Lydia Goehr and Gregg M. Horowitz, Editors

Advisory Board
Carolyn Abbate
J. M. Bernstein
Eve Blau
T. J. Clark
John Hyman
Michael Kelly
Paul Kottman

In memoriam: Arthur C. Danto

Columbia Themes in Philosophy, Social Criticism, and the Arts presents monographs, essay collections, and short books on philosophy and aesthetic theory. It aims to publish books that show the ability of the arts to stimulate critical reflection on modern and contemporary social, political, and cultural life. Art is not now, if it ever was, a realm of human activity independent of the complex realities of social organization and change, political authority and antagonism, cultural domination and resistance. The possibilities of critical thought embedded in the arts are most fruitfully expressed when addressed to readers across the various fields of social and humanistic inquiry. The idea of philosophy in the series title ought to be understood, therefore, to embrace forms of discussion that begin where mere academic expertise exhausts itself; where the rules of social, political, and cultural practice are both affirmed and challenged; and where new thinking takes place. The series does not privilege any particular art, nor does it ask for the arts to be mutually isolated. The series encourages writing from the many fields of thoughtful and critical inquiry.

For a complete list of titles, see page 279.

SOCIAL APPEARANCES

A PHILOSOPHY OF DISPLAY AND PRESTIGE

BARBARA CARNEVALI

Translated by Zakiya Hanafi

Columbia University Press / New York

The translation of this book has been funded by SEPS - Segretariato Europeo per le Pubblicazioni Scientifiche; Via Val d'Aposa 7 - 40123 Bologna - Italy; seps@seps.it, https://www.seps.it.

Columbia University Press wishes to express its appreciation for assistance given by Il Mulino and the Centre de Recherches sur les Arts et le Langage (CRAL) of the Ecoles des Hautes Etudes en Sciences Sociales (EHESS) Paris, France in the publication of this book.

Columbia University Press
Publishers Since 1893
New York   Chichester, West Sussex
cup.columbia.edu
Copyright © 2020 Barbara Carnevali
All rights reserved

Library of Congress Cataloging-in-Publication Data
Names: Carnevali, Barbara, author. | Hanafi, Zakiya, 1959– translator.
Title: Social appearances : a philosophy of display and prestige / Barbara Carnevali; translated by Zakiya Hanafi.
Other titles: Apparenze sociali. English
Description: New York: Columbia University Press, 2020. | Series: Columbia themes in philosophy, social criticism, and the arts | Translation of: Le apparenze sociali. | Includes bibliographical references and index.
Identifiers: LCCN 2019052351 | ISBN 9780231187060 (cloth) | ISBN 9780231187077 (paperback) | ISBN 9780231546980 (ebook)
Subjects: LCSH: Appearance (Philosophy) | Prestige. | Aesthetics.
Classification: LCC B105.A66 C3713 2020 | DDC 177/.4—dc23
LC record available at https://lccn.loc.gov/2019052351

Cover design: Lisa Hamm

Cover image: Andy Warhol, *Ethel Scull 36 Times*, 1963. Copyright © 2019 The Andy Warhol Foundation for the Visual Arts, Inc. / Licensed by Artists Rights Society (ARS) New York.

It is only shallow people who do not judge by appearances.
The true mystery of the world is the visible, not the invisible.

—Oscar Wilde

Society, in the last analysis, is a work of art.

—Georg Simmel

CONTENTS

Acknowledgments ix

Prologue xi

PART I APPEARING: ON THE AESTHETIC FOUNDATIONS OF SOCIAL LIFE

1. Life as a Spectacle: Self-Display, Reflexivity, and Artifice 3

2. Masks and Clothes: Medial Surfaces and the Dialectic of Appearing 20

3. Aesthetic Mediation: A Theory of Representations 28

4. Figures: Social Images 34

5. Out of Control: The Alienated Image 41

PART II VANITY AND LIES: ON THE HOSTILITY TOWARD APPEARANCES

6. "Vanity Fair": The Frivolity of Worldliness 57

7. Against the Mask: The Rise of Social Romanticism 69

8. Against the Spectacle: The Crusade of Romantic Anticapitalism 81

9. Against Aesthetic Values: Aestheticism, Aestheticization, and Staging 96

10. Two Baptisms and a Divorce: *Homo Economicus* Versus *Homo Aestheticus* 111

PART III TOWARD A SOCIAL AESTHETICS: ON THE SENSIBLE LOGIC OF SOCIETY

11. The Opening: Aesthetic Foundations of the Common World 131

12. *Aisthesis*: Senses and Social Sensibility 150

13. Social Taste and the Will to Please 166

14. Aesthetic Labor and Social Design: The Value of Appearances 175

15. Prestige and Other Magic Spells 190

Conclusion: Social Immaterialism or the Philosophy of Andy Warhol 209

Afterword 231

Appendix: Illustrations Mentioned in the Text 233

Notes 235

Index 271

ACKNOWLEDGMENTS

The first version of this work was published in Italy at the end of 2012. This new edition has been enlarged and reworked to the point of becoming a very different book, with substantial original sections added and the ambition of being more complete and better argued than its predecessor. For the new version I am particularly grateful to Luca Savarino, who discussed it with me at all stages, and to Carlos Otero Álvarez, who participated remotely in the editorial process through continuous dialog: the current result would not have been possible without his contribution. To Zakiya Hanafi I owe not only the elegant translation into English but also a series of critical observations that were precious for honing and updating the content.

Among the people who contributed to the publication, I'd like to mention Barbara Faedda and David Freedberg, for two stays at the Italian Academy for Advanced Studies at Columbia University, where I was able to work under ideal conditions. I'd also like to thank Wendy Lochner and Lydia Goehr, who welcomed the volume into the Columbia University Press collections, as well as Biagio Forino for his generous support. I'm grateful to Fred Neuhouser and Giulia Oskian for so many things, including ushering me into the world of

American universities. Finally, I'd like to thank Carl Pierer for his careful reading of the entire manuscript.

During the first few months of 2019, Jean Starobinski and Alessandro Pizzorno passed away, only a few weeks apart. My thought on social appearances owes so much to their teachings. I'd like to dedicate this book to their memory.

PROLOGUE

non ridere, non lugere, neque detestari,
sed intelligere.
—Spinoza

SOME VIEW PHILOSOPHY as its own time apprehended in thought; others think of it as a challenge and battle with its time. Whichever conception is adopted, one thing is certain: a philosophy of social appearances has never been needed more urgently than today. This is only partly due to the growing importance that our Western, late-modern form of life gives to images and aesthetic experiences. The main problem resides in the intellectual attitude marked by moralism and denial: at the same time when self-representation and self-display are mass behaviors, when politics seems increasingly dependent on media spectacle and staging, when social and economic dynamics are intensely, explicitly aesthetic and connected more than ever to sensibility, taste, publicity, fashion, and lifestyles, what prevails in moral and social philosophy is simply reprehension. The conceptual apparatus used by philosophical thought to tackle these phenomena is for the most part still firmly anchored in the great Platonic-Christian-romantic dichotomies (being versus appearing, interiority versus exteriority, depth versus surface, authenticity versus alienation) and in an often ingenuous, hasty use of notions such as narcissism, aestheticization, and spectacularization. When it comes to analyzing and judging a phenomenon associated with appearing, what prevails almost unfailingly is the attitude Spinoza defined in opposition to true ethics and political philosophy as *satire*: the attitude of those who conceive of human beings not for what they are but for how they would like them to be, and who thereby turn their backs not only on understanding but also on acting effectively in their reality.

The aim of this book is to fill this lacuna, by laying the groundwork for an interpretation of appearing in human life and in social relations that measures up to the demands of our age and from which new critical and normative perspectives can develop in the future. We need to renew our theoretical and analytical tools so that we can seek, as Spinoza suggested, *to understand* social appearances, without fear of dismantling established commonplaces or of correcting—or even outstripping—old explanations. While the romantic theory of authenticity and of the primacy of use value over display value, for example, may have served as useful devices for critique in the past, they have now had their day. The fact remains that in contemporary social philosophy and cultural critique the subject of appearances is still viewed through a "pathological" lens, as a target for denouncing the inauthenticity of social relations and the commodity fetishism propagated by capitalism. As I will show, these concepts responded to political and moral exigencies that certainly still need to be recognized and discussed, in order to seek the possibility of agency and self-mastery, to counteract the tendency of social images to escape subjective control, and to establish the conditions for demystification against the domination of the market and ideologies of power. But these exigencies can no longer be pursued using traditional tools, which have proven to be outworn or simply unrealistic. Their effect is to subject contemporary individuals to a double bind, in which real social practices and phenomena are condemned by the system of values inherited from the Christian-romantic metaphysical paradigm even though these social practices and phenomena are in reality still at work: similarly to what happened with sexuality before Freud, as long as repression prevails over the will to understand, the power of appearances will continue to triumph as readily as they are devalued. This is why we must complete the process of "mental modernization" (Peter Sloterdijk) begun by the modern masters of suspicion and call into question the relationship between center and periphery, seriousness and frivolity, giving proper due to what has been unjustly denigrated as marginal, accessory, and insignificant.[1] My claim is that the pathological approach must, first of all, be integrated with a "physiological" one. The only way to confront the issue of the specific aestheticization and spectacularization of modern society is to determine more exactly the role that display and appearances play in social life in itself.

While Western metaphysics and morals have consistently disdained appearances and expelled them from their domain, there does exist a branch of thought whose task is to methodically address this lesser, debased sphere of reality (the others avoid it for the most part or speak about it only to condemn it). I am referring, obviously, to *aesthetics*, the philosophy of sensible appearance.[2] Only recently—no more than two and a half centuries ago—did an overly restrictive notion of the discipline relegate aesthetics to an autonomous sphere that was separate from social reality. The sophisticated interpretative and analytical tools reserved today for the realm of art criticism or for a mysterious "aesthetic experience" are too often viewed as a simple negation of the real, social world: on the contrary, they should be used to analyze *all* sensible manifestations, including those related to the communications and forms of shared life. For this reason, those who want to approach society as spectacle will have to follow the route of aesthetic sensibility: they will have to gain expertise in forms and sensible qualities and, in a certain sense, become art critics themselves. Nietzsche, who set out to relearn this wisdom from the ancient Greeks, was well aware of the fact that the way out of the Platonic-Christian impasse comes from aesthetics, which teaches us to rediscover the substance of phenomena through the love and "worship" of their sensible surface: "Oh, those Greeks! They knew how to *live*: what is needed for that is to stop bravely at the surface, the fold, the skin; to worship appearance, to believe in shapes, tones, words—in the whole Olympus of appearance! Those Greeks were superficial—*out of profundity!*"[3]

My book develops this insight systematically and articulates it in tandem with the ideas of other authors who have inspired me (in particular Georg Simmel, Helmuth Plessner, Hannah Arendt, Erving Goffman, and Pierre Bourdieu) in order to lay the foundation for a philosophical theory that I call "social aesthetics." Specific to my approach is the *immanent understanding* it develops, which explains the world of social appearances precisely qua appearances, by considering them as sensible entities that count and act fully rather than as inessential and ephemeral "foams" of movements occurring in a deeper sphere of reality. I am convinced that the only method for dealing with social appearances is to approach them *iuxta propria principia* (according to their own specific principle): by calling into play the senses, sensible forms and qualities, pleasure and taste; and by making use of the wealth of conceptual and analytic tools put at our disposal by the philosophies of perception and art.

Social aesthetics is thus an inquiry into the aesthetic dimension of social life. The term *aesthetics* should be understood here as occupying a semantic space between the meanings that have historically characterized the philosophical discipline of the same name: between the field of studies that focuses on the realm of sensation and perception (*aisthesis*), baptized "Aesthetica" by Alexander G. Baumgarten in the mid-eighteenth century, and that pertaining to the theory of the arts—major and minor—as well as those techniques used to shape and transform the sensible world.

This reference to a branch of philosophy that is seemingly remote from knowledge of the social world might at first glance seem surprising. If so, a simple observation may help to demonstrate the relevance of examining society from an aesthetic perspective. Some of the conceptual lexicons of the social sciences and of the vocabulary of everyday language already, or might easily, belong to the vocabulary of aesthetics: images, figures, lifestyles, representations, display value, ceremonies, rites, publicity, prestige, luxury, fashion, politeness, civilization, manners. All these notions are at heart aesthetic notions, because they refer to the sensible, qualitative, and formal aspects of social reality. The phenomena they identify share at least two fundamental properties: they appear in the social sphere, that is, they manifest themselves publicly and are thus perceptible through the senses; and they are capable of being transformed and elaborated by means of specific techniques or arts.

The expression *social aesthetics* struck me as preferable to an "aesthetics of the social" (which was suggested to me as more perspicacious) because it is analogous to "social philosophy": social aesthetics designates a specific area of aesthetics—a determinate branch of philosophy in its turn—whose specific object is society and social phenomena. When I began working on this book in the mid-2000s, the expression was not in circulation or, at least, I was not aware of it. I later discovered that "social aesthetics" has been talked about by scholars who work from a perspective that in some respects converges with the one presented here, as "everyday aesthetics." My research shares an interest in the sensible dimension of ordinary life; but it does not articulate the same approach and the same normative purposes of this focus.[4] In fact, my conception of social aesthetics develops in closer dialog with philosophical anthropology and social and critical theory. From this point of view, it includes the "sociological aesthetics" defined programmatically in 1896 by Georg Simmel in an essay of the same name and then applied in all his works, starting from his masterful analysis of the modern *Lebensstil* in *The Philosophy of Money* (1900).[5] Simmel's pioneering perspective on the chiasm between sensible forms and social forms and on the aesthetic lifestyle of modernity inspired the work of his greatest pupils, from Walter Benjamin to Ernst Bloch, and from György Lukács to Siegfried Kracauer. But since more than a century separates us from these revolutionary studies, it behooves us to update them in the *spirit* with which they were created rather than apply them literally. This spirit is encapsulated in a famous aphorism by Kracauer:

> The position that an epoch occupies in the historical process can be determined more strikingly from an analysis of its inconspicuous surface-level expressions than from that epoch's judgments about itself. Since these judgments are expressions of the tendencies of a particular era, they do not offer conclusive testimony about its overall constitution. The surface-level expressions, however, by virtue of their unconscious nature, provide unmediated access to the fundamental substance of the state of things. Conversely, knowledge of this state of things depends on the interpretation of these surface-level expressions. The fundamental substance of an epoch and its unheeded impulses illuminate each other reciprocally.[6]

These words could serve as a manifesto for social aesthetics: in order to bring to completion the process of philosophical modernization started by Nietzsche and carried forward by Simmel by reasserting the value of appearances and a new role—cognitive, ontological, and moral—for aesthetics, my work proposes to plumb the depths of surfaces, to affirm the centrality of the peripheral, and to bring to light the subtle influences that act beneath our conscious awareness. (The word *influence* will prove to be more apt than *unconscious*, which would seem to presuppose a vertical and still dualistic dimension.) Kracauer's aphorism will also serve to judge the attitude that I hold toward historical manifestations of today's society that are "apparently" the most frivolous and superficial, such as social media communications, fashion, and pop culture.

Given the importance of the "critique of critique" in my book, the work could have been arranged in the traditional order, putting the *pars destruens* ahead of the *pars construens*. To defend a conception of philosophy that does not overlook experience and things themselves, and to ensure that the book will not be read above all as a criticism of books written by others (an intra-academic or intratextual polemic), I have preferred a less conventional order structured in three parts. The second part—a historical section that lays out the critical genealogy of the tradition whose prejudicial condemnation of social appearances prevented them from being examined as a serious philosophical subject—is set between two more theoretical sections. However, no harm will come to the argumentation from inverting this order: readers who prefer to become familiar with the issues from a genealogical approach, through the lens of the history of philosophy and ideas, can start directly with the second part and then connect back up with the beginning of the book. Proceeding from this vantage point, the path laid out in the first and third sections provides a positive theoretical alternative to the tradition reconstructed and critiqued in the second.

Accordingly, the first section, "Appearing," opens at the heart of social appearances: it presents several anthropological cornerstones of social aesthetics, starting from an analogy that is more substantial than a simple metaphor, between human life and a spectacle. Key issues dealt with in this first part include self-display, reflexivity, representation, and aesthetic mediation. An initial reflection on the problem of the alienation of the social image, to which the negatively framed romantic approach owes a great deal of its force and success, introduces the problems addressed in the second part.

The section that follows, called "Vanity and Lies," reconstructs and discusses critically a centuries-old tradition of hostility toward appearances, starting from the metaphysical theory of the two worlds of Platonic and Christian descent and culminating in the social romanticisms of Jean-Jacques Rousseau and Guy Debord. My critique of this paradigmatic pathological approach extends to the contemporary current of aesthetic anticapitalism, which shares unsuspected points of contact with metaphysical and moral dualisms and with the romantic myth of immediacy.

After this parenthesis, in "Toward a Social Aesthetics," now unburdened by prejudices and dichotomies, the argument picks up again on the plane of philosophical anthropology and social theory. By questioning the disciplinary separation between aesthetics and economy, a divergence inherited from the eighteenth century, a social aesthetics is developed in the persuasion that social appearances have their own way of being, their own partly autonomous "sensible logic," and their own specific grasp of the human psyche, which alone can explain their force of seduction and social-ontological power. This insight is best elucidated through the notion of "prestige," that is, the sensible aspect of status, which coincides with the aesthetic manifestation of social relevance in the public sphere and which requires aesthetic labor to achieve its effectiveness.

The final chapter summarizes the main themes of the work, tracing out a picture of contemporary social aesthetics, paradigmatically represented by the art of Andy Warhol. It connects up again with the beginning of the book, with a reflection on the figure of Marilyn Monroe: her emblematic relationship with social romanticism and her lack of "freedom of the mask."

If I had to condense the idea of this work into a single sentence, I would paraphrase Hegel's definition of the beautiful: social aesthetics aspires to be a *theory of society as it appears in sensible form*. Its object is society as an aesthetic phenomenon, in both meanings that the history of philosophy has given to the term *aesthetic*: as an object of sensation and sensible perception, of *aisthesis*; and as a product of work on appearances, the "aesthetic labor" that acts on the sensible surfaces of social representations through "social arts." Everything that is social appears sensibly and therefore aesthetically. Far from being a diminished form of reality, this semblance has an inestimable value. The stunning thought that opens Hegel's *Aesthetics* can be adapted to convey the expressive and constitutive significance that this value has for the forms of human life: "So far as concerns the unworthiness of the element of art in general, namely its pure appearance and deceptions, this objection would of course have its justification if pure appearance could be claimed as something wrong. *But appearance itself is essential to essence.*⁷ My hope is that the echo of these words will resound throughout the reading of this book.

Paris, June 2019

SOCIAL APPEARANCES

PART I
APPEARING

*On the Aesthetic Foundations
of Social Life*

1
LIFE AS A SPECTACLE

Self-Display, Reflexivity, and Artifice

Compelling Appearances

What we know about others and what others know about us are based essentially on appearances. None of us has direct access to the inner states of others—to their thoughts, desires, and emotions. None of us can present ourselves directly to others without resorting to a sensible mediation, to something that manifests itself to the senses and that can be sensibly expressed and perceived. Like all living beings, when relating to their fellow creatures, human beings have no choice but to take things as they appear. And, paradoxically, the more importance they give to the hidden reality—the more they focus their attention on the meaning of a gesture, on the ambiguities of a character, and on the mystery of a mind—the more they have to focus their attention on what is visible and perceivable to the senses.[1]

The reason human beings cannot communicate and connect with one another without resorting to sensible appearances is that there is no such thing as a disembodied mind—perhaps because, speaking in Spinozist terms, what we call mind, soul, spirit, or consciousness is simply an idea of the body or a particular way of living in and with corporeality, as

4 Appearing

I will argue by introducing a few fundamental concepts from philosophical anthropology. Be this as it may, one thing is certain: when bodies find themselves side by side, sharing a common space, their minds "sense" each other and they mutually perceive one another; when they are not in each other's presence, because they are separated in space and time, the senses, through their media extensions, are still what create relations through the exchange of perceptions and sensations. This leads us to conclude that, as our first tools of communication, the senses are also our first *social media*, without which society itself would be neither possible nor even conceivable. The word *medium*, which, in relation to the senses, can also be understood as environment, atmosphere, or milieu, is primarily intended here as a means of communication.[2] The senses are *passeurs*, ferrymen, go-betweens. They are bridges and doors: entranceways for the sensible that allow impressions from outside the body to pass inside it and exits through which inner states are transformed into expressions. But they are also footbridges for the intersubjective bond—a sort of overpass that allows individuals to cross over the boundaries of bodily finitude to traverse the spaces that separate them from others and unite with others. So that this metaphor does not lead us astray, and to prevent any misunderstandings arising from the words *impression* and *expression*, we might just as well dive immediately into what will become the main theme of this book: what I will call the "medial" dimension is what makes the opposition between inner and outer and subject and object possible in the first place. In other words, there are no such things as inner states or qualities that are givens from the outset and then only later expressed outwardly. Like all mediums, the senses are a priori conditions that, in making a relationship possible, form not only the relationship itself but also its parts. In the same way that no distinction exists between inside and outside before there is a door, and no perception of the possibility for connection and, hence, for separation exists between two shores before there is a bridge, there is no individual interiority and exteriority before there are senses.

Inasmuch as the senses are a priori forms of communication, they are also a priori forms of sociability: that is, they must be viewed as conditions of possibility for the social bond, without which no relation between individuals would be possible. This explains why it is impossible in human interchange to clearly distinguish reality from appearance and the inner from the outer: in the social reality, which is necessarily founded on relationship and mediation, depth always requires surface and essence its own phenomenal manifestation. This paradox, which is inherent in the very nature of the social relationship, does not grow out of a perversion in the legitimate order of communication—a conclusion often reached by the current of thought I will call "romantic." According to romantic thinkers (such as, paradigmatically, Jean-Jacques Rousseau) social appearance is a potentially distorting or alienating dimension that corrupts and impedes transparency and sincerity. It blocks any authentic exchange between individuals, an exchange that can bring one inner world into contact with another, with no filters or need for mediations. (From now on, I will use "romanticism" in this specific sense, to designate conceptions of the social world and subjectivity that defend a radical notion of authenticity and thus reject the value of mediation and representation by appealing to myths such as faithfulness to origins, transparency, naturalness, immediacy, or presence-to-self.)[3]

The way people appear to one another is the unavoidable medium of their mutual relations that constitutes the shared substance of the social world. Through its appearance, the *I* addresses another *I* and connects with it. Everyone who lives in the world is in actuality a *public* being; the appearance we transmit and project around ourselves accompanies us in every situation, surrounds us, and exposes us, but at the same time it protects us, like the atmosphere that, significantly, we call a person's *air*. Similar to the visiting cards of the past or the profiles we now create on social media sites, this sensible appearance *publicly represents* us and *presents* us to others before we meet them, influencing our relations with them. For now, we will keep to the perspective that seeks to understand the basic mechanism of human communication and sociability apart from any prescriptive moral or political considerations: it does not matter whether this aesthetic presentation is expressed unconsciously and spontaneously or whether it is the product of strategic calculation and a manipulative attitude. Whatever the "intention" behind it, appearance is what creates an intersubjective bond and establishes and represents that bond, making society a complex web of sensible relations.

6 Appearing

"Appearingness" and Self-Display

Appearances are thus anything but naturally morbid or pathological phenomena; indeed, they must be viewed as the physiological conditions of sociability itself. This is the conclusion Hannah Arendt reached in the dazzling first pages of her last book, *The Life of the Mind* (1978), in which she compares the world to a theater and living beings to actors on a stage. Arendt develops her aesthetic-political theory starting from a phenomenology of the way living beings (all living beings, not just humans) present themselves, based on the original idea of *appearingness* (the ability or capacity to appear that creates the conditions for political life to exist), and identifies this primacy of the sensible through a novel variation of Heidegger's "ecstasis": human beings are ecstatic, in the sense that they are "outside themselves," open to the world in which they live and to those with whom they share it, because they are aesthetic—endowed with an appearance and a sensorial apparatus that allow them to express themselves and perceive the appearance of others. Arendt also observes that living beings have the capacity to transform their public display—something that for lifeless things is a substantially passive way of being, a helpless, uncontrollable surrender to the perception of others—into the most active and enterprising form of *self-presentation* or *representation of self*: "To be alive means to be possessed by an urge toward self-display which answers the fact of one's own appearingness. Living things *make their appearance* like actors on a stage set for them."[4] While a stone is constrained by how it looks, as if chained to its appearance, a human being dons its appearance like a stage costume. The actor is someone who acts in appearance and through appearance, as the fundamental condition of his or her performance in the world. These premises of Arendt's theory—an anthropology of appearingness and theatricality—form the bases of my social aesthetics, but they require further explanation.

In reality, not all things are condemned to total passivity. Some human artifacts seem to possess the powers of display and seduction that are proper to living beings. These include commodities—which Marx aptly compared to fetishes, for the very reason that they seem to be animate, and which the anticapitalist tradition (discussed in depth in the second part of this book) has long held responsible for the spectacularization processes of the social world. Commodities are endowed with a conspicuous power of self-display: their labels, their packaging, their arrangement on shelves and in store windows are all ways that products present themselves, by communicating their qualities and merits, making themselves desirable and attractive to customers, putting themselves forward in the best light. Similarly, other highly communicative accessories like ornaments, jewelry, and clothes can be viewed as animate objects, as actively contributing to their wearers' presentation and effectively influencing external situations.[5]

But for commodities or jewelry to take on life and act through their appearance still requires human intervention to lend them a symbolic dimension: human hands must nevertheless arrange the display and create seductively designed computer graphics; their staging must target the sensibility of the human eye. Clothes and a pair of earrings come to life when wrapped around a human body and a human face: even when these inert items are displayed in a museum case, they tend to be put on a mannequin's body; and when contemplated, the goals of a human relationship are still projected onto them. In a nutshell, the "social life" and "agency" that these sorts of things enjoy are anthropomorphic; they are willed into being by humans in order to serve human relationships. To display themselves requires the play of human beings. "Showing is a practice" that follows the human rules of representation[6]—even if, as I will argue, this practice is not necessarily intentional and personal but can also act through impersonal and unconscious factors of social stylization. Or to put it another way, *the life of things is human life*, which creates culture through things and itself becomes culture in things.

For living beings, the representative dynamic is immanent to their social nature to the point that *there can be no shared life without spectacle*. This explains why theater has always been considered the privileged metaphor of our life in common, but also why concepts like *self-display* dominate the terminology of disciplines that share an interest in sociability and communication—above all, sociology and particularly Erving Goffman's dramaturgy, which focuses on the *presentation of self* (to which I will return often in this book) and rhetoric.[7] Even zoology has the notion of *Selbstdarstellung* (more accurately translated as "self-representation" than as "presentation"), which was developed in the mid-1900s by the Swiss-German biologist and anthropologist Adolf Portmann.[8] All these studies illuminate one another by defining the world—the public sphere inhabited and shared by social beings—as a theatrical backdrop against which individual representations are silhouetted and interact with one another. For the actors, then, being in the world is being on stage, a form of self-manifestation and self-representation with a strong aesthetic dimension: it's a public appearingness, a becoming-image and becoming-object of *aisthesis*, or a sensible perception for the eyes of a spectator. Ordinary language, with its customary wealth of phenomenological insights, reveals this idea in many everyday expressions, such as "to make a spectacle of oneself," "to make the right impression," "to look good (or bad)," and in the eloquent ambiguity of the term *public*, not to mention countless references to losing or saving face, masks, and the social game of parts and roles.

Spectators of Ourselves: Aesthetic Reflexivity

Adolf Portmann, the biologist and anthropologist mentioned earlier, developed the concept of self-presentation in order to critique functionalism. He argued that there exist appearances without a spectator, intended exclusively for their own purposes, for nobody's eyes, as pure images immanent to their own gratuitous self-expression.[9] This idea, also dear to Merleau-Ponty's phenomenology and revived in part by Arendt, is a fascinating notion that may help in learning how to view the realm of nature from the perspective of disinterest and gratuitousness, as opposed to reducing animal appearance exclusively to economic ends (reproduction, survival, and self-defense, through camouflage, for instance). From this point of view, the peacock's tail and the luxuriant colors of deep-sea creatures that live at depths where light cannot penetrate and that will never be perceived by their own species can be viewed as "unaddressed phenomena"—phenomena that contain the mystery of a gratuitous splendor that makes nature akin to a gift. The same idea of spectator-less appearances can help to relativize the weight of the economic in human behaviors and to critique the empire of instrumental rationality in moral and political philosophy.[10] However, this perspective will necessarily remain peripheral to our investigation into the role that appearance plays in the world of sociability, since by definition the social relationship, whether human or animal, can only be interactive and communicative.

For this reason, even if we keep the hypothesis that there is some degree of gratuitousness in appearance, appearance must be at least partially functional, performative, and strategic.

Still, the issue at stake philosophically in the difference between spectator-driven and non-spectator-driven appearance is not really reductionism. What distinguishes the appearance of human beings from that of other forms of organic life is actually its eminently *reflexive* nature, based on the intrinsic relation that humans entertain with the possibility of a public. This reflexivity makes a completely spontaneous, immediate, and self-centered presentation of the human being impossible: the actor who acts always "knows" that there is a spectator ready to react to his or her representation. Even before the real reaction of the public, the anticipation of its possibility influences the actor, who must necessarily take into account the effect that his or her self-presentation will have on the external world.[11] Of course, the degrees of this awareness can vary widely in intensity. At the top of the scale, on a clinical level, we find the pathological forms of hyperreflexivity studied by psychiatrists, which can lead to devastating syndromes such as alienation and schizophrenia.[12] On a more ordinary level, we all know the inability to act that cripples people who observe themselves too much (the idea expressed so meaningfully in the word *self-consciousness*); or the awareness of potential judgment from others, the source of many social emotions, such as awkwardness, shame, modesty, and embarrassment, but also pride, vanity, and arrogance.[13] At the other end of the scale, there is the insouciance of those who are able to forget about the existence of their spectator, which allows them to recapture a form of second-degree immediacy, of "spontaneous affectation" or "artificial naturalness." These are the problems raised and illustrated in an exemplary way by Heinrich von Kleist in the apologues described in his essay "On the Marionette Theater" (1810) and by Italian modernist writers of the last century, such as Italo Svevo or Luigi Pirandello.[14]

We will not look into the question of whether there are higher animals endowed with reflexive capacities (primates and other animals are known to recognize themselves or at least to react to their reflected images in a mirror)[15] because this would just extend these capacities to potential non-human corollaries and go against the "thesis of the human exception" rather than change the makeup of social aesthetics.[16] What matters for us in this context is that *within the limits of the human condition there are no appearances without a spectator*. The public that observes us may not be physically present even, but, in reality, it always remains implicit in our reflexive faculty: it is a sort of "transcendental spectator." This is a crucial issue that merits being stated and clarified from the beginning. Even isolated, solitary individuals who are physically removed from the sight of their fellow human beings never stop being spectators of themselves—primarily because their reflexive attitude is already produced ontogenetically by the mechanisms of social interaction, that is, by introjecting the gaze of others. This is the hypothesis of the *social origin of reflection*, which, with varying normative overtones, we find in many modern social theories: in Rousseau's philosophy, which traces it to our first discovery of the judging gaze of another human being; in Adam Smith's idea of an "impartial spectator," who supposedly guides our moral development by forcing us to view our own actions with the attitude of a judge, an attitude acquired gradually by taking on the perspective of others; in Hegel's theory of recognition, which attributes the rise of self-consciousness to the relation with the other; or in the analyses of symbolic interactionism, which explain the objectification of the "me" as a process of assuming a second persona, as when a child begins to see itself from its mother's point of view. Psychoanalytic or Nietzschean-inspired theories on the sense of guilt can conceivably be included in this family as well: the gaze of the other makes me feel guilty because I project onto it the blame that is supposedly directed at me from a morally authoritative person or law. Arendt herself considers reflexivity to be a social dimension. No "cogito ergo sum"—she writes—would have been able to convince Descartes of his own existence if he had been born in the desert.[17] All these theories make reflexivity (the capacity we have as subjects to observe, analyze, and judge ourselves) dependent on intersubjective experience: we learn to be spectators of ourselves thanks to our relations with other human beings, thanks to the real gaze of one or more external spectators who are accommodated little by little inside us and introduced into our way of viewing ourselves until, at last, they are "represented" in our inner world, regardless of whether the person involved is physically present or not. According to proponents of the intersubjective, "exogenous" origin of reflexivity, human beings feel watched and judged even when they are alone, owing to the introjection of the social gaze, which becomes a spectator-actor in the drama of our conscience.

Alongside the hypothesis that views individuals as always already immersed in social relations, of which they are not the presupposition but the product (*pace* Hegel), the idea that human representation is impossible without a spectator is also suggested by another, more radical hypothesis. This alternative approach states that human beings are *already* reflexive and mediated *by themselves*, independently of their being immersed in social relations. This inherent, "endogenous" reflexivity, rooted in our relationship with our bodies, interacts with the reflexivity produced by the social gaze, intertwining with it and multiplying its mediations and effects. This is the thesis that I intend to develop, while drawing inspiration liberally from the notion of "eccentric positionality," elaborated by Helmuth Plessner. Plessner was one of the leading figures of twentieth-century German philosophical anthropology, a contemporary of Martin Heidegger and the author of a masterpiece titled *Levels of Organic Life and the Human* (which has only recently appeared in English, almost a century after the date of its original publication, in 1928).[18] The theory of eccentric positionality that Plessner developed in his most important work is also summarized in the first chapter of a book he wrote in 1941 called *Laughing and Crying*.[19] In it, he develops a theory of human expressivity that is the core of his anthropology. This essential idea is what I will trace out now.

Plessner's persuasive explanation posits individuals as the first spectators of themselves, by virtue of the double relationship they maintain with their own bodies: the individual is capable simultaneously of *being* a body (a living, subjective body, what Plessner defines as *Leib* in German, a language that distinguishes between two types of body) and *having* a body (a thing among other things, an objective part of nature, or *Körper* in German). A similar idea was to be found already in the work of Arthur Schopenhauer, and Maurice Merleau-Ponty would arrive at the same conclusions in his turn. In Plessner, though, this idea acquires a novel significance by becoming the anthropogenic principle, which generates and explains the specific, constitutively open, indeterminate structure of human life. Indeed, it is owing to this ambivalent bodily position that human beings are able to live while at the same time seeing themselves live, act while watching themselves act, *be actors and spectators in a single person*. Playing with film vocabulary, we might say that human beings always have the capacity to simultaneously film their lives from two points of view:

from inside, in a "subjective" shot, and from an exterior panoramic view, in an "objective" shot. As Plessner notes, animals lack this dual perspective. In order to avoid being drawn into the question of anthropocentrism again, and to grant animals (and perhaps even machines like Kubrick's Hal) the capacity of eccentric positionality (as I would like to do), I will limit myself to saying that there is an important distinction between "reflexive" and "nonreflexive beings." Nonreflexive beings can live in a centered, immediate perspective, expressing and manifesting themselves instinctively and spontaneously through their corporeity, without this expressivity being perturbed by the mediation of an objectifying gaze on their bodies. The expression of reflexive beings—human beings preeminently—is always articulated from this dual perspective, which is mediated and ambivalent.[20]

Now, these two explanations—that of the social origin and that of the positional origin of reflexivity—are neither hierarchically ordered nor mutually exclusive; on the contrary, they must be taken together in order to account for the reflexive entanglements in which we find ourselves enmeshed: in addition to watching ourselves live, we see ourselves as others see us; we can even think that others are watching us while they are watching themselves, and so on. Nonetheless, compared to explanations centered on intersubjectivity, Plessner's theory of reflexivity has the specificity of being founded exclusively on the perception that the individual has of his or her own body—and, thus, on a biological, materialistic, and aesthetic dimension—without slipping into the ethical and political implications of our relationship with others. Rousseauians and romantics view the introjection of the other's gaze as a factor of inauthenticity (when I begin to see myself as others see me, I am also tempted to be how others want me to be and to stray from my "true" nature). Smithians, Hegelians, and interactionists like George Herbert Mead insist instead upon the socializing and propaedeutic effects of the other's introjected gaze on the development of morality (when I start to see myself as others see me, I learn to control my egotistic inclinations, to treat myself as I treat others and others as I do myself). Plessner, on the other hand, favors the aesthetic dimension of *self-display*: at stake in reflexivity is the physical image of one's persona, its sensible appearance; because the sensible appearance is rooted in material corporeity, the conception of alterity that accompanies it is devoid of idealistic associations. Plessner does not view the human being's certainty of self and self-awareness as acquired through a spiritual and moral relationship with a "you," the alterity of another individual who is different from me but at the same time, as human, is similar to me. Rather, he thinks it comes through the relationship with *radical alterity* that is embodied in the natural, uncanny materiality of the physical body.[21]

Before this analysis is brought to a close, a brief but necessary digression on gender is called for. Reflexivity is a form of relation with the self that is valid for all human beings, because it is founded on the embodied dimension of the human condition and on the reflexive attitude that is characteristic of human beings both biologically and socially. However, while from a transcendental point of view men and women are equally subject to what I have defined as endogenous reflexivity—the watching oneself live that ensues from the dual relationship with the body—from the empirical point of view, specifically from the perspective of Western history, women have always been much more subject to the pressures of reflexivity introjected from the environment, to social reflexivity. In the context of an age-old patriarchal culture that has relegated women to the status of objects of perception rather than that of subjects with agency, it is hardly surprising that the propensity to look at oneself and devote obsessive attention to one's appearance has become a primary characteristic of the female *habitus*, giving rise to a particular historic form of pathological hyperreflexivity, that of female narcissism. In addition to the masterful and still valid observations by Simone de Beauvoir, there is also John Berger's synopsis: "One might simplify this by saying: men act and women appear. *Men look at women. Women watch themselves being looked at.* This determines not only most relations between men and women but also the relation of women to themselves. The surveyor of woman in herself is male: the surveyed female. Thus she turns herself into an object—and most particularly an object of vision: a sight."[22] While it might be that reflexivity has no gender from the anthropological perspective, in historical and social terms, as Nietzsche would say, "appearance is a woman"—and, culturally, even the relationship with the aesthetic realm has acquired a feminine component. This problem will not be tackled systematically in this book (my intention is to produce an entire study on the topic) but it will cross our path explicitly in several discussions in parts 2 and 3.

14   Appearing

Actors of Ourselves: Life as Staging and Artifice

In aesthetic reflexivity the *I* splits into two and perceives itself as an other. *Ego* refers to *Alter*, and they are never merged. This point deserves further exploration in order to understand why the romantic tradition so often associated reflexivity with a harrowing experience of alienation and dispossession (a question that helps explain the diffidence surrounding the realm of appearing, to which I will return continually in this book). One of the most powerful representations of this tradition are to be found in romantic German tales of the *Doppelgänger*, such as Adelbert von Chamisso's character Peter Schlemihl (1814) or "The Story of the Lost Reflection" from *The Adventures of New Year's Eve* (1815) by E. T. A. Hoffmann, which describe the tragedy of those who have lost their shadow or reflection. The image that represents the body (projected in the form of a shadow or reflected in a mirror) is emancipated from the subject and becomes a diabolical entity, autonomous and independent, capable of harassing and persecuting the individual to death. The interpretation of these tales often brings up the question of exogenous reflexivity: the lost shadow or reflection would be metaphors of social identity, which the individual dreads because he or she can no longer master and control it. Following the path of endogenous reflexivity, on the other hand, one can interpret the philosophical power of these romantic anxieties as a metaphysical problem related to the profound splitting of the *I*.

The ending of *Film*, the celebrated movie written by Samuel Beckett and directed by Alan Schneider (1965), suggests this very idea. The character played by Buster Keaton seems to be crushed by the agonizing experience of being perpetually watched: he cannot find safety even by fleeing the social world encountered in the street or in the vestibule of a building. Closing himself up in a room, alone, he gradually shuts out any possible gaze from the outside: the eyes of other human beings, animals (a cat, a dog, a parrot, and a gold fish), the inanimate eyes of simple representations (such as the disturbing primitive picture hung on the wall, some photographs he is carrying with him, and even the envelope that contains them, whose two buttons can be viewed as a pair of eyes).[23] This torment, emphasized by the quiet of the silent film, does not arise (or does not arise solely) out of a sense of guilt;[24] it is not a product of Christian introspection and the gaze of God. It issues apparently from the protagonist's simple awareness of having a bodily appearance and of being able to be depicted in images. In a vain attempt to obliterate his own figural representation, Buster Keaton tears up photographs of himself and nervously covers the mirror with a rug. Despite these defensive efforts, his own image materializes like a disturbing double and starts to watch him—we don't know if it is a dream or the simple concretization of his inner gaze. The idea of the individual being split into two, of the double nature of the *I*, is accentuated by the fact that one of the protagonist's eyes is covered by a patch. As a last resort, with the gesture children make when they think they can hide from the gaze of others by shielding their face with their hands, he covers his eyes. However, the implacable beating of his heart continues to testify to the alien, ineffaceable existence of his body and its reflexive perceptibility: acoustic self-perception (which, worthy of note, is one of the most original subjects in Plessner's writings on aesthesiology) ends up taking the place of visual self-perception.[25] Like the pendulating movement of the rocking chair, the heartbeat reproduces the deep pulsation of life in all its disturbing and "obscene" alterity.

This reading of Beckett's film is in full conformity with the negative romantic tradition, which has historically dominated the interpretation of reflexivity. By assuming the point of view of the subject who feels dispossessed of an essential part of herself, it accentuates the anxiety-provoking aspects of material reflexivity, which has become synonymous with expropriation and alienation. It is no coincidence that the images at the heart of *Film*—the eye and the camera—are recurrent in accounts of patients who have developed schizophrenia from hyperreflexivity. The fact that this is not due to simple social experience makes any form of return to self-correspondence solely through solitary authenticity impossible. It's useless to flee the gaze of others, as Rousseau does in *Reveries of a Solitary Walker*; it's useless to close oneself up in a room to escape worldly alienation, as does the narrator of Proust's *In Search of Lost Time*. A spectator's look will continue to persecute us, given that the splitting is located already inside the self, in its depths, and the first look to break its unity and mediate it belongs to the subject herself. This romantic, tragic version is too unilateral, however, and does not take into account the positive, creative, emancipatory potential of reflexivity. Like the diabolical potential, this positive potential is anchored in the double endogenous and exogenous structure: in the self-spectatoriality rooted in the body and in the social spectatoriality rooted in relationship with others.

In the philosophy of Plessner, who will serve as a guide for elaborating an anthropology of aesthetic artifice and staging, the result of the divide between the two perspectives that run through human beings and mediate each of our expressions and creations remains ambivalent. This ambivalence is well expressed by the three fundamental laws of anthropology on which the analysis that ends *Levels of Organic Life* is based, which I will briefly recall here. The law of *natural artificiality* refers to the way the absence of any given definition or essence of the human leads us to break away from nature and compensate for this lack with the compensatory construction of culture. The law of *mediated immediacy* refers to the tendency of humankind to create mediations at all levels of reality, but also to the autonomy of the objective dimension, its tendency to escape human control, prefiguring the later critique that Plessner would formulate against the notion of alienation and its equivalents, such as Simmel's "tragedy of culture." And finally, the law of *utopian standpoint*, which refers to the perpetual tension in human beings between realism, awareness of limits, and aspiration toward the absolute.[26]

Between these poles in tension, the human condition separates itself from nature, to which it belongs and yet from which it "naturally" takes leave because it was never in a position to coincide with it: in denaturalizing, in becoming artificial, the human condition opens itself to the unreal and the imaginary. Expressivity (understood in the nonromantic and nonimmediate sense) assumes the anthropogenic role of a creative, formative force of the human, and the aesthetic dimension, which was already central in this sensorial rootedness of social anthropology, becomes the essential medium through which the human condition blossoms and expresses itself. The opening to cultural artifice coincides with a continuous representation of new possibilities of existence, among which the concept of mimesis is crucial, understood as the imitation of an image or, more precisely, as images, which become the guide for the inner construction of the person, transforming the individual who is imitating from inside. One need only think of the most frequent reactions we have when we look at ourselves in the mirror: the "play" with our appearance, which we do through facial expressions, gestures, disguises, makeup, fancy clothes. The structure of reflexivity becomes at the same time, both the creative and critical faculties.

This existential structure finds its powerful mise en abyme in Plessner's texts on the actor.[27] Play-acting, that is, the representation of a human possibility by means of the body, is the form of art that, as Plessner puts it, makes the structure of the human condition "transparent." This is not only owing to the reasons I have already mentioned—the display of the human being in the world through the intermediary of the senses and appearance, as well as the theatrical structure of the public sphere—but also *because play-acting seems to embody the inwardly dramatic and fictional dialectic of the self*. This structure divided in two ensures that all human life ends up appearing as a "staging of itself"—an infinite play between expression and distancing, action and judgment, representation and spectatoriality, constantly subject to the possibility of reinvention and adjustment thanks to the critical potential of self-reflection.[28] A passage from Plessner's article "On the Anthropology of the Actor" elucidates this point:

> It is here, in this being-present-to-oneself, that the rupture is constituted, the "place" that makes it possible to differentiate-from-oneself, that gives human beings—within the constraint of choice and as a force of know-how—their particular way of existing, which we have called eccentric. It [this particular way of existing] is an advantage and a weakness at the same time. It exposes human beings, and thus exposes them to a particular danger, which they know how to handle through particular means, in the corrections and compensations of culture. . . . Philosophy is faced immediately, and paradigmatically, with the opening into the actor's protean art of metamorphosis, which, through figuration, makes human beings enter into play-acting.[29]

In the following chapters, I will develop primarily the social aspects of these premises, leaving those related to the self to a future work. However, at least one aspect related to the self needs to be addressed right away. A *representational* (I prefer this term to the by now hackneyed *performative*) conception of the self derives necessarily from a philosophical foundation that does not allow for a presupposed human nature or essence.[30] Personal appearance is not deeply rooted in being, expressing its substance, but rather emerges in an intrinsically mediated dimension; it does not "spring forth" immediately from an essence that precedes it ontologically and logically, but rather *becomes* being through a reflexive expression, a fiction, a play. This is an insurmountable consequence of the anthropology of the actor, something that Nietzsche commented on magnificently in his aphorism 51 in *Human, All Too Human*: *How appearance becomes being*: "If someone obstinately and for a long time wants to appear something it is in the end hard for him to be anything else. The profession of almost every man, even that of the artist, begins with hypocrisy, with an imitation from without, with a copying of what is most effective. He who is always wearing a mask of a friendly countenance must finally acquire a power over benevolent moods without which the impression of friendliness cannot be obtained—and finally these acquire power over him, he is benevolent."[31] As in Roberto Rossellini's film *General Della Rovere* (1959), a vile, small-time criminal can become a heroic resistance figure and even die as a martyr thanks to his faithful devotion to his part and total adhesion to the image that he imitates.[32] But this becoming-reality must not be confused with the establishing of a new essence in the traditional, Platonic sense. This temporary representation becomes concrete in a historical, mediated, and temporary form—a *habitus*, therefore, not an essence—that can always be modified and transformed by way of the eccentric mechanism of taking distance and self-alienation: appearance becomes being, but being will dissolve in its turn because of a new mimesis, thanks to a new effective representation. In this view, the critical distancing is ensured by the theatrical splitting of the sense of self that is articulated in a formal, nonidealist anthropology.

Of course, the normative consequences of this conception of "ontological hypocrisy" and the question of whether there is still space in a theory of appearances for the moral value of authenticity remain to be seen. For now, I will confine myself solely to social aspects. As Plessner stresses in other writings on the public sphere and its "representative" nature,[33] to appear by giving oneself a form also means to play a role and fulfill a social function. When individuals stage themselves, they become "characters," public personas, and give up on bringing into the world their unique, fragile, secret individualities, and on being considered on the basis of them. The only thing to be openly displayed and publicly scrutinized is the "persona," the "mask" performed for us and for others.[34] This apparent, fictional, artificial personality exercises a function of representation for the psychic interiority, which gives social interaction the theatrical consistency of a play. This game of roles has a strong ludic component—since representation enables active, free, and playful creation of the self—but it is also a theater of war, because social success and failure, visibility and invisibility are decided through and by means of appearances, not underneath them.

It is in these *aesthetic and purely formal* anthropological foundations—which conceive of the human starting from the empty form of reflexivity, as a pure "eccentricity," a capacity to fashion oneself and take distance from oneself—that my philosophical project of a social aesthetic is rooted: a theory of representation in a sensible form of the persona and of the forms of shared life.

2
MASKS AND CLOTHES

Medial Surfaces and the Dialectic of Appearing

The Freedom of the Mask

If social life is a representation and human beings are actors on a stage, appearance can be thought of as a mask. An ambiguous object par excellence, the mask shows by concealing, because the instant it reveals an aspect of the personality, by displaying and communicating to others, the mask covers up another aspect with its own substance and opacity. What shows through the mask seems to exist but may not. Like a mask, appearance is always suspect, lending itself to the accusation of concealing, deforming, disguising, or distorting a more profound and authentic reality. Without masks, though, there could be no knowledge or social communication, because the spiritual world is invisible and formless, and without appearances human beings would have no reference point in social exchange: they would not be able to represent themselves or understand and interpret the behavior, or the representation, of others.[1]

Hence masks and appearances are mediating entities, and their role is always a medial one: they are the vehicle through which reciprocal relations between people are established and regulated, but also those between the psyche and the world—between the subjective, private inner world and the objective, accessible, public reality. The mask is like a diplomatic mediator between distant and potentially incompatible entities, because they are made of different, incommensurable, and indeterminate substances. The mask is a filter, a shock absorber: through its porous surface, resistant and flexible at the same time, the stimuli coming from the inside are transmitted to and manifested in the outer world, while those coming from the outside are received, selected, and adapted for the purposes of subjective assimilation.

The function of the mask is therefore always dual. It is *exhibitory* and *ecstatic*, drawing outward and leading outside itself, while at the same time also being *protective*: the mask is useful for opening up a crack in the inner space, for revealing interiority and communicating it to the outside, but also for safeguarding its fragile content and hiding it from the gaze and intrusions of the outside world. A beautiful German expression, *Maskenfreiheit*, accentuates this ambivalence: it signifies the freedom enjoyed when donning a mask or playing a role, the *ludic freedom of representing oneself* and, therefore, also of creating a fictional character, of giving oneself a new form (a freedom symbolized by the euphoria of carnival, when we try out identities and actions that would be unthinkable in "normal life"). But it also denotes *the freedom of hiding behind a mask*, of shielding oneself and protecting a part of oneself that is inaccessible to the gaze of others, to the demands and intrusions of the public social world, and hence a shadowy space for preserving a secret and a moment of intimacy. Not that behind the mask there necessarily lies an authentic face, an *I* that is different and more true than the one on display. On the contrary, it is more likely that there is actually no substantial reality at all, just a cocktail of possibilities waiting to be actualized behind the mask, or just a negative identity, *the possibility of a no*: the possibility of throwing down the mask to say, "I *am not* what appears like this" or "I am not *only* what appears like this." In developing this insight, in my future work I intend to develop a theory of the self that is founded on the concepts of *self-representation* and *negative authenticity*. The representation of self is the capacity of the subject, as an actor on the world-stage, to represent his or her "person," in the etymological sense of "personage" or "mask," and to negotiate it with the other subjects in the dynamics of recognition and conflict. Negative authenticity is the faculty of withdrawing from social representation to throw away the mask and draw on one's still unexpressed possibilities of identity in order to bring out new self-representations. It consists in the *epoche*, the act of retreat that protects the irreducibility of the self from the social and opens the subjects' space of freedom and creativity, their capacity to free themselves from given social constraints and, above all, to produce novelty.[2]

One of the anthropological characteristics in which human autonomy finds its ultimate expression is the capacity, always available to us, to modulate these two forms of freedom—one affirmative, the other negative; one creative, the other recessive—by measuring out the degree of display, the exposed public surface behind which there always lies concealed an invisible part, a dark side of the moon. Without this covering, there would never be any shade under which the self could protect itself and find relief from the blinding illumination of the public sphere: it would risk "spiritual burnout."[3] Conversely, one of the worst acts of brutality is to force people to strip themselves, literally or metaphorically, by forcibly denuding or unmasking them, to reveal their private parts in public—whatever they simply do not want or prefer not to show. Even prior to the physical act of sexual assault, the cruelty of rape consists in the preliminary act of denuding the victims by ripping off their clothes and, along with them, the "dignity" of their self-presentation. Erving Goffman has shown brilliantly that the inaugural—and most unbearable—act performed on new arrivals by "total institutions" such as insane asylums, hospitals, monasteries, and military academies is that of depriving them of their habitual "identity kit," the set of objects (mirrors, combs, tools for hygiene, makeup, and hairstyling) and practices (hiding, privacy, secrecy) that form the precondition for self-presentation. He has also shown that resistance to institutional power and recovery of a form of self-governance consist precisely in the most varied attempts to recapture a space of free representation and the freedom of the mask.[4] On the same note, Hans Blumenberg has warned on several occasions of the potential for violence that even apparently innocuous hermeneutic activities such as physiognomy (and, by extension, graphology or even psychoanalysis) can inflict on the subjects involved: in reaction to a relentless pursuit of transparency, a "right to one's own obscurity" was theorized early on from within the psychoanalytic movement itself. The loss of opacity, continues Blumenberg, can give rise to a specific form of distress, such as the one experienced by the character in Pirandello's novella *A Call to Duty*: Paolino Lovico has the "misfortune" of being transparent and incapable of hiding or controlling his emotions.[5] Simmel, who defined secrecy as one of "humanity's greatest spiritual conquests," a prerequisite for the precious vital substances—which could never tolerate absolute transparency—to reveal themselves, has similarly talked about a "right to secrecy" that should remain inviolable even in the most intimate love relations: the residue of mutual ignorance with which lovers should engage with each other ensures the permanence of desire but also the living dynamics of the relationship itself. We might understand these reflections as an antidote to the ideals diffused by the romantic culture, especially that of Rousseau and Rousseanism, which resurged during the second half of the twentieth century along with the existentialist culture of authenticity and sincerity and still exert a profound influence on our moral scene.[6] The capacity to keep people "at the right distance," preserving an individual's "sacrality," is also one of the functions that Goffman attributes to the rules of behavior such as the norms of tact and etiquette.[7] The culture of liberalism has formulated the same insight in the regulatory sphere through the concept of privacy, viewing it as a right worthy of protection. Special laws have been created in defense of this value and it is one of the reasons the social norms of discretion and tact came into being: to discourage us from trespassing across the boundary line erected by other people in order to limit confrontation with us, and to encourage us to respect the image they use to represent themselves and to publicly exist.[8]

Appearance is basically a fabric caught between two conflicting, equally powerful impulses: displaying versus concealing, public versus private, vanity versus shame and *decoration* versus *decorum*. Whatever displays also conceals; whatever seeks to cover up is often precisely what exposes and highlights: a veil over a face, the strands of hair combed over a bald spot, or the blushing and stammering of someone who is intimidated, all end up calling attention to exactly what they seek to conceal. In 1930, when analyzing the psychological function of clothes and comparing it to the function of neurotic symptoms, the psychoanalyst John Carl Flügel proposed this brilliant definition: "clothes resemble a perpetual blush upon the surface of humanity."[9]

Concealment and Exposure

The dialectic of appearing is found in everything we will define in this book as *medial surfaces*, that is, the interfaces that articulate the relation of human beings with display and concealment. The skin, the outermost layer of our bodies, is the first surface to be perceived by others; it can be seen, touched, sniffed, and kissed, but it also serves as a barrier and as an envelope that contains and protects the internal organs. We feel and communicate with our skin, we open ourselves up to the world and its sensations, we brush against others and perceive them; but thanks to our skin we are also protected from contact with things and people that might lead to blows, injuries, and infections. The skin is hidden and displayed in its turn by other medial surfaces, like makeup, tanning, tattoos, clothing, mutilations, and scarifications, which Hegel (in a passage whose very unexpectedness made it famous) saw as the origin of the aesthetic dimension and the original gesture of human *freedom*:

> And it is not only with external things that man proceeds in this way, but no less with himself, with his own natural figure which he does not leave as he finds it but deliberately alters. This is the cause of all dressing up and adornment, even if it be barbaric, tasteless, completely disfiguring, or even pernicious like crushing the feet of Chinese ladies, or slitting the ears and lips. For it is only among civilized people that alteration of figure, behaviour, and every sort and mode of external expression proceeds from spiritual development.[10]

This is a crucial insight, but it needs to be reframed, to go beyond not only its superseded universalist presuppositions about culture and history, but also its idealistic conception of aesthetic expression. The freedom expressed in the sovereign gesture of permanently decorating and adorning one's figure is not the freedom of the spirit as it begins to emerge out of the nature from which it emancipated itself in order to progress toward civilization. Rather, this is the *freedom of decoration and decorousness*, the aesthetic embodiment of the freedom of the mask, which does not seek to transform the dimension of natural alterity by spiritualizing it through the artistic gesture, as in Hegel, but instead *plays with it using different formulas of display and concealment*. This is not the freedom to "digest" the material body in the spirit, but the freedom *to represent the body on the threshold between concealment and exposure*, without ever seeking to eliminate and negate its natural dimension.

Along with the mask, the most popular metaphor for the constitutive relationship between human beings and their social image is clothing—perhaps the first and most important of appearances with which we socially express ourselves, and from which we gain an impression of our fellow human beings. Today, as in the past, clothing is the privileged form of representing the self in a sensible form, with the difference that, in a status society, prior to the rise of the purely modern phenomenon of fashion and the development of social differentiation, a piece of clothing did not so much express the individuality and originality of a person as it classified him or her—according to rank, gender, age, and economic standing. In modern, differentiated societies, in which traditional models of action no longer provide a stable, unchangeable foothold, and in which fashion gives form to the uncertainty of contingency, the two dimensions overlap, with the former claiming a cultural primacy.[11] The clothes we wear primarily express an image of ourselves more than they indicate the category to which we belong or our obedience to a code—although in the various social roles we occupy, especially professional ones, individual expressive needs must in any case be subordinated to or harmonized with those of the group.[12] What results from this are sophisticated adaptations intended to individualize uniforms and dress codes: from nurses who customize their scrubs with bright colors and accessories, to flight attendants who play with jewelry and hairstyles, to the virtual limit cases of tattooed priests and police officers with piercings or long hair, like Al Pacino's Serpico. The growing number of expedients used in Muslim countries to wear the hijab in creative ways and the invention of "burkinis" (appropriately adapted bathing suits) and other uniforms for practicing women's sports are similar examples of how the modern tendency toward individualization gives rise to the most ingenious compromises, even in contexts where traditional actions persist.

Finally, medial surfaces also extend beyond the dressed body, in acts of courtesy, for example. Although rituals and ceremonies often have an exhibitionist or affected aspect and they serve to create social distinctions, they also preserve modesty, discretion, and dignity. They extend to the ceremonies with which we exhibit our openness and welcome toward others while at the same time holding up a shield to keep us distant from them: the ambivalent function of the ceremonial is to include the newcomer but also to separate the initiated from the uninitiated.[13]

As Flügel suggests in another quotable definition, once again in the language of psychoanalysis, appearingness should be defined as a *compromise formation* between conflicting impulses. In its intimately dialectical nature, the way human beings experience their relationship with their appearance perfectly illustrates the principle of ambivalence, or "overdetermination," which allows us to gratify competing needs and desires in a single action. This dialectic, which governs the conflict between individualizing urges and mimetic drives or conformist obligations, as in the cases mentioned earlier, is demonstrated exemplarily by the clothing we wear, in which the tension is smoothed out between an expository or exhibitionist drive and a sense of modesty, both of which are partially satisfied without mutually excluding each other. The function of clothing to protect us from the cold and other climate aggressions, a function that is more utilitarian and less communicative in nature, is only the third factor at play. It comes after and is subordinate to the essential conflict between two primary, contradictory drives: the open versus the closed, the visible versus the invisible. The well-known theory of "shifting erogenous zones" could be included in this dialectic. According to the fashion historian James Laver, who was influenced by Flügel's psychoanalytical interpretation, this theory explained transformations in fashion and quick variations in the appearance of women's clothing: these changes were thought to draw attention to perpetually new areas of the female body, such as the back during the 1930s, in order to attract the gaze and keep alive male desire. Clothes thus served to fulfill a "framing" role, performing a crucial dialectical operation of separating and connecting, displaying and concealing.[14]

Another dialectic that is reconciled in the compromise formation offered by appearance is that between attack and defense—between aggression and protection in the face of other social subjects and the dangers of shared life. In this case, appearance creates distance and protects us from contact with otherness while at the same time creating a *facies* appropriate for combative encounters—which works actively to distinguish between friends and enemies, gain recognition and threaten, and ritualize and ceremonialize conflict. Uniforms, sports outfits, and war dances are essential appearances in agonistic encounters, whether for play or war. In this regard, it should be stressed that the antagonistic function of appearances is just as important and fundamental as its representative function, with which it is intertwined and by which it is completed. As I have already noted, the social world is at once a playground and a battlefield—we put on our uniforms to play and fight on both types of "fields." Social life is permeated by conflicts, and communication with other people is always fraught with risks: for this reason, appearingness cannot be conceived solely as the vehicle of an innocuous self-display or gratuitous, aesthetic self-representation.[15] It must also be understood as a weapon for attacking and defending, with which we confront dangers and battles, asserting ourselves while at the same time protecting ourselves from any potential external threat. In no way therefore can the emphasis on the aesthetic dimension and the specific logic of appearing cancel out this aspect and diminish the conflictual character of interaction. From now on in this book, the concept of display will be understood in the double meaning of displaying oneself by opening up creatively to the world and of making oneself vulnerable, by exposing oneself to potential attacks from the outside. Stressing the violence that always confronts the individual who inhabits the public sphere, Plessner rightly compares appearance to a suit of armor that protects us against the wounds of social relations: "The individual at first must give himself a form that makes him unassailable, an armor that he can wear entering the battlefield of the public sphere. After having become visible in this manner, the individual demands corresponding relationships to (and answers from) other persons." However, he continues, "the human masks himself with the unreal compensation; he renounces his becoming respected and seen as an individual to produce, at least, representative effects in a representative meaning—that is, in a particular function—and to be respected for them."[16]

3
AESTHETIC MEDIATION

A Theory of Representations

The Irreducibility of the Medium

Sensible appearance is the medium, the necessary route of all communicative relationships, which take place in an endless exchange between expression and impression. Expression can be thought of as the systole of social communication, the process by which the internal—an intelligible state by itself devoid of phenomenal substance—makes itself external by appearing in the world and taking on qualities and forms, by assuming a sensible guise, for example, in a gesture or a facial expression through which states of mind or passions are manifested. With impression, which represents the diastolic moment, the external phenomenon is captured and absorbed; it is distilled from a sensible form into a subjective state. Here the represented image creates its own inner intelligibility: the instant the beauty or sadness of a face, the brilliance of a jewel, the misery of an environment, the lavishness of an evening gown, or an unpleasant aspect of a situation is perceived, it provokes sensations and emotions of love, pity, desire, shame, disgust, or suffering. In expression, aesthetic mediation occurs in an extroverted fashion; in impression, mediation intervenes in the form of introversion.

It bears repeating that the concepts of expression and impression must not be understood according to a romantic notion of communication—as if they allowed for direct, *immediate* translation from interiority to exteriority and vice versa.[1] For thinkers like Rousseau, who aspire to transparent communication in the relationship between individuals, and even before that in the relationship between inner states and the outer signs that represent them, the expression must immediately manifest the content and faithfully materialize it, without leaving anything unaccounted for and with no opacity. A perfect correspondence reigns between the ideal meaning and the appearance designated to express it, because the realms of the ideal and the sensible are seen as parallel and commensurable. However, what also ensues is a precise ontological hierarchy: the idea is superior to its sensible form, which is the secondary and subordinate instrument of its expression. In my view, on the contrary, a mediated relationship of a *representative* type exists between the spiritual content and appearances.

In representation, the sign *is not* the meaning; rather, it is, as we would expect, its "representative," which must speak in the absence of what it represents. As Jacques Derrida put it, the phenomenon can never be reduced to a presumed ideal and "present" voice in which it is expressed; instead, it preserves the depth of its medial and mediated nature and the opacity of its sensible consistency.[2] The aesthetic dimension of communication lies in this *irreducibility of the medium*, from which social philosophy should also draw its conception of the relations between form and content. Compared to the romantic conception of expression, the representative view breaks the immediate communicative relationship, inverting its principle and logical order, so that it is not the intention that makes use of the medium (as a subordinate and derivative instrument) but rather the mediation itself that makes communication possible: mediation incorporates internally, as its intrinsic possibility, the principle of noncorrespondence that the philosophy of the 1960s was fond of defining as "difference." Although the representative may look similar to what it represents, in its nature it maintains an unbridgeable distance—that which separates, for example, the spiritual from the sensible, the ideal content from its material sign—and an equally irreducible expressive independence. Precisely because the spirit is not endowed with a phenomenal surface, it cannot appear or be perceived without going outside itself and making use of something else; it cannot express itself unless it has itself been embodied by a representative that can always speak in *its* way. Always implicit in this "standing-for" is a *gap/difference*: the possibility of a dispossession or an alienation.[3]

As will be explained more fully in the second part of this book, on the genealogy of social romanticism, romantic philosophers think of communication as a problem, which is ultimately a moral one: they are concerned about the *authenticity* of the content communicated, that is, its faithfulness to the meaning and to the original intention, and about the *sincerity* of the exchange, namely, its socially nonmanipulative function. Both concepts are loaded with normative judgment. My philosophy of appearance, or social aesthetics, is initially neutral toward these concerns and must necessarily place itself ahead of them. It does not seek, nor should it, to put these issues aside indefinitely, by any means, but prior to addressing what are, in effect, nothing but the consequences of an anthropological and social structure that precedes and influences them, we must delve into *social appearance as appearance, and into its peculiar logic*: what social aesthetics needs to understand before anything else is the philosophy of the mask qua mask, of the social image qua image, of representation qua representation. The expression of grief on my face may reflect the pain I truly experience from the death of a loved one, or it could be a "funeral face" that I put on as demanded by the circumstances: the difference is certainly significant from the moral point of view but from the perspective peculiar to social aesthetics this issue has a lower priority. Regardless of whether I am sincere, tactful, or hypocritical, regardless of whether my inner feeling corresponds to the image that publicly displays it or not, *this apparent image is in any case what represents it* and thus mediates my relationship with others.

To put it another way, the mistake of the romantics is not so much that they aspire to authenticity and sincerity, or that they cultivate a normative attitude toward social representation (human beings *are* normative beings, and they will inevitably feel the need to take a moral attitude toward their mutual relations). What the romantics get wrong is the idea (rooted, as we will see, in a tradition that goes back to the rise of Christianity and before that still to Plato) that appearances are intrinsically lying, and that in order to arrive at these values one could too readily circumvent their aesthetic mediation. This mistake is rooted in the metaphysical premises and method of their analysis, not in their moral preoccupation. Appearance is a given and in no way can it be eliminated from social life. Only a careful analysis can tease out *the evaluative and normative dynamics already implicit in the aesthetic logic* in which the truly moral dimension is rooted and entangled.

There is no harm in asking, then, as romantics do, if degrees of intimacy exist in appearance, if differences occur in the way we wear our masks when communicating with strangers or friends—but it bears stating from the outset that none of us will ever be able to remove our mask completely and communicate with others in our nakedness. More than as a myth of origin and decadence (the original nature awaiting our return, the golden age or paradise that we lost), the desire for authenticity should be understood as the regulative ideal of those who are aware of the inescapability of the social-aesthetic realm in which we are necessarily implicated as social subjects. In this realm, the metaphysics that starkly opposes reality and appearance do not apply, there are no transparent signs or voices devoid of phenomena, there are no people without masks, and sensible appearances mediate all forms of communication and shape them. Only after understanding and fully accepting the inescapability of aesthetic mediation will it be possible to consciously take up one's place in it and reflect, among other things, on a normative use of appearances. And no matter how greatly these appearances may differ in depth or artifice—their degree of opacity lies in a virtual spectrum ranging from the presumed spontaneity of an infant's face to the melodramatic mask, from the conformism of "good manners" to courtly sophistication—they all share the lowest common denominator of their phenomenal being and public perceptibility. No social image can be completely transparent.

The Form Is the Content

Beyond the communicative sense, however, the concept of aesthetic mediation must be understood in a constitutive sense that we might also define as transcendental (and this second sense is the most important aspect, which, philosophically, should precede and found the first one). More than simply *conveying* the communication within preexisting and preconstituted social relations, appearances *form* these relations—they are their condition of possibility and formation. Sensible appearance is a medium that transmits its message by shaping it from inside. In representing the spiritual meaning, the sensible appearance not only communicates the meaning (transmits it from one place to another), but also gives it a structure and a sensible aspect that allow the meaning to *exist as a phenomenon*. Neither a copy nor a mere instrument, appearance is the condition that simply allows social reality to exist and become real in a social sense. Things show themselves and become perceptible in the public sphere—in other words, they become real in the world—through appearance. This is why the form cannot be separated from the content without destroying the phenomenon itself, *along with its specific meaning.*

This principle, which is familiar to the discipline of aesthetics proper, also applies to its social version. Just as poetic content can never be separated from its metrics, its rhetorical figures, and the sound of the syllables, all of which make a poem a poem, there is no such thing as the content of a novel that can be separated from the plot, the dialog, and the system of characters and descriptions—in other words, from everything that characterizes the novel-form. Similarly, there is no content of a portrait that can be distinguished from the colors, the drawing, and the stylistic conventions that determine it as a painting or as a sculpture or as something else. In the same way, form and content are mutually dependent and, indeed, indistinguishable in social-aesthetic phenomena.[4] If the constitutive principle of social appearances is no different from the principle that forms lyrics or a painting, it becomes understandable why artists so often grasp and express the essence of a social phenomenon thanks to their sensitivity to the language of forms.

The nature of aesthetic form is such that no content sensibly conveyed by it can be extracted from its shell, like a gold nugget from its veinstone. The explanatory-interpretive activity performed by aesthetic disciplines, then, including social-aesthetic ones, cannot consist in providing a simple explanation of content, which eliminates the forms in order to work back to the ideal content that they convey. The work of aesthetic disciplines is rather the delicate task of translating from the sensible to the conceptual: thought tries to transpose what is communicated in the mode of appearance into the mode of the discursive mediation, without ever forgetting—this is a consequence of the mechanism of representation—that this translation will be a *metabasis eis allo genos* (a jump from one dimension to another) in which, inevitably, something changes or gets lost. From this point of view as well, then, social philosophy comes close to philosophy of art in seeking to explain discursively that which is represented sensibly in society and in focusing on that which the aesthetic experience always preserves of the irreducible in relation to the discursive: the relationship with sensibility, with forms, and with sensible qualities; subjectively, with the senses and with taste.

4
FIGURES

Social Images

Snapshots of Appearing

Appearance is everything that we express in the public sphere and offer to the perception of others through exchange and social communication: from the words we pronounce to the clothes we wear, from facial expressions and gestures that we draw in the air to the accessories with which we adorn ourselves, passing through all those minor features, more subliminally emitted and perceived, such as tics, bodily postures, smells, sounds, blushes, quick glances, and modulations of the voice, which, more often than not, are all the more significant the more they are considered to be inconspicuous. Produced by each minimal perceptual interaction, appearances are layered in perpetually differing combinations and are transformed according to the changing circumstances of time and space and to the points of view of the perceiving subjects; they are volatile by definition and difficult to pin down. Their specific mode of being is flow—the flight of phenomena, with all its instability and inconstancy. Such fleetingness does not prevent us from studying them analytically, though, by using the philosophical equivalent of a photographic snapshot or freeze-frame image. By stopping the single frames of appearing, we arrive at what we will call *social images*: sets or agglomerates of features that mediate the relationship between individuals and make up the aesthetic substance of the social reality. Despite their static nature, social images retain the memory of the fluid dynamic from which they were generated: rather than points, they are centers of aggregation, sets charged with force and dialectical tensions.

The choice to use the concept of image as a metonymy for the more general concept of sensible form, following a usage of medieval philosophy that still holds theoretical potential,[1] is also justified in my view by the greater social significance that sight possesses compared to the other senses. The primacy of the eye is also suggested by ordinary language, when image is spoken of as a synonym for "what others perceive about us," as well as the cluster of idiomatic expressions in various languages that describe the experience of social recognition in unabashedly aesthetic tones. In Italian, Spanish, and French, phrases such as *fare bella, brutta figura, figurare, sfigurare, hacer buena figura, figurar, desentonar, faire bonne, triste,* and *piètre figure* evoke a spectacular, representative vision of society that still resonates in the English expressions *to cut a fine figure* or *to cut a poor figure*. The key lies in the original Latin term, *figura*, which denotes a formative activity and, at the same time, an idea of visibility and public perceptibility. A good term of comparison is the German word *Gestalt*, which has the same meaning as the Latin. The German word *Bild* suggests similar allusions to the formative and social dimension of the figure. Indeed, the peculiar relationship that binds together the pedagogical and aesthetic thought of German idealism is founded on a series of words that derive from *Bild*, starting with the crucial *Bildung* (formation, creation, education) or *Vorbild* (example, model). Both suggest the idea that it is essential to "make oneself into an image," to cultivate a relationship with an image (real or ideal, one's own or that of others). This image shapes individuals through a strict reciprocity between inside and outside, and, through their apparent form, connects them socially to others through education, imitation, exemplarity, and so forth.

Individuals "figure" in public and, even before that, in the reflexive relationship that they entertain with themselves—in the sense that they give shape to a sensible representation of themselves, or to a "self-design." We offer these figures of the self to the gaze and appreciation of the social spectators who surround us as much as we do to our inner spectator. Society itself, with its dynamics of representation and recognition, demands this figure from individuals, only to then snatch it away from them.

At the center of the social image stands the face: the fulcrum of human appearing and its relationship with otherness. The face is the facade we project outward, the most exposed aspect we offer the world—in the sense of self-display as well as that of vulnerability, of opening to injury and violence (Latin, *vultus/vulnus*).[2] In it are concentrated the two main communication processes: the presentation of self and the interpretation of the presentation of others. Both these practices are strictly "aesthetic" because they have to do with the creation and processing of sensible qualities and forms. This aesthetic work takes place in the two complementary senses of social communication, expression and impression, never to be understood as immediate flows but always as representative dynamics, influenced and instituted by the medium that makes them possible.

The face is the first thing that talks about us and, in many cases, represents the focal area of one's social image. It is the place where the character of the passions and the individual's history are revealed, a wax tablet on which are engraved the signs of experience and the layers of life, in which the flight of time becomes visible and concrete, fragile in its nudity, isolated in its peculiar position, projecting out from the rest of the body. Simmel likened it to a peninsula, but another appropriate metaphor for the face could be an expression dear to the Italian poet Antonella Anedda, "the balcony of the body." The face is one of the main mediums of communication and on its ductile and malleable surface is focused much of the aesthetic work demanded by social life: techniques of the face include physiognomy, mime and acting, the control of expressions, makeup, piercing, tanning, and plastic surgery, but also the counterpractices of defacing, like scrawling across posters and disfiguring the faces of advertising models or election candidates, or the game that magazine readers play with the help of experts to unmask the cosmetic "touch-ups" of celebrities. Acid throwing or "vitriolage" is a form of facial rape that is perhaps even more serious than the sexual one, owing to its more visible and indelible nature, and especially to the fact that our faces are the compendiums of our social identity. Using acid to disfigure people's faces, primarily those of women, in order to punish them or exact revenge is a practice that has grown in recent years with disturbing symmetry in Western and non-Western countries. As Thomas Macho points out, these and other "facial skills," valuable in every form of communication, seem to have gained further importance in today's *faciale Gesellschaft*, or society of the face.[3] At the macro level, the same techniques take on Orwellian dimensions in star systems and advertising methods similar to political propaganda: a spectator from abroad who tours our cities with an unfamiliar gaze might very well perceive the enormous faces that dominate our billboards and the windows of our pharmacies and makeup stores as murals of dictators.

The figure transcends the face, however, and extends to the entire bodily appearance, encompassing our entire *air*: everything that others can perceive about us, starting from the personal leitmotiv of the voice. Developing the theatrical metaphor, we might say that, in addition to the mask, the social stage setting includes an array of sounds, gestures, postures, costumes, accessories, and sets. While this array plays an important role in any interaction, it is crucial in status settings, such as prestige (or glamour, its reincarnation in mass society), or in the particular social icons of charismatic figures and role models. From the iconology of Christian saints to that of the pagan or Christian virtues, from political leaders to stars, the construction of a public figure (whether real or fictitious) with the capacity to influence the public imagination always involves the creation of a specific representative apparatus, intended to stylize the personality and construct a "type."[4] If the figure to be represented is expected to be easily recognizable within its group, then the apparatus focuses on distinguishing marks: just as all saints sport the symbols of their martyrdom (wheel, grill, sword), all stars have their look, gestures, and individual accessories: a pompadour or peekaboo hairstyle, a wobbly walk on high heels or a leather vest. Like a Cesare Ripa in Hollywood, researchers with a historical sense of iconology can indulge themselves by creating a classificatory and structural analysis of the star system. Even the figure of the philosopher, seemingly remote from the public scene, has been subject to figural design from its very beginnings: the staff and the lantern are as vital to the icon of Diogenes as they are to his philosophical thought, for which they provide a representation in symbolic form. Images translate a style of thought, the same way that the preaching of John the Baptist (which owes many of its features to the iconography from the tradition of the Cynics) receives its sensible translation in a garment of camel's hair, a cross-staff, and a leather belt around his waist. Obviously, the greater the public and media involvement of philosophers—a phenomenon that had already acquired its specifically modern traits in the mid-eighteenth century—the more stylized their figure appears: in Rousseau's Armenian kaftan and Voltaire's worldly elegance, which were the first figures of modern intellectual celebrities, we already recognize the mannered self-design of French theorists and *nouveaux philosophes*.[5]

Depth, Distance, and Reciprocity

The social image produced through public interaction coincides with the appearances that arise out of a given situation but it also has a historical depth, an evolution, and a duration. In addition to a look that matches our stage setting or the face we put on in response to circumstances, our social image includes those we perpetuate regardless of the circumstances of individual encounters. These never abandon us, either because they are permanent features of our physical appearance or because we have gradually assimilated and incorporated them into our *habitus*. These earlier appearances are composed like architectural layers of a city: some have existed for decades, others for a few months; some of them disappear or are destroyed to make room for new appearances, while others are constantly renovated and refurbished. (Contrary to the commonplace notion that thinks of surfaces as necessarily "flat" and attributes this layered type of composition only to the deeply vertical structure of the unconscious, we should therefore acknowledge that the uppermost layer of the person also has its own specific form of depth, articulation, and stratification.) Because appearances have their own expressive autonomy, they may very well communicate at cross purposes to whatever mask has been donned for a specific occasion, even to the point of blatantly contradicting the intended message or sabotaging the effectiveness of the entire performance. This possible discrepancy founds the humor and suspense of everyday gaffes, which happen when the stage setting prepared in the wings clashes with the unexpected hitches and incidents of real interaction. (And these unexpected events are what give back the thrill of the unpredictable and a taste of freedom to the script of social performance.) The dramatic potential of these moments, when the mask drops or threatens to drop, has been widely exploited by the most successful theater and film scenes, in which spies, undercover agents, or imposters are threatened with being unmasked.

If the concept of social image has thus far seemed similar to that of *face* theorized by Goffman, the following remarks will clearly delineate the most important differences between the two. Unlike in Goffman's use, the medial function of the social image is very broad, since it is not necessarily confined to face-to-face interaction or relations of simultaneous and symmetrical reciprocity—in a situation of copresence, reciprocity is immediately evident from the fact that all the participants influence one another: to every action there corresponds a reaction that follows or has mentally anticipated it. Like the portraits exchanged between royal families of the Renaissance to allow betrothed couples who had never met to get to know each other, or like the images of celebrities collected and exchanged by fans, social images also create connections between people who are not yet, may have never been, and may never be in immediate physical contact. Another example of a social image that connects at a distance is the home page that users of social networks create: ironically overstepping Goffman's restriction, the most famous social network of all has retained the word face in its name. Finally, what we might define as *nonmimetic social images* represent the public persona like all other social images but through a highly symbolized and stylized process—coats of arms, emblems, signatures, trademarks, logos, stamps—and do not require contact or reciprocity because they are created for the purpose of circumventing that limitation.

In reality, when scrutinized under a more powerful philosophical lens, even these distinctions appear to be undermined by a dialectic. A form of presence is always implicit, especially where there is the greatest distance: in the photographs of the dead or in the posters that populate the bedrooms of teenagers a presence materializes that can have a greater effect on our real lives than the gazes of real people. Conversely, face-to-face interaction cannot be excluded from a form of mediation at a distance. People never interact in an unmediated fashion, even when they touch each other: even in the embrace of two lovers there are countless medial surfaces separating them (the presence or absence of clothing, lights and shadows, a sense of modesty, and respect for the other person's self-representation) that bring them closer while distancing them, by establishing specific spatial and temporal limits: not now; not here.

A fan who collects images of his or her idol without the celebrity knowing anything about the collector, or even that he or she exists, or a child who collects baseball trading cards shows how a sensibly mediated social relationship can be established in a communication that is predominantly one way. In reality, no social relationship mediated by images is completely unilateral, and a form of mutual action, more mediated in time and space, can be discerned in even the most apparently asymmetrical cases: politicians are very careful to calibrate their public figure to the preferences of their constituents, promptly adjusting them whenever the need arises; cases of celebrities who redeem themselves with their outraged fans after some unpopular behavior are not uncommon. The asymmetry that constitutes the very definition of celebrity—being known by someone you do not know—must not mask the persistence of an interaction that characterizes, as Simmel defined it, any social relationship: even the most anonymous and insignificant of groupies is a partner in *Wechselwirkung*, or reciprocal effect.

5
OUT OF CONTROL

The Alienated Image

Objectivity, Estrangement, and Alienability

The primary characteristic of the social figure is its *public* nature. The social image exists in the space of *Öffentlichkeit*, "the public sphere" or, literally, "publicity"—an open space where everything, in principle, should be accessible to all, exposed to the eyes or senses of a public, the object of possible perception and therefore also for the evaluation and criticism of the public. From this first characteristic derive the other fundamental attributes of the social image, all strictly interdependent: its *objectivity*, its *estrangement*, and its *alienability*. By objectivity I mean its nature as an object: although produced by a subject, and more specifically by several subjects who interact among themselves, the image is an *objective entity* that exists as a kind of thing. By estrangement I mean the fact that social images are perceived by the represented subjects as *other(s)*, as *different from themselves*: something they are too (their images, perceived by others and by themselves) but, at the same time, something they are not. Alienability, finally, is *the faculty of being able to be transferred elsewhere*, as in legal language, just like a property that passes into other hands. In the concept of *Entfremdung*, for instance, in the Hegelian and Marxist traditions, all these various meanings tend to overlap in a single idea of *alienation* that alludes simultaneously to a nonthing becoming a thing, to the distancing and defamiliarization of what was close, and to the loss of a property that originally belonged to the subject.[1]

The social image does not belong to whoever is represented in it and by it—the person who also contributes to producing it with his or her expressive self-presentation and self-reflection—which is why it appears alien or even threatening. This is my image, *Ego* says to itself, yet it is not mine and that is not really me portrayed in it, because this is the way someone else sees me. (As we have noted, this holds true first and foremost in the sense of Plessner's eccentric positionality: the image does not belong to the subject because the subject always has a spectator, and the first, alien spectator is the subject itself.) However, neither can we say that the figure belongs to the subjects who perceive it and vouch for it, contributing in their turn to shaping it. I see you and I make an image of you for myself, *Alter* responds, but in reality your image does not belong to me any more than it belongs to you, who is represented in it. The alienation of the social image is not a transfer into the hands of specific individuals but a form of ontological desubjectivation and autonomization, of *independent life in an alien dimension*.

This multiple unbelongingness reveals the fatal autonomy of the social image, which has the power *to emancipate itself from the interaction that generated it and migrate through the social ether*, moving through distant times and places, well beyond the contingent circumstances that gave rise to it. Like all images, social images are also suited to migrate to posthumous lives and to survive in other forms and with other features. Produced by intersubjective relations, they transcend these relationships so as to exist in an independent dimension—the realm of social appearances—inhabited by entities that tradition has largely judged as inferior to tangible and material ones, but that indisputably have their own form of reality. And this reality is also and primarily evidenced by their effectiveness: the best proof of the reality of a social image is its ability to powerfully influence human behavior.

Publicity, objectivity, estrangement, and *alienability* make social appearances a full-fledged sphere of reality, endowed with characteristics similar to those Hegel attributed to the "objective spirit," but with a difference. From the point of view of social aesthetics, objectivity is embodied not in culture and in institutions but in sensible entities, which, precisely because of their aesthetic nature, that is, their rootedness in corporeality, sensoriality, and perception, allow the spirit to be "naturalized."[2] Hannah Arendt spoke in this regard about "world": the objective dimension that transcends subjects, forms the framework and the environment of their relations, and has the capacity to endure and remain (for her, artwork was the paradigm of this worldly persistence). This world that connects and separates comprises material things but also more unstable sensible appearances, leading to a crucial problem in Arendt's theory: How can vain, volatile appearance be stabilized in order to transmit the world and allow it to survive? Arendt went on to define this stabilizing force as "power": "without power, the space of appearance brought forth through action and speech in public will fade away as rapidly as the living deed and the living word."[3]

From our perspective, however, which seeks to understand why the Western tradition so forcefully rejected the laws of social aesthetics, it is the other side of the capacity described by Arendt that causes a problem: the autonomy and persistence in time of social images, which manage not only to endure beyond the contingency of the action and speech that generated them but even to transcend the individual's biological life. The images we produce during our appearance on the worldly scene under particular contingent circumstances will be fixed, thanks to the media that capture them in a variety of different substrates, and transmitted in all sorts of modes (from "rumors" to stories, pictures, photos, and sound and film recordings).[4] They will also accompany us throughout the various phases of our lives, to a time when we are very different from how we were, when (as Proust observed) we will have other selves, other lives, and other identities. And they will remain behind us even after we have passed away and vanished from the sight of other human beings. It is curious, then, to think that appearance, the most despised of realities, owing to its ephemeral and insubstantial character, has the capacity to persist longer than the human beings who originate it. The social image is not the physical body of the living individual, which represents only one of its possible mediums; the social image has even less to do with the subject's passions, thought, and inner states; and yet, the images of this individual are what the world will perceive, preserve, and protect in the memory. The mortal being vanishes from the public sphere before its sensible likenesses, which, although not immortal, are more durable and can endure beyond the death of the physical body thanks to their properties of objectivity and alienability. Thus, the life of a social image surpasses that of a human being. Not to be confused with eternity, its particular temporality seems to be *persistence*—the form of persisting in life, of surviving or *Nachleben*, persevering through effort and resistance, like ghosts, to which images are often likened.[5]

Human beings produce images that, once perceived and witnessed by other people, represent their social reality. And this reality has the power to escape control and take off on its own, in space and time, to become part of worlds that will remain unknown, even to those who produced them. Its double bond with exteriority—the first being introduced by the witnessing and respect of others, which can always be denied, and the other being produced by the tendency of images to break free and migrate—makes the figure a reality that is lost the instant it is created. Figures are ingenious. They tend to slip away through all possible mediums and can be stolen from us through betrayal, as with gossip and photos taken surreptitiously by paparazzi (a contemporary reincarnation of the diabolic figure that appears in the nightmares of the German romantics who can steal away our reflection),[6] or stolen from archives and mobile phones. It is one of the reasons individuals perceive their own image as unstable: "face" is by definition what one "loses" the instant one makes a gaffe, and the constant tension between gaining and losing is what distinguishes all social images, all the "goods" produced by recognition—honor, glory, respect, reputation, and their counterparts, such as shame, humiliation, and dishonor—which, for this reason, are the object of perpetual struggle.[7] Visual likenesses, but also those created through different sensible mediations, such as voice and hearing (the social image has an acoustic matrix in the concepts of fame, glory, honor, name, and hearsay), are all forms of existing in appearance and therefore in the public sphere of publicity, in objectivity, in estrangement, and in alienation. The existence of regulatory techniques and protections—such as charges for defamation or breach of privacy, which afford a measure of control over media processes that encourage the production of more "official" public images—is an attempt to respond through legal means to this sense of dispossession and violation.

The disorientation arising from the fact that something that constitutes our identity and social reality is constantly destined to elude us is one of the reasons romantic thinkers fought so tenaciously against social images. They accused them of the most obvious and at the same time most banal offence: *of being what we are and what we are not; of simultaneously belonging and not belonging to ourselves; of not representing us adequately and eluding our control.* In the name of freedom and moral autarky, the ancient philosophers, especially the Stoics, spared no sallies against the ephemeral nature of the external goods produced by *doxa*. However, in the romantic tradition, exemplified by the philosophical and literary work of Jean-Jacques Rousseau, the Stoic conception of freedom that motivated the rejection of forms of social recognition (because they make individuals into the slaves of others) fused with the typically modern demand for personal identity and subjective truth and was concretized in a new, specific value: the ideal of authenticity.[8] The ethics of authenticity urge us to emancipate ourselves from the burden of our social image *so that we are able to be ourselves*: in other words, so that we are able not to be how others would have us. The law of the other that is asserted most aggressively is precisely the *Entfremdung* (alienation) of the social image. Romantic moralists condemn estrangement and alienability—characteristics of the social image inasmuch as they are objective entities—by putting themselves in the position of the subject who experiences them: they feel betrayed and threatened by so much autonomy. By disparaging and discrediting a priori the social experience of alienation, and by defining estrangement and alienation in an existential and moral sense, *they refuse to accept the law of objectivity that develops necessarily according to its own logic.* In the impossibility of condemning the image per se, which by itself has no morality, they end up condemning both the society in which the image is generated (whence the romantic–existentialist idea that the social dimension is in itself hypocritical and misleading and that solitude is nobler and more moral than being with others) and the individual, who, instead of remaining true to his or her authentic (not social) self, has agreed to be alienated and lost in it. Romantic philosophy thus tends to interpret the social experience negatively, even independently of particular historical circumstances of exploitation and injustice. From this point of view, social life is an experience of dispossession—a way of being that is necessarily false and inauthentic. This is not solely because, as the existentialists showed so well, the gaze of the other alienates us by reifying us and turns a subject into an object, something that is deprived of freedom.[9] The real reason is that *social images themselves make us exist elsewhere*, outside ourselves and remote from ourselves, in an inherent state of alienation.

Learning from Pirandello: In Front of the Mirror

Luigi Pirandello has left us a profound meditation, tinged with desperation and humor, on the social image and its innate tendency to become estranged and alienated—to the point of becoming another, even threatening, entity. Although Pirandellian philosophy is no longer studied outside the classroom and rarely transcends the confines of Italian culture, its topics are more relevant and ineluctable than ever. Its great value for a philosophy of social experience was noted early on by Karl Löwith and Walter Benjamin and, more recently, by Hans Blumenberg, who has also reevaluated its insights for an anthropology of visibility.

Pirandello's most emblematic text is his last novel, *One, No One, and One Hundred Thousand*, published in 1926. It all starts when Dida, wife of the protagonist Vitangelo Moscarda (whom she calls by the pet name Gengè), points out to her husband that his nose has a visible flaw that he had been unaware of until then: "'Tilts? My nose?' And my wife said, serenely: 'Of course, dear. Take a good look. It tilts to the right.'"[10] Suddenly, Moscarda, an ordinary man who had always lived peacefully and spontaneously in his own skin, discovers that he has a social appearance and that he exists differently in the perception of others from how he had imagined himself to be until that moment: "I didn't know well even my own body, my most personal possessions: nose, ears, hands, legs. And I began looking at them again, to re-examine them. This was the beginning of my sickness. . . . *I was obsessed by the thought that for others I was not what till now, privately, I had imagined myself to be.*"[11]

Through the eyes of his wife, from the perspective of a second person, then, Gengè discovers a disturbing difference, a fracture, between the way he lives in his body and the way his body is seen by others. In Plessner's terms, Moscarda discovers that he has a *Körper*, and that he is not just a *Leib*.[12] However, unlike in Plessner's theory, in Pirandello's this discovery, which leads to a splitting and rupture, is not attributed to an original, eccentric experience of self-reflection but to the gaze of others: reflexivity is turned entirely outward, as in Rousseau, and an element of relativism and perspectivism (probably deriving from Schopenhauer and Nietzsche) is introduced. Moscarda's discovery of the *Körper* is disturbing to him and then, bit by bit, it shatters him with the thought that other people have an image of him that belongs to him and yet, at the same time, is impenetrable to him, from which he is necessarily excluded: "The idea that the others saw me as one who was not I as I knew myself, one whom they could know only through watching me from outside *with eyes that weren't mine, giving me an appearance fated to remain always an outsider's to me*, though for them it was inside me, mine (*a 'mine' therefore that didn't exist for me!*); a life which, though for them it was mine, I couldn't penetrate: this idea allowed me no peace."[13] The awareness of having a social image shreds the integrity of the individual and, along with it, his inner peace: it breaks up the unity and coherence of the *I*, now split into an *I* "for itself" and an *I* "for others." Like an unwelcome and invasive intruder, it also expects to move in permanently with the host who rashly welcomed him in, and even to take his place: "How could I bear this outsider inside me? This outsider that I was for myself? How could I live without seeing him? Without knowing him? How could I remain forever doomed to carrying him with me, inside me, visible to others and beyond my vision?"[14]

The series of thoughts to which Moscarda abandons himself in his long and increasingly tormented monologue offers a brilliant compendium of the different approaches with which philosophical analysis can treat the problem of the social image and the discovery of its estranging, alienating power. Pirandello first highlights a cognitive perplexity: the awareness of the tragedy of eccentric positionality is expressed in a paradoxical way. I, to whom I am so close, whom I sense as alive by perceiving myself from within, who am always and continuously *with myself* and *at home with myself*, have to admit that I know myself less than anyone who observes me even distractedly from outside: the reflexive view, which is "objective" by definition, prevails as more meaningful than the individual's "subjective" view. It would even seem—and this is the premise of all forms of objectifying knowledge—that the degree of objectivity of self-knowledge is directly proportional to the distance involved. This suspicion fuels Moscarda's desperate hunt: placing himself in front of a mirror, he wages a comic war with his reflected image as he tries to surprise it and capture it the way it appears exclusively in the eyes of someone else:

> As long as I keep my eyes closed, we are two: I here, and he there, in the mirror. I must make sure that, opening my eyes, he doesn't become I, and I don't become he. I must see him and not be seen. Is it possible? The moment I see him, he'll see me and we'll recognize each other. Thanks a lot! I don't want to recognize myself; I want to know him outside of myself. Is it possible? My supreme effort must consist of this: not seeing myself *in me*, but being seen *by me*, with my same eyes but as if I were another: that other whom everyone sees, except me.[15]

This is how the Pirandellian conscience passes through its mirror stage. However, it is an alternative, different mirror stage from the one theorized by Lacan. The latter, as will be recalled, coincides with the phase when the child masters the totality of its body image for the first time by seeing it reflected in its entirety, by *recognizing itself* in this mirror image and therefore finally feeling like a subject, a self: "We have only to understand the mirror stage as an identification, in the full sense that analysis gives to the term: namely, the transformation that takes place in the subject when he assumes an image—whose predestination to this phase-effect is sufficiently indicated by the use, in analytic theory, of the ancient term *imago*."[16] Lacan's is a peculiar version of the *Bildung* model—to "make oneself into an image," to imitate an ideal image of the self: "This jubilant assumption of his specular image by the child at the infant stage, still sunk in his motor incapacity and nursling dependence, would seem to exhibit in an exemplary situation the symbolic matrix in which the I is precipitated in a primordial form, before it is objectified in the dialectic of identification with the other, and before language restores to it, in the universal, its function as subject."[17]

In Pirandello's view, instead, what the conscience seeks in the mirror is its *social* image. Not the *I* as the *I* sees it, watched and mastered by me; but the *I* from someone else's point of view, as others see it, who looks at me from an external point of view that does not coincide with the subjective one. And when Moscarda finally catches his own image, unlike the

Lacanian infant, *he does not recognize himself*: he fails to identify himself in this appearance because it no longer belongs to him; it seems produced by the hands of strangers, completely devoid of a "self-design." This is why the relationship between the *I* and its image can have none of the developmental or formative "jubilant" effects that Lacan would later attribute to it. For the French psychoanalyst, the plastic power of the image is kindled specifically by the tension that the apparent form—an estranged and transcendental entity—inspires in the subject, causing it to attempt to identify with the fictional, superior identity, to live up to the imaginary idea of itself. The mirror stage works by prompting the child's development because the image is recognized and desired by the subject as a goal of identification. According to Pirandello, however, the social image neither permits nor promises any possible identification, not even in an ideal and projective dimension. Rather than form, the social image *deforms*: it disfigures, deceives, betrays, dispossesses the *I*, by condemning it to perpetual exile from itself, by multiplying its painful divisions—between mind and body, between my *I* and that of others, between the *I* of today and those of yesterday. Every look coming from the outside is a blow to the subjective integrity:

> It stood there before me, almost non-existent, like a dream apparition, that image. And I could very well not recognize myself. What if I had never seen myself in a mirror, for example? Wouldn't my same thoughts, perhaps, still be inside that head, there, unknown to me? Yes, yes, and many others. What did my thoughts have to do with that hair, that color, which could also not be there or could be white or black or blond: and with those greenish eyes, that could also have been black or blue; and with that nose which could have been straight or snub? . . . And yet, for everyone, summarily, I was that reddish hair, those greenish eyes, and that nose; that whole body there, which for me was nothing. Nothing! Anyone could help himself to it, that body there, and make of it the Moscarda he felt like making, in one fashion today and another tomorrow, according to circumstances and moods. . . . Once the moment I stared at him was past, he was already another; in fact, he was no longer what he had been as a boy, and was not yet what he would be as an old man; and I tried to recognize him today in the him of yesterday, and so on.[18]

In Exile from Ourselves: The Others, the Modes, and the Media

Pirandello's thoughts on appearance made a strong impression on Karl Löwith, who saw the merits of Pirandellism in having developed a "monomaniacal" thought on the relationship between the human condition and the *persona*, the social mask. During the same period that Pirandello was publishing his pieces and novels, Löwith devoted a chapter of his habilitation dissertation, *Das Individuum in der Rolle des Mitmenschen* (The individual in the role of fellow man, 1928), to it. The chapter in question is focused on the theme of the *bare mask*, which summarizes the key philosophical questions at the heart of Pirandello's theater works. Löwith, taking an interest in the play *Right You Are, If You Think You Are* (performed for the first time in 1917) and reflecting on the meaning of the title, writes:

> Someone *is* defined in the first place as he *appears* to someone (another or himself). The accent is not placed on appearing as "mere" semblance, but rather on a being's mode of appearance. And since in Pirandello the existence of man rests on appearance, it follows that for him it is a matter of showing *that* and *in what way* someone appears to another but also to himself, *as* [als] someone; only in this way can appearance be seen as a masked appearance and thus in the nakedness of its authentic being. Only in this way is it possible to arrive at the question: what is someone in himself? To ensure that the question has a concrete ground, someone must already be there in some way for another person, and someone must in some way "appear" as that which someone "is."[19]

In this passage Löwith emphasizes the *modal* consequences of appearance, the fact that the act of appearing is always perspectival and relative to someone (the modes in which the individual appears to herself or to others are always different) and that this perspectivism is potentially infinite. The passage also stresses that the problem of authenticity stems from relativism: the relativity of the modes of appearingness is what generates the question about authentic being, about what is *in itself* and not *for someone*.

Even stronger than this cognitive perplexity, though, and more tragic in its consequences, is the moral perplexity. As emphasized in popular Pirandellism, individual identity splits and multiplies in proportion to the number of facets produced in the social perception, which depend equally on the various perceiving subjects and their different perceptive modes, since the same person can see me in different ways according to different circumstances and moods. The mass of ungovernable identity creates an unresolvable dilemma for the *I*. What is my true reality? The one that I sense I possess in any case, or the one conveyed by the images that others make of me? Or both? Moreover, how can I match my inner value, what I am, or believe, or claim to be, with the outer value, attributed or attested to by those who judge my social images? In other words, how can I act on the social recognition process to manipulate it and ensure that others see me how *I* want myself to be, so that my images in circulation correspond to how I want to appear, to the value I feel that I possess—or so that they at least produce a single coherent picture? In the situation encapsulated in the formula *One, No One, and One Hundred Thousand*, each new social perception produces a new image of Moscarda; but this new image does not necessarily erase the previous ones, many of which continue to roam the public space, indifferent to the existence of their siblings, becoming stratified and entangled with one another in no particular order and with no hierarchy, producing potentially inconsistent meanings. The head spins, as we know well, when we think about how many different images of ourselves we have produced in different situations and with different spectators, and how these images not only clash with the idea we have of ourselves but often mutually contradict one another. Once Moscarda becomes used to this thought, he surrenders himself to the *cupio dissolvi* (I wish to be dissolved), almost taking pleasure from pitting the figures against one another, enjoying the explosive fragmentation of his substance (for example, when he first evicts his tenants, playing the part of a skinflint, and then welcoming them back as a generous benefactor). In the end, what triumphs is the overwhelming magma of social images. Faithful to the contrast between life and the forms typical of the *Lebensphilosophie* of his time, Pirandello winds up giving a romantic, existentialist twist to his story, which ends with the choice of monastic solitude: feeling deprived of any authentic personal reality, obsessed by the masks that imprison and condemn him to incommunicability, threatened by madness, Gengè ultimately abandons the social world and withdraws into a home for the poor.

With the same dizzying radicalism, Pirandellism also invites us to reflect on the power exercised by the media, which not only are delegated to capture, transmit, and freeze social appearances but, by the same token, can also edit, develop, efface, and retouch them. The individual may thus feel doubly expropriated: by conveying and shaping the social image, the medium amplifies estrangement and alienation; it adds a further gap and layer of mediation to the reality of the image that is already reflexively mediated, thereby making it even more alien and threatening. No wonder, then, that in another novel closely allied with *One, No One, and One Hundred Thousand*, called *Shoot! The Notebooks of Serafino Gubbio Operator* (published separately the first time in 1916 with the title *Si gira . . .* and then in 1925 as *I Quaderni di Serafino Gubbio operatore*), Pirandello is interested in the relationship between the social image and the motion picture, seen as a hostile device that amplifies the alienation that is always looming in social life, reproducing it at a further level of estrangement. According to Pirandello, unlike a theater actor who performs directly and immediately in front of a public that is present, a film actor surrenders his or her facade to a mechanical device that freezes it, edits it, and takes it apart, ultimately transporting the facade to invisible and indefinitely distant spectators. Separated from a living, immediate relationship with the theater public, deprived of a clear consciousness of their role, because of the filmmaking practice of shooting scenes out of chronological order and the editing process, film actors are therefore doubly alienated. They live "in exile from themselves": "Here they feel as though they were in exile. In exile not only from the stage but also, in a sense, from themselves. Because their action, the *live* action of their *live* bodies, there, on the screen of the cinematograph, no longer exists: it is *their image* alone, caught in a moment, in a gesture, an expression, that flickers and disappears."[20]

This is why (putting Pirandello's observations in dialogue with the anthropology of reflexivity described at the beginning of this book) film actors are perceived in the public imagination as exemplary representatives of the human condition and of its dialectical relationship with appearing. As actors in the most mimetic and popular genre, they embody par excellence the representative form of life, the play with possibilities that come into reality through the body and its staging. But at the same time, by virtue of their increasingly mediated and distancing relationship with spectators and the means of communication, they are exposed most intensely to the eccentric tendency, to a constant centrifugal force that makes them the very emblems of dispossession and alienation. The acuity of Pirandello's observation did not escape Walter Benjamin, who returned to it in his essay "The Work of Art in the Age of Mechanical Reproducibility" (1936) with these comments:

> The representation of human beings by means of an apparatus has made possible a highly productive use of the human being's self-alienation. The nature of this use can be grasped through the fact that the film actor's estrangement in the face of the apparatus, as Pirandello describes this experience, is basically of the same kind as the estrangement felt before one's appearance [*Erscheinung*] in a mirror—a favorite theme of the Romantics. But now the mirror image [*Bild*] has become detachable from the person mirrored, and is transportable. And where is it transported? To a site in front of the masses.[21]

Benjamin's formulation is fitting, partly because it takes the metaphors literally: the medium "separates" the specular images of human beings—the reflected image, the one retransmitted by the mirror, which, in its turn, reproduces the gaze of other people and that of the internal spectator—and "transports" it over infinite distances. Paraphrasing Simmel's expression, the "tragedy of culture"—namely, the tragedy of a second nature that develops following an objective logic, thereby eluding the subject's will and control—is what romantic thinkers might call the "tragedy of the social image." However, the social image is only tragic from the subjective point of view of those who feel expropriated, and for romantic thinkers who react by fantasizing about a return to immediacy, to the "aura" of live presence and absolute self-possession that converges with our first nature. From the point of view of social aesthetics, there is nothing tragic about it: what prevails is simply the implacable law of objectivity, of social reality, and of *the specific logic of social images*.

PART II
VANITY AND LIES

On the Hostility Toward Appearances

6
"VANITY FAIR"

The Frivolity of Worldliness

The Metaphysics of Two Worlds

Our investigation into appearance is bound to run into several areas of resistance, or at least chronic suspicions, that may discourage readers from treating this essential dimension of social life as a serious philosophical concern. In the following chapters, through a variety of deep dives into the history of thought and culture, we will examine primarily three of these prejudices. First, that of ancient classical and Christian genealogy, which is founded on "the metaphysics of two worlds"—on the series of oppositions deriving from the ontological and moral distinction between appearance and reality and on the consequent condemnation of vanity. Second, the quintessentially modern paradigm epitomized in the tradition I will define as "social romanticism." And third, the contemporary current of "aesthetic anticapitalism," which grew out of the romantic heritage and is aligned with (neo-)Marxist or Frankfurt critical theory. This last approach reduces social appearance to a mere manifestation of the competitive mechanisms of the market economy and, in particular, to the phenomenon of commodity fetishism. As will become clear, despite diverging aims and guiding principles, not only are these three thought traditions closely related (they all meet up in

Rousseau's keystone work), they also share a few basic metaphysical and anthropological premises. Only after summarizing and discussing their arguments and history will we be able to continue our investigation in a way that is truly free of encumbrances.

The tradition of thought that has been most hostile to appearances ever since its beginnings—and the most successful in the history of philosophy—is the one that came under continuous fire from Nietzsche, who defined it as "Platonic-Christian." The hypothesis that inspired Nietzsche's philosophical battle (which tends toward stereotyping and verges at times on caricature, as do all great summaries intended to reconstruct a venerable genealogy of thought only to subvert it) is that Platonism and Christianity converged precisely in their common hostility toward sensible appearances: their incapacity to adequately relate to aesthetic phenomena is rooted in the metaphysical dualism that subordinates appearance to reality, like body to soul, outside to inside, and surface to depth. In step with Nietzsche's polemic, attacking dualisms and metaphysical hierarchies, Jacques Derrida spoke about a "logocentrism" that he saw afflicting philosophy from Plato on. This centrality of logos implies the ontological and moral superiority of the ideal over the sensible, of the spirit over the flesh, and of immediacy over mediation. In a passage that dovetails meaningfully with our inquiry, Derrida compares the contempt with which metaphysics has regarded writing to the even more explicit disdain with which it has condemned sensible appearances and all forms of clothing or masks:

> Writing, sensible matter and artificial exteriority: a "clothing." It has sometimes been contested that speech clothed thought. Husserl, Saussure, Lavelle have all questioned it. But has it ever been doubted that writing was the clothing of speech? For Saussure it is even a garment of perversion and debauchery, a dress of corruption and disguise, a festival mask that must be exorcised, that is to say warded off, by the good word: "Writing veils the appearance of language; it is not a guise for language but a disguise." Strange "image."[1]

In this tradition, which has permeated Western thought and survived for more than two millennia, appearance is considered to be an inferior reality, diminished and discredited, relegated to the illusory sphere of *doxa*—a concept that Platonic philosophy associates with the irreducible ambiguity of sensorial knowledge but also with an inherent, inevitable mystification. Indeed, there are two worlds: the uncertain world of sensible appearance, which is immersed in the deceptiveness of the senses, where what seems real and authentic is actually a copy and an illusory imitation; and the stable, truthful world of being, which transcends the first because it lies beyond the illusions of appearances. And since communication between human beings is necessarily linked to a sensible medium, this metaphysical subordination of appearance has often been accompanied in Western thought by a devaluation of certain fundamental characteristics of sociability. Plato's condemnation of rhetoric, for instance, is exemplified in *Gorgias* and *Phaedrus*: the tricks of psychagogy—the art of seducing the human psyche by "making us believe" through the skillful play of verbal and visual appearances—are accused in the final analysis of being sophistic. By distinguishing between good and bad rhetoric, Plato draws the art of manipulating *doxa* under the rigid, instrumental domination of dialectics, the true method of philosophy, so that it will only be used for the ends of truth and good. Contrary to this doctrine, Aristotelian philosophy has instead always championed the importance of rhetoric in public life and has generally valued the function of social appearance, recognizing it as an insuppressible condition of the ethical and political life of a community: Aristotle considers "endoxa"—opinions and customs that appear plausible and reputable in social common sense—to be a legitimate and authoritative starting point for the study of human affairs. Since human affairs are unstable by definition, they must be judged according to criteria of probability and likelihood rather than being submitted to the mathematical criteria of certainty.[2]

Although cursory, this sketch helps to understand the perspective that led Hannah Arendt to launch her passionate defense of appearances in a polemic against Western metaphysical dualism, which she saw as obstructing an accurate analysis of the human condition (something that in her Heideggerian framework can only be thought about beyond metaphysics). It also explains why her personal and idealized reinterpretation of the model of the Greek polis—converging with the Aristotelian model but not reducible to it—gave so much emphasis to the issue of appearingness that the latter became in her thought the "political transcendental": the condition necessary for human beings to realize the vocation proper to them. Without appearance, without the aesthetic dimension as the "ecstatic" medium in which individuals can present themselves on the world stage—opening themselves up and exposing themselves in the public sphere of living and acting together—there would be no individuation or political action, and therefore no possibility for a properly human life as such: "A life without speech and without action, on the other hand—and this is the only way of life that in earnest has renounced to appearance and to vanity in the biblical sense of the word—is literally dead to the world; it has ceased to be a human life because it is no longer lived among men."[3] By provocatively reversing the biblical condemnation against "vain appearance," this fragment from *The Human Condition* suggests tacitly an original approach for retracing the history of the dualistic paradigm that has undermined Western thinking: through the vicissitudes of *vanity*. This moral concept that originated in the classical world became a fundamental concept in Christian theology. Later, via Montaigne and Pascal, in the anthropology of the *âge classique* it ended up playing a crucial role in the moral and political thought of modernity, which preserved it until the twentieth century. A few important moments in this history are worth recalling.

Two Senses of Vanity

From a subjective point of view, understood as a motive or as an attribute of social subjects, vanity is the attitude of those who are obsessed with their own appearance and with what I will later define as the "will to please," that is, the desire to please themselves and others. Although this is an egocentric attitude, it necessarily involves uninterrupted social exchange, since the *I* that is concerned about its image has to seek validation through reflections of itself in the mirror of other people's minds and evaluate itself, through comparison, in relation to other social subjects. As Simmel expressed in a maxim worthy of La Rochefoucauld, the paradox of vanity is that it "needs others in order to be able to disdain them."[4] This attitude embodies emblematically the passion that Thomas Hobbes defined as *glory* (or *vanity* and *vainglory*) and which he made central to his political anthropology. Although it arises from an entirely undue feeling of superiority (since all human beings are substantially equal when it comes to their mental and bodily faculties) and is concerned purely with "trifles," vanity is a universal motive and one of the causes of the endemic state of competition in which human beings live, the proverbial "war of all against all." Because everyone wants to be considered the best, vanity triggers a violent struggle for the recognition of honor and leads people to attack one another "for trifles, as a word, a smile, a different opinion, and any other signe of undervalue, either direct in their Persons or by reflection in their Kindred, their Friends, their Nation, their Profession, or their Name."[5] Even though vanity is concerned with trifles and, indeed, precisely because nothing is at stake, according to Hobbes it is destructive and destined to annihilation. This intimate bond with death reveals one of its most persistent cultural traits. In the wake of Hobbes's assertions, other modern thinkers gave a prominent place to vanity in their social philosophies, making it the principle of both subjective corruption and social conflicts: hence the eighteenth-century French moralists, who attributed all human weaknesses to the wiles of *vanité* or *amour-propre*; Bernard de Mandeville, who gave *self-liking* the role of a universal vice stimulating rivalry and competition; and Jean-Jacques Rousseau, who made vanity the principle of all forms of personal and collective alienation.

In the objective perspective, complementary to the one that views vanity as a subjective motive, vanities are seen instead as social phenomena linked to appearance that bring into play individuals' "figures"—the images that people make of one another: publicity, honors, ceremonies, fashions, signs of prestige, success, and reputation. Characterized by an ephemeral temporality, destined to fade over time, vanities are considered by the Western tradition to be valueless and unworthy of pursuit as moral purposes. The link between vanity and death thus proves once again to be decisive, because it is precisely when faced with the inevitability of the end (of futile worldly satisfactions but also of individual existences) that the frivolity of social appearances and the need to aspire to a form of superior, transcendent, and eternal stability is revealed. The most adamant words on the topic are undoubtedly to be found in Pascal's Augustinian assertion: "You do not need a greatly elevated soul to realize that in this life there is no true and firm satisfaction, that all our pleasures are simply vanity, that our afflictions are infinite, and lastly that death, which threatens us at every moment, must in a few years infallibly present us with the appalling necessity of being either annihilated or wretched for all eternity."[6] Yet despite, or perhaps precisely because of, their transient and varied nature, vanities have always exercised an extraordinary, seductive force on human desires, arousing reactions charged with blame and morbid curiosity. The deeply ambivalent attitude that Western culture has adopted toward this entire sphere of phenomena can be summed up in the expression "Vanity Fair," the fair of the vanities, whose success summarizes the whole history of social appearance from Ecclesiastes to today's glossy magazines.

The name of the glamour magazine founded in New York in 1913, revived in 1983, and still published in many European editions picks up on that of a weekly satirical publication that appeared in Britain between 1868 and 1914, which critiqued the customs and fashions of the Victorian era. The title of the two magazines is inspired by William Makepeace Thackeray's most popular novel (*Vanity Fair*, 1847–48), which narrates the adventures of the social climber Becky Sharp and a group of dismal characters, all of whom are caught in the grip of vanity. Thackeray took his inspiration for the title of his book in turn from the great classic of Puritan literature, *The Pilgrim's Progress* by John Bunyan (1678 and 1684), the allegorical tale that is perhaps the most widely read religious work in the English-speaking world after the Bible. "Vanity Fair" is the title of an episode in the first book describing one of the stations where Christian, the Everyman pilgrim in search of redemption, stops along with his traveling companion, Faithful—who loses his life there from brutal torture. He is first lashed, then stabbed repeatedly, and, finally, burned: "Then I saw in my dream that when they were got out of the wilderness they presently saw a town before them, and the name of that town is vanity; and at the town there is a fair kept called Vanity-Fair. It is kept all the year long; it beareth the name of Vanity-Fair, because the town where 'tis kept is lighter than vanity; and also because all that is there sold, or that cometh thither, is Vanity; as is the saying of the wise, *All that cometh is vanity*."[7] Governed by Beelzebub, Vanity Fair is the sinful city where humankind runs the risk of straying from the straight and narrow; it is the kingdom of valueless things, illusion, and distraction; but it is also a "fair" or a show, a space for display, for exhibiting goods, with boisterous advertising of wares and irresistible seduction: "houses, lands, trades, places, honours, preferments, titles, countries, kingdoms, lusts, pleasures, and delights of all sorts, as whores, bawds, wives, husbands, children, masters, servants, lives, blood, bodies, souls, silver, gold, pearls, precious stones, and what not. And moreover, at this Fair there is at all times to be seen jugglings, cheats, games, plays, fools, apes, knaves, and rogues, and that of all sorts."[8]

Bunyan alludes to the book of Ecclesiastes and its famous adage that warns against the transience of earthly experiences: *vanitas vanitatum*. Thackeray, too, mentions it several times during his story, in his typically moralist tone, censuring the vacuous ambitions of his characters. In his novel, the theme of the spectacle of human vanity provides a moral frame for the stories that he tells, connecting the prologue, called "Before the Curtain," to the edifying reflection that brings the book to a close. The show begins: "As the Manager of the Performance sits before the curtain on the boards, and, looks into the Fair, a feeling of profound melancholy comes over him in his survey of the bustling place.... Yes, this is VANITY FAIR: not a moral place certainly; nor a merry one, though very noisy. Look at the faces of the actors and buffoons when they come off from their business."[9] The curtain closes: "Ah! Vanitas Vanitatum! which of us is happy in this world? Which of us has his desire? or, having it, is satisfied?—come, children, let us shut up the box and the puppets, for our play is played out."[10]

The arc taken by the expression "Vanity Fair," which passes from moral theology to society journalism by way of the satirical novel, can be traced in parallel with the secularization of the words in Romance languages that derive from the Latin *mundanitas*. *Mundanitas* was originally a theological concept that signified the degraded earthly life that followed after the fall of original sin, the so-called postlapsarian life: in contrast to the original paradisiacal perfection, in the earthly "world" humankind lives deprived of grace, in a condition of corruption and desperate misery. In modern languages, this theological significance became secularized into a social meaning: in Italian, Spanish, and French, the words *mondanità*, *mundanidad*, and *mondanité* signify the practice of playful and casual sociability, *worldliness* as the aesthetic way of life of fashionable people and socialites.[11] These terms, like their English cognate *mundane* (from Old French *mondain*, from late Latin *mundanus*, from Latin *mundus*, "world"), still retain a negative moral tone in their everyday use: as in the idea we associate with Proust's *In Search of Lost Time* or Fellini's *La dolce vita*. When *mondanité* is talked about, the insinuation is that it is equivalent to time wasted; and people who are *mondains* are depicted almost without exception as vain, hypocritical, and superficial. Or, another example that will prove to be crucial for our reflections on contemporary social aesthetics is the blame surrounding celebrities, party people, or their digital reincarnation in the media socialites of "Facebook society."[12] This semantic history, which testifies to the powerful bond that modern social criticism maintains with its Christian origins, has been accompanied by a progressive softening of the moral judgment: harsh Puritan condemnation evolved first into secular satire, which moralizes with a smile (*castigat ridendo mores*), and finally into casual gossip. But the basic attitude remains one of ambivalence, charged simultaneously with disapproval and voyeuristic curiosity: human vanity is always viewed as *spectacle* par excellence.

Saving Appearances: The Logic of Vanity Fair

The charm that Vanity Fair has exercised over the past few centuries has not been limited to society journalists, readers of celebrity news, and fashion victims—it has also seduced artists like Marcel Proust, F. Scott Fitzgerald, Truman Capote, Federico Fellini, and Andy Warhol, whose works have celebrated the ambiguous spell of the social spectacle. The constellation of voices that have dissented from the Platonic-Christian paradigm even includes a few philosophers who have worked against the current of the dualist tradition of Western metaphysics. Those who are most sensitive to the specific characteristics of worldliness and human sociability have gone so far as to attribute a positive role to vanity. Alexandre Kojève certainly deserves mention. The Russian-born French philosopher built an entire theory of humankind and history based on the passion of vanity. Interpreting Hobbes's pages on *glory* in the light of Hegel's reflections on the struggle between master and slave,[13] and provocatively switching their value from negative to positive, Kojève attributed a progressive and even *anthropogenic* role to the most fatuous of subjective motives. The passion of vanity acquires an explicitly warlike connotation; it is identified with the virtues of courage, selflessness, and the desire for great, spectacular feats: it would actually embody a noble, idealistic motive—the exclusively human ability to transcend the realm of animal needs and material economic necessity in the name of a spiritual value, the desire to win a beautiful image for oneself and, especially, to have it publicly appreciated and acknowledged by others. Going against the instinct for self-preservation and making the impalpable and evanescent social figure more precious than life itself, this desire for recognition alone pushes human beings into the "fight to the death for *pure prestige*," producing full-fledged human beings: beings free from natural necessities and instincts and capable of triumphing over the animal they bear inside, thanks to their love of appearances. The radical nature of this idea, as a limit case, prompts us to reflect on the fact that all modern thinkers who have worked on the question of recognition have had to engage more or less directly with the topic of vanity and grant appearingness some constructive role in the dynamics of social esteem.[14] What is at stake in the relation of recognition is actually the value of the individual, but for this value to be defined it must be conveyed by a sensible image, by something that can be publicly perceived on the world stage and judged accordingly by others.[15]

Kojève's move calls for another brief digression on "gender." According to the anthropological approach that inspires my book, vanity is a form of relation with the social world and with temporality that is valid for all human beings, because it is founded on reflexivity and rooted in the sensible dimension of the human condition. From a cultural point of view, however, specifically from the perspective of Western history, vanity has primarily been associated with the negative value of effeminacy. The reasons for this association are the same as those mentioned in the first part of this book regarding reflexivity and—empirically speaking, based on social history—women's greater penchant for checking how they look. Because women were excluded from the world of serious activities and were bereft of agency, relegated to the role of objects of perception and brought up, consequently, to look at themselves and keep a close watch on their appearances at all times, they were viewed as particularly vain and inclined to frivolity and superficiality. The commonplace is that feminine preoccupation about appearance is synonymous with merely caring for one's beauty and elegance, while men who are interested in their physical image are accused of abdicating their virile nature. It is interesting to note, then, that the author who dared most greatly to reevaluate vanity philosophically tries to nobilitate it by spiritualizing the reflexive dimension (the central focus shifts from bodily appearance to spiritual appearance, from the physical image to that of the soul) using masculine cultural values of heroism and war. This would seem to usher in a new hierarchization: between "noble vanities," having to do with politics, honor, heroism, and war, and "ignoble vanities," such as fashion, shopping, and gossip, for which there is no better definition than the formula from Ecclesiastes—"vanity of vanities." Further accentuating the virile and aristocratic tones of his thought (from this perspective, vanity clearly ends up coinciding with glory and honor, the passions of the aristocratic *habitus*), Kojève absolutizes the connection between vanity and death, by showing that the capacity to sacrifice oneself for one's image is indeed the specific difference of the human being—its nobility and dignity. His diagnosis provocatively inverts that of Pascal: no animal would risk its life in a duel, or commit suicide because of lost honor, as did Ajax; no animal can be a snob, that is, capable of going against economic interests and natural instincts for aesthetic, purely formal reasons. Herein lies the greatness, not the misery, of the human condition:

> Man realizes (=creates) and "manifests" his humanity (=freedom) by risking his life, or at least by being able and willing to risk it, solely "for glory" or for the sake of his "vanity" alone (which by this risk, ceases to be "vain" or "nonexistent" and becomes the specifically human value of honor, fully as real as animal "values" but essentially different from them).... No animal commits suicide out of simple shame or pure vanity;... no animal risks its life to capture or recapture a flag, to win officer's stripes, or to be decorated; animals never have bloody fights for pure prestige, for which the only reward is the resulting glory and which can be explained neither by the instinct of preservation (defense of life or search for food) nor by that of reproduction; no animal has ever fought a duel to pay back an insult that harmed none of its vital interests, just as no female [animal] has died "defending her honor" against a male. Therefore it is by negating acts of this kind that Man realizes and manifests his freedom—that is, the humanity which distinguishes him from the animals.[16]

In less idealistic philosophical perspectives, which diverge and yet resonate, others thinkers like Simmel and Arendt have attempted to formulate a positive philosophy of *doxa*. They do so by reappraising the set of phenomena and experiences that, precisely because they are ephemeral and superficial, show to advantage what is most irreducible and fascinating about human life: its finitude, its relativity, its melancholy, yet also its euphoric levity—its bond with time, play, and art. But apart from these exceptions, the prevailing view in Western philosophy is certainly that founded on the "metaphysics of the two worlds," which opposes the phenomenal sphere (comprising everything that is subject to corruption and that consequently corrupts the interiority of those who dedicate themselves to it, people labeled as trivial and "vain") to the substantial and lasting core of the real. This substance has been named in a variety of ways: God, Being, the realm of Ideas, but also the economic-political laws of the modern era, significantly defined by Marxism as the "structure" of social reality. Whether theological, metaphysical, or even economic, structures are always characterized by consistency, stability, and immutability, and philosophy sees them as its most legitimate object, describing them as primary from every point of view: logical, ontological, and moral. Everything that cannot be related to this armature is considered to be shallow appearance, simple play, and *illusio*; and superior disciplines of thought are discouraged from venturing too deeply into its facile territories. The opposition between seriousness and frivolity, like that between necessity and play, falls within the same system of metaphysical hierarchies that devalued the sphere of appearance by identifying it with illusion in the negative sense and with vanity.[17]

But if metaphysics and morals have disdained vanity and expelled it from their domain, must we come to the conclusion that there is no way to arrive at a philosophical understanding of vain appearance? As anticipated in the introduction of this book, such a way does exist: it is the one marked out by the discipline of *aesthetics*, as sensible knowledge, and as a form of "taste" in relation to everything that appears. No wonder the most revolutionary insight has been shared not only by the artists that have been mentioned earlier but also by several major art historians. In an essay titled, significantly, "The Logic of Vanity Fair" (1974),[18] Ernst Gombrich asked what method is best suited for studying social phenomena in which the aesthetic dimension is absolutely crucial, such as changes and transmission of fashions, tastes, and lifestyles. In polemic against the Hegelian-Marxist method, judged to be "holistic," Gombrich called for a Popperian approach—but his specific response is not what interests me so much as the insight underlying the entire text: yes, it is possible to study the Kingdom of Vanity Fair, provided that its autonomous "logic" is respected. And this logic is a "sensible logic," a logic of an aesthetic nature. We will return to these issues in the third part of this book. Before setting out our *pars construens*, however, we must continue our genealogical exploration into the history of the dualistic paradigm, which, by establishing an overly stark opposition between being and appearing, and giving the latter realm the status of a deceptive mask, blocked the possibility of understanding the world of social appearances *iuxta propria principia*.

7
AGAINST THE MASK

The Rise of Social Romanticism

From Moralists to Romantics

The idea that the social world resembles a theater and that a strong affinity exists between the art of acting and the art of shared living is an ancient *topos*.[1] The *theatrum mundi* motif has resurfaced regularly in the history of Western culture, leaving its mark especially on the literature of the Baroque age and in particular on the works of the modern moralists. The contemplative and anatomical approach typical of the moralist tradition was born out of a strong appreciation for the championing of visual perception implicit in the metaphor of the human spectacle, whose forms and specific laws the moralists sought to decipher from their position as "spectators of life."[2] The most incisive compendium of this line of thought—which was fond of comparing society to a comedy or a drama, and which proliferated metaphors of the mask, the theater curtain, the stage, wings, and theatrical illusion—is perhaps Baltasar Gracián's *Oráculo manual* (*The Art of Worldly Wisdom*, 1684). In its dazzling aphorisms, the social world, in which we recognize the historic space of the court transposed to a universal key, fills our view like a kaleidoscope of appearances. Its internal laws are gradually revealed by Gracián, in a style that translates the political realism of Machiavelli into a uniquely "aesthetic" sensitivity that is attentive to the modes of expression proper to the sensible realm: "*Reality and appearance. Things pass for what they seem, not for what they are. Only rarely do people look into them, and many are satisfied with appearances. It isn't enough to be right if your face looks malicious and wrong* (XCIX)." And also: "*Do, but also seem. Things do not pass for what they are, but for what they seem. To excel and to know how to show it is to excel twice. What is invisible might as well not exist* (CXXX)."[3]

The writers of the moralist tradition devised a method for analyzing social appearances that became their hallmark, developing into two complementary but divergent approaches. On the one hand, there is *the art of perspicuously observing and describing* the external signs of human behavior, which were viewed as meaningful for what they expressed by themselves, qua appearances. This approach developed into the genre of characterology—the phenomenology of moral types in the style of Theophrastus—and into a similar genre known in France as "peinture des mœurs," the description of the customs and the habits of different countries or social groups. The masters of this first style, in some respects a sort of morphological method applied to the human ethos, were Montaigne, La Bruyère, Molière, and, after the *âge classique*, the great novelists who were heirs to the moralists, such as Balzac and Proust.[4] On the other hand, there is *the art of unmasking appearances*, representative examples of which include the famous treatise by Jacques Esprit *De la fausseté des vertus humaines* (*Of the Falsity of Human Virtues*, 1677-78), a manifesto for systematic demystification, to which the moralist is expected to subject every perceived appearance. Another example of this approach from the French moralist school is the maxims of La Rochefoucauld (first edition 1665, fifth edition 1678), which take aim at the wiles of self-interest and pride that lurk behind every honest appearance.[5]

What unites these two approaches—perspicuous description and demystifying suspicion—is a refined aesthetic sensibility, close in spirit to the sensibility that Nietzsche (an admirer and self-proclaimed heir to the moralist tradition) associated with the "worshipers" of sensible forms.[6] Moralists approach the social world with the curiosity of artists: they are attracted by the phenomenal surface, which presents itself seductively to the senses, and they are eager to devote careful study to it, dissecting or reproducing it in a mimetic form. (The reverse explanation, according to which the moralists' perspective is said to have prepared the ground for the birth of the aesthetic attitude, would also be legitimate.) A further distinction needs to be made, though: while the first attitude stops at the outer membrane of things, seeing it as a dimension charged intrinsically with meaning, the demystifying attitude tries to lift it off like a lid in an attempt to arrive at the deepest layer of reality, which is assumed to be concealed by the outer surface. In the first case, *the meaning lies in the appearance* itself, in the way things present themselves and not underneath their surface, because the phenomenon is already considered to be substance. In the second, *the meaning lies beyond the appearance*: either as an essence concealed by the mask (the *iconoclastic tendency*: we need to rid ourselves of appearance in order to recapture truth), or as the revelation of an interiority that precedes and is superior to the appearance (the *expressionistic tendency*: appearance should be interpreted as a manifestation of essence but should nevertheless remain subordinate to it, as its expressive medium). In the case of the French moralists, this is purely a hermeneutic distinction; in other words, it serves to delineate two ideal types of approach that often coexist in works by the same author. Nevertheless, in a theoretical perspective this distinction has to be reinforced in order to fully elucidate the alternative between two ways of examining the social reality and the relationship between inside and outside and depth and surface. The unmasking method actually descends genealogically from the Platonic-Christian paradigm (with which many of the seventeenth- and eighteenth-century French moralists were imbued through their readings of Augustine and Augustinian writers) and would garner its greatest modern interpreters in Pascal, Rousseau, and their heir, Guy Debord. The method of perspicuous description links up again with the Aristotelian heritage of *ethopoeia*, the mimetic representation of manners and characters, such as Montaigne's *Essays* ("Of Custom," for example, in which the author expounds an interminable list of manners and habits) and La Bruyère's *Characters*.[7] This current widened to include the Wittgenstein of the "forms of life" period, the phenomenology of Merleau-Ponty and Alfred Schütz, Simmel's sociological aesthetics, and even the philosophical anthropology of Hannah Arendt and Hans Blumenberg. For this second family of authors there is no such thing as dualism: the face of things consumes their meaning in its entirety. Our knowledge of phenomena is exhausted already by describing appropriately how they present themselves, without presuming to dig under their skin or strip them of their external appearance in order to unearth an underlying truth. What there is to know is already in full view, on the surface, exposed to the eyes of everyone, and it asks only to be examined with more tact and attention.

On the Origin and the Foundations of Appearances Among Men

At the height of the moralist tradition, in the mid-eighteenth century, Jean-Jacques Rousseau formulated what is rightly considered to be the first modern social philosophy. He inherited the moralists' spirit, their interpretative subtlety, and their legacy of phenomenological observations, but he reworked them with great originality into a more ambitious theoretical synthesis. At the center of Rousseau's system stands the issue of social appearances. In his founding text, *Discourse on the Origin and the Foundations of Inequality Among Men* (1755), in which the problem of inequality is integral to the origin of social relations, the beginning of society proper coincides with the emergence of the "spectacular." This event stimulates the awakening of the reflexive attitude in the consciousness of individuals, while it foments attitudes of seduction, simulation, and rivalry in social relations.[8] According to the hypothetical-mythical reconstruction posited by Rousseau, the episode that began the process of historical decadence, and marks the human race's definitive abandonment of natural innocence, took place the instant a harmless rural festival put on by a peaceful gathering of the first families was transformed into a frenzied show. As these human beings participated in the entertainment, dancing and singing, they had the experience for the first time of acting in public while knowing they were being observed. They began to exhibit themselves and to perform in front of others *for* others; they began to think about the possible reactions of their spectators, attempting to anticipate the audience's responses and to satisfy its expectations—in fact in Rousseau's view there is no representation without "le désir de plaire" (the desire to please). Not unsurprisingly, the process had already been triggered by the amorous passion, which—because of its obvious connection with seduction and the problem of appearance—heralded on a small scale the representative dynamics of spectacularity. In this way the *center of gravity of subjectivity shifted inevitably from inside to outside*, from spontaneous expression to a pursuit of effect (or affectation), thus creating a disastrous inner imbalance. As a result of this socially induced off-centeredness, or eccentricity, a communicative form founded on *fiction and performance* came into being.

Let me resume the issue by putting it into dialogue with the problems examined in the first part of this book. In a condition of nature, the Rousseauian *I* is insensible to the gaze of others, because it enjoys a form of cognitive and emotional self-sufficiency that shields it from reflection on itself. The expressiveness of the *I* is immediate and immanent and its mode is absolute presence, which is free of representative tension (representation always projects image ahead of itself). The only natural and original human passion is what Rousseau defines as *amour de soi,* or the feeling of existence, through which "every individual human being views himself *as the only Spectator to observe him.*"[9] In Plessner's terms, it is as if Rousseau denied, or, better yet, as if he relativized the experience of eccentric positionality. He does this by making reflexivity the product of a historical transformation (which is therefore contingent and capable of being reformed), caused by the development of intersubjectivity, instead of an original given of the human condition—an anthropological a priori. Indeed, in the state of nature individuals seemingly lived in perfect correspondence with themselves, in an eternal present and in absolute closeness with themselves, still unaware of their phenomenal nature and incapable of seeing or observing themselves from outside and of self-projecting themselves.

Although Rousseau explicitly mentions an internal "spectator," in this instance it would be inappropriate to speak of reflexivity, because the gaze of this observer doesn't represent a form of otherness: it coincides, that is, with inner feeling and does not produce an *image of self* (objective representation, difference from the self) so much as a *feeling of self* (subjective presence to the self, identity with the self). Its positionality is therefore *centric* and *nonecstatic*, making it indistinguishable from that of animals. In the state of society, the opposite is true: the spectator role, which in nature is delegated to the inner self-contemplation performed by *amour de soi,* is assumed by otherness and by the outside world, and reflexivity develops in proportion to the number and intensity of social exchanges.

Consciousness makes itself external; it goes out into the public sphere; it experiences *social ecstasy and estrangement*: "The Savage lives within himself; *sociable man, always outside himself.*"[10] And while the *I* first gains awareness of having an appearingness, inside itself it conceives of *amour-propre*, the narcissistic desire to see its appearance reflected positively in the consciousnesses of other human beings. (In other words, vanity cannot be defined as a feeling; the fact that it passes through the mediation of an image implies a reflexive attitude.) In order to make a good impression on others, to cut a fine *figure* for itself, consciousness then throws itself into the fight for recognition: it opposes rival consciousnesses in a relentless competition, which takes place before an audience of judging spectators. Social esteem will be equivalent to the conquest of status, of a place in the sun in public life:

> Everyone began to look at everyone else and to wish to be looked at himself, and public esteem acquired a price. The one who sang or danced best; the handsomest, the strongest, the most skillful, or the most eloquent came to be the most highly regarded, and this was the first step at once toward inequality and vice: from these first preferences arose vanity and contempt on the one hand, shame and envy on the other; and the fermentation caused by these new leavens eventually produced compounds fatal to happiness and innocence.[11]

For the *I*, this experience is the loss of innocence: all the passions of rivalry, opportunism, glorification, and the pursuit of prestige will derive from this reflexive turn of subjectivity, which Rousseau compares to the opening of Pandora's box.[12] In the narrative structure of the *Discourse*, this turning point performs the role of a secularized original sin. For the community, it is the beginning of the degeneration of morals but, more than anything, it inaugurates the *social institution of sensible appearances*, the formation of a homogeneous space of images that are perceived and recognized by everyone: "publicity." The dividing up of this space will be at the origin of the first hierarchies of the symbolic order.[13] Human beings who lived in a sort of immediate and unaware uniformity in the state of nature, who perceived themselves as equal and indistinguishable from one another, now become classified by social opinion in order of importance, according to their success and prestige. Their rank depends on the social evaluation of the public image, on the way the individual's *figure* is perceived and appreciated by the spectators, whose taste is far from being disinterested—mostly it is arbitrary or subject to strategies of power and the logics of opportunism and distinction, such as fashions. And this is how the apparently inoffensive game of social appearances leads to the scandal of inequality: all the economic, legal, and political disasters of social life will develop with an avalanche effect from a problem of an aesthetic nature—*Which social image is more seductive? Who makes the best impression and is the most powerful in the public sphere?*[14]

The Invention of Authenticity

The *Discourse on Inequality* should always be read in parallel with the essential text that complements it: Rousseau's harangue against shows and the theater, formulated in the *Lettre à M. d'Alembert sur les spectacles* (*Letter to M. d'Alembert on Theater*, 1758). The following passage from the letter rails against the actor's craft, but it can also be read as a criticism of the *homme social*: "An actor on the stage, displaying other sentiments than his own, saying only what he is made to say, often representing a chimerical being, *annihilates himself*, as it were, and is lost in his hero."[15] Apart from denouncing individual alienation, Rousseau also highlights the simulative, seductive, and agonistic mechanisms by which the "Society of Spectacle" works and is perpetuated. In order to create a positive image in the eyes of others, individuals will go so far as to deceive and betray one another, multiplying strategies of flattery toward the public: they live steeped in hypocrisy and pretense. This description is the same as that of Hobbes's state of nature—a state torn apart by the passions of vanity and by the struggle to capture an ephemeral moment of glory in the show of social appearances. But in contrast to Hobbes, with a philosophically decisive gesture, Rousseau transposes the kingdom of Vanity Fair from the state of nature to the civil state, bringing social theory back under a theological-moral paradigm: submerged in the illusion of false worldly appearances, human beings do not live by nature due to a universal, innate vanity; the fault lies rather with a perversion of history—the "sin" of reflexive narcissism that arose during the socialization process. Although Rousseau also alternates in his various works between an explanation that attributes the evil to specific material factors in the historical experience of the modern age—such as private property, the division of labor, and economic inequality—his social anthropology remains profoundly Christian, since he attributes original sin to the vice of vanity. In other words, evil arose from the same pride that led to Lucifer's downfall and to that of Adam after him, and that Augustine considered to be the most unforgivable sin.[16]

Rousseau's analysis does not stop at the act of describing and demystifying, though. As the last of the modern moralists, Rousseau was also the first of the romantics, and the epoch-making condemnation he issued against spectacle—understood in the double meaning of sociological category and artistic genre, form of life and form of art—is founded on what is perhaps the most peculiar value of romantic culture and thought: the value of authenticity.[17] To save ourselves from society, which forces us to perform as actors in a theatrical setting, we must have the courage to come back to ourselves; we must learn to live according to our spontaneous feelings rather than by catering to the taste of spectators. Authenticity, as in being at one with our deepest nature, becomes the counterconcept of alienation. This pair of values—articulated in a philosophy of history that opposes decadence to redemption—is what enabled romantic social critics to frame their denunciation. The *I*, which came outside itself in order to expose itself in the public sphere, is distorted and "annihilated" and must now retreat back inside itself: be yourself (warns the romantic), forget your social image, despise it even, reject it as different from you, as if it were not even your own image, and do not worry about how others see you and judge you—close your eyes and forget that you are on stage in the social theater. The Augustinian warning *Noli foras ire, in te ipsum redi* (Do not seek to go outside yourself, the truth dwells within) continues to resound in romantic authenticity. This normative ideal has such a strong influence on Rousseau's judgment that it prevents him from accepting the hypothesis that representation and spectacularity are not so much pathologies of an alienated communication as they are constitutive and inescapable aspects of living with others.

Rousseau's thought offers a still relevant diagnosis of the psychological mechanisms of performance, of competitive society, and of the fragmentation that the modern social experience inflicts on subjectivity. But, despite its modernity, his system continues to rest on the archaic structure of the

Platonic-Christian paradigm: its foundation is the metaphysics of two worlds, which opposes authentic, stable, and profound beingness to inauthentic, vain, and superficial appearingness, to which is grafted a conception of history founded on a secularized version of the theological fall. Rousseau inherits many of these themes from the Augustinian tradition that was brought to the fore in France by Jansenism. In Rousseau's theory of social appearance it is easy to recognize the ontological dualism of Pascal and his condemnation of vanity, which is inseparable from a mythical-religious vision of the origins of evil. It is summed up in these extraordinary thoughts from *Pensées*: "We are not satisfied with the life we have in ourselves and in our own being: we want to lead an imaginary life in the minds of other people, and so we make an effort to impress [*paraître*]. We constantly strive to embellish and preserve our imaginary being, and neglect the real one." Also: "And so human life is nothing but a perpetual illusion; there is nothing but mutual deception and flattery. No one talks about us in our presence as they do in our absence. Human relationships are founded only on this mutual deception."[18]

This immense theological and metaphysical legacy imposes a series of axiologies on Rousseau's system, in the areas of morals and aesthetics. Nature is the realm of authentic being and life, where immediate and sincere communication reigns; authenticity is valued in proportion to the proximity to nature and the degree of immediacy of relations; society is the realm of alienating appearances, in which opacity, deception, and falsehood dominate. In fully developed civil life, human beings relate to one another only through masks, which falsify the truth of inner feelings and betray the sincerity of communication.

With a revealing choice, starting from his first *Discourse*, Rousseau addresses the concept of *art* in a polemical tone: art is the artifice that enables us to manipulate sensible appearances in order to produce and reinforce the social illusion. Recognizable in his polemical definition is the morality of *honnêteté*, a "substitutive morality," according to Jean Starobinski's insightful take on it, which moralists like La Rochefoucauld opposed to the negative anthropology of *amour-propre* and universal vanity.[19] From this perspective, although human beings are corrupt by nature and powerless to act in line with Christian virtues, there remains the possibility of artificially re-creating a harmonious intercourse of pleasing appearances. While it is useless to attempt to abolish appearances, they can always be played with and transfigured to create the same taste and the same *style* of life and thought within a close-knit community: an artificial "second nature" in which the aesthetic values of elegance, refinement, and courtesy are substituted for moral values, and the sought-after normative ideal is a synthesis of nature and artifice. This is the idea that Rousseau forcefully rejects in favor of a different conception of morality. All the arts come under his condemnation because, by definition, they are practices that transform the "natural": from the metaphysical point of view, art is guilty simply for being artificial, for not being nature. But the most suspect of all the arts, owing to its effects on communication, is the "art of pleasing," the art of seducing by appearing, which includes, for example, the artifices of rhetoric, fashion, etiquette, and courtesies: "Before *Art had fashioned our manners* and taught our passions to speak in ready-made terms, our morals were rustic but natural; and differences in conduct conveyed differences of character at first glance. Human nature was, at bottom, no better. But *men found their security in how easily they saw through one another.*"[20] Well-turned phrases, codes of elegance and presentation of self, good manners, worldly formalities, the duties of civility, all the diplomatic mediations that promise to bring human beings closer to one another, to seduce and not offend and wound them in the image they have of themselves, are in reality obstacles that act as buffers. They are barriers that make impossible communicative *transparency*—the "seeing through one another," which, according to Rousseau, is the only thing guaranteeing mutual trust and, through it, the development of the social virtues: "*One no longer dares to appear what one is. One will thus never really know with whom one is dealing.* What a train of vices must attend upon such uncertainty. No more sincere friendship; no more real esteem; no more well founded trust. Suspicions, offenses, fears, coolness, reserve, hatred, betrayal, will constantly hide beneath this event and deceitful veil of politeness, beneath this so much vaunted urbanity which we owe to the enlightenment of our century."[21]

Against the backdrop of an idea of decadence charged with religious values and a poignant regret for a lost immediacy, by problematizing the issue of appearingness in metaphysical terms, this is how Rousseau founded the *romantic approach to social philosophy*. With varying arguments but a constant inspiration, it has continued to resurface up until our own century. Faced with the *illusio* of the social game, with its artificial, spectacular, and representative dimension, and faced with its system of mediations, distances, and vanities, romantics (existentialists, situationists, spontaneists) immediately think in terms of true or false, good or bad faith, sincerity or falsehood, origin and fall, nature and artifice, face and mask, nudity and veil, transparency and obstacle, *authenticity and alienation*. And since the first term of these oppositions is always positive by virtue of its proximity to the guiding values of origin and nature, their social philosophy results in a moral indictment. The goal of romantic criticism is to restore the immediacy compromised by artifice, on the fronts of both individual and collective life: eliminate appearances, take off our masks, and abandon the medial role of images, in the name of transparency and honesty with oneself and others.[22] Under the guidance of the value of authenticity, the romantic pursues the innocence of the original life, oscillating perpetually between the two poles of rebellious individualism: the myth of the "beautiful soul" and that of radical communitarianism. While the romantic's longing sways between two ideal goals that are irreconcilable (one must choose between the human being and the citizen, between loneliness and the organic community), her contempt focuses on a single target: society as a system of mediations, which are not only economic and political (the market, money, political representation) but also *aesthetic*. The romantic condemns all forms of exchange in which images intervene, as medial surfaces, in the contact between subjects of society.

The romantic critic takes aim at the heart of "worldliness," inside of which Rousseauian romanticism was actually born and where it developed its virulent, reactive protest. As Norbert Elias realized, rebellion in the name of spontaneity and individual originality can also be explained historically as a reaction to the superfetation of ceremonies, forms, and other social mediations in the court and "salon" society.[23] The worldly sphere is the domain of sociability where the game of images is conspicuous and blatant, the distance between subjects can never be eliminated, and people relate to one another in full awareness of publicity, artificiality, and the representative nature of communication. The romantic hostility toward mediation—toward "what separates and is artificial," to use the words of Helmuth Plessner, someone who has always shown a diffidence toward immediacy equal only to that of Hegel or Derrida—will always arouse the desire to annihilate the obstacle and return to nature. But this romantic temptation does not take into account the paradox by which *the only possible "nature of the social" consists precisely in artifice.* I will thus close this first chapter of criticism of social romanticism with a phrase from Plessner's *Limits of the Community*. His words were originally addressed to rising political radicalism in Weimar Germany but we can also imagine them being directed against Rousseau's cult of authenticity: "belonging to the basic character of societal ethos is a longing for the mask behind which all immediacy disappears."[24]

8
AGAINST THE SPECTACLE

The Crusade of Romantic Anticapitalism

Debord: The Pathology of Appearances

"The spectacle is not a collection of images; rather, it is a social relationship between people that is mediated by images": the fourth aphorism of *The Society of the Spectacle*, published in 1967, paraphrases Marx's well-known analysis of commodities in *Capital*.[1] With this analogy, which would become the leitmotiv of his entire work, Debord gave life to the most important form of contemporary social romanticism. Its specificity lies in its grafting of the Rousseauian moral metaphysics of transparency and authenticity onto the Marxian critique of capitalism. This synthesis, which blends the two most powerful critical paradigms of modernity, is an ideal embodiment of the contemporary "pathological" approach to the issue of social appearances. It proceeds by mobilizing a whole arsenal of polemical arguments, both ancient and modern: the atavistic Platonic–Christian condemnation of the mask fuses with the "absolument moderne" suspicion of the market, media, and phenomena of consumption. And the spectacle, which is equivalent in Debord's view to *the mask of commodities*, becomes the principle of falsehood and universal corruption: a sort of monstrous polemical idol or radical evil from which all the distortions of contemporary life derive. Partly owing to this layered rootedness in the moral and political imagination of the West and to its evocative power, Debord's work is an obligatory reference point for examining the peculiar relationship that capitalist society entertains with appearances. For this reason, it deserves careful and thorough review.

It bears stating from the outset that a philosophical reading, such as what I offer here, does no justice to the work of Debord, whose thought takes the form of great avant-garde art. When the ideas of *The Society of the Spectacle* are stripped to the bare bones of their arguments and deprived of the defamiliarizing effects created by Situationist montage and an extremely seductive rhetoric (one of the distinguishing features of Debord's style is the striking contrast he creates by expressing brutal content in a language of classic eloquence and elegance), they lose much of their poignancy. And perhaps some of their persuasive power, too. A "theoretical" approach also makes itself vulnerable to the accusation of depoliticizing Debord's discourse, by neutralizing the primacy of praxis on which he insisted. He did this by choosing to define himself as a "strategist" instead of as a philosopher, for example, and by proclaiming his revolutionary vocation with an appeal to number eleven of the *Theses on Feuerbach*: "For obviously no *idea* could transcend the spectacle that exists—it could only transcend ideas that exist about the spectacle" (§203).

The perspective we take here is unavoidable, however, if our aim is to refound a new theory of social appearances that is not only philosophically solid but also politically responsible. *The Society of the Spectacle* is still intriguing from many points of view, beginning with the way it took the Marxist paradigm in a novel direction, toward the superstructure, in order to demonstrate that "the social-aesthetic question" plays an increasingly important role in the historical evolution of capitalism. In the late 1960s, when French society was undergoing the huge transformation of the postwar period, Debord had the prophetic insight to alert social criticism to a series of phenomena that an orthodox follower of historical materialism would have viewed as ephemeral and secondary; he also recognized that these phenomena were deeply allied, despite their apparent dispersion and heterogeneity. These included advertising, television and other media (ever more present in the lives of individuals), the star system, journalism and communications, the entertainment and leisure industries, the culture of commerce, cinema, tourism, architecture, and urbanism: the sphere of sensible appearance was assuming unprecedented proportions and proving to be the new barycenter of social life. Debord gives a unique name to this sphere—"the spectacle"—and reveals a systemic logic behind it, a coordinated and strategic movement of the new capitalist economy that constitutes its secret machinery. If Debord's analysis shows an affinity with social aesthetics in its desire to reexamine the dimension of appearances from a general perspective and attempt to understand the latter's principles and dynamics, it diverges from it because of its dual will to reduction. On the one hand, by replicating the Platonic-Christian-romantic gesture, he unmasks appearance and diminishes it, viewing it as a simple derivative of the profound substance of the real, thereby reproducing the theory of two worlds and rekindling the Christian-Rousseauian myth of authenticity. On the other hand, using the scissors of the reductionist materialist in the context of the capitalist regime, he denies any autonomy to the sensible dimension by making aesthetics the simple ideological instrument of the economy. The pathos of demystification ends up dissolving the same aesthetic–social sphere that the eye of Debord, as observer, had perceived so acutely.

History, Alienation, Commodity: Longing for the Authentic

Let us piece together the argumentative structure of *The Society of the Spectacle*—the series of theses that Debord uses to explain both how the capitalist spectacle originated and functions and the necessity of critiquing it. His thought can be summed up in three fundamental theoretical assumptions.

1. The point of departure is an epochal historical diagnosis of the state of capitalism and its destiny. Debord refers openly to Marx's critique of political economy and philosophy of history—a humanist, dialectical Marx, read through Lukács's *History and Class Consciousness*, whose Hegelian roots are fiercely asserted against French structuralist-type interpretations such as Althusser's.[2] The original aspect of this reading of Marxism is that the analysis of capital is transplanted into a metaphysical framework that is remote from the framework of historical materialism and in many ways in contradiction with its foundations. Indeed, Debord

adopts a dualistic ontology, traceable to Rousseau (and therefore indirectly to the French moralists and even to Plato), founded on a drastic separation between two spheres of reality: an authentic one of being and an illusory one of sensible appearance. In this mix of Hegelian Marxism and social romanticism, the society of the spectacle is defined as the last evolutionary stage of bourgeois–capitalist society, during which a growing ontological process of degradation comes to completion. From an earlier era of *being* (the stage of full ontology, which Debord also defines as "real life"), passing through an era of *having* (the stage of materialistic ontology, in which reality is reified as an object of exchange and consumption, as a "commodity"), we arrive at an era of *appearance* (the stage of spectacular ontology, of reality as "image"). This progressive process of derealization runs parallel to an impoverishment of human beings' cognitive and moral potential. Accordingly, the form of knowledge that dominates in the spectacular era is *doxa*, ideology that passes appearance off as reality by distorting the truth of things and whose purpose is not to understand the world but to legitimize its only existing form: its cannot-be-otherwise. For the individual, all this translates into the loss of experience, into the impossibility of living an authentic life and of deriving some meaning or a feeling of satisfaction or fullness from it: "All that once was directly lived has become mere representation" (§1).

It should be noted that the Rousseauian, romantic emphasis on the immediacy of lived experience in Debord's text is opposed to the negativity of representational mediation (a mediation, as we know, that is an indispensable principle of social aesthetics). Following the degradation on the plane of being as well as on the plane of knowing and experiencing, the spectacle looms as the terminal stage of civilization's fatal disease. Both the tones and the content of Debord's prophecy seem to be taken directly out of Rousseau's *Discourses*:

> The first stage of the economy's domination of social life brought about an evident degradation of being into having—human fulfillment was no longer equated with what one was, but with what one possessed. The present stage, in which social life has become completely dominated by the accumulated productions of the economy, is bringing about a general shift from having to appearing—all "having" must now derive its immediate prestige and its ultimate purpose from appearances. At the same

time all individual reality has become social, in the sense that it is shaped by social forces and is directly dependent on them. Individual reality is allowed to appear only if it is not actually real. (§17)

2. This leads us to the second theoretical pillar of *The Society of the Spectacle*, the concept of alienation. Like Rousseau, Debord, too, is compelled to rely on what Paul Ricoeur has brilliantly defined as "modernity's hospital-word,"[3] the seemingly obligatory keystone of any social or existential analysis that views itself as "critical," whose aim, that is, is to denounce social pathologies. This is indicated by a quotation from the *Essence of Christianity* by Feuerbach, which serves as an epigraph to the work: "But certainly for the present age, which prefers the sign to the thing signified, the copy to the original, representation to reality, the appearance to the essence, ... illusion only is sacred, truth profane. Nay, sacredness is held to be enhanced in proportion as truth decreases and illusion increases, so that the highest degree of illusion comes to be the highest degree of sacredness." The role that the concept of *spectacle* plays in Debord's theory is the same as that played by *religion* in Feuerbach. It is the domain in which humankind estranges all its best and highest qualities, its dreams of redemption and happiness. The spectacle is the mirror in which human beings who live in the era of capitalism represent themselves and contemplate their own sublimated image, without realizing, however, that it is an upside-down image, which diabolically escapes their control, to the point of enslaving them. In Debord's view, the example par excellence of this illusion is the media worship of celebrities. Stars, like the gods of Olympus, are "total" false personalities: onto them are projected all the perfections of which the miserable earthly existence of real individuals is deprived.

As in every romantic critique, the reverse side of the concept of alienation is that of authenticity—the way of being of those who are still at home with themselves, still close to uncorrupted nature and faithful to the origin: a life lived in harmony with the essence; a life that is still ontologically full, cognitively true, and morally intact. The condemnation of the society of spectacle thus appeals to the existence of a mysterious "real life," a life evoked by Debord through a hazy, epiphanic memory that provokes surges of nostalgic yearning. This mirage of the authentic life provides the yardstick for social criticism and is at the same time the origin and goal of the philosophy of history: this mythical origin began to be corrupted with the rise of capitalism, only to be definitively lost with the advent of the society of the spectacle. A coveted mecca, it acts as a magnet for those who still reject the existing world and who find the pathos they need to attempt a revolt in the flashes of memory that conjure up an age of innocence. Melancholy nostalgia is thus converted into a desire for rebellion and revolutionary hope. The tension between these two normative poles, between the alienation of the false spectacular life and the integrity of lost innocence, is what holds Debord's condemnation together and ensures the unity of his thought and his symbolic system.

The authenticity-alienation opposition is well exemplified by the complementarity of Debord's two most important films. The theme of the first, *La société du spectacle* (1973), which was inspired by the book of 1967, is a critique of alienation. The second, *In girum imus nocte et consumimur igni* ("We wander in the night and are consumed by the fire," 1978), is a memorial that combines the condemnation of spectacular society, presented with the usual montage of dismal images of the capitalist form of life, with a series of snapshots of authentic life, whose appearances create the effect of poignant epiphanies of happiness. They include stills taken from other films using the technique of *détournement*, autobiographical documents and memories of the 1950s, and, most notably, a long and beautiful sequence of the Fondamenta of Venice filmed from a moving boat. The intensely romantic tone of the film is evident in passages like the following, which describes the lost Paris as an idealized cradle of youthful rebellion: "When they lived in their own city, no one would have dared to make them eat or drink the sort of products that the chemistry of adulteration had not yet dared to invent.... Governmental corruption had not yet darkened the clear sky with the artificial fog of pollution which now permanently blankets the mechanical circulation of things in this vale of desolation. The trees were not yet dead from suffocation; the stars were not yet extinguished by the progress of alienation."[4] Its lyricism recalls the revolt of the English romantics against modernity, comparable, for example, with the imagination of William Blake, with whom Debord shares an anti-industrial polemic and a messianic view of history.[5] But the romantic interpretation is already suggested by the title of the film, in the solution of the riddle contained in the Latin palindrome: the creatures that live at night and are consumed by fire are moths, whose ephemeral but passionate existence is a metaphor for the scorched youth of the revolutionaries: "Midway on the journey of real life we found ourselves surrounded by a somber melancholy, reflected by so much sad banter in the cafés of lost youth."[6] In commenting on this work, whose piercing romanticism probably makes it Debord's masterpiece, he has said that "The theme of the film is not spectacle but, on the contrary, real life."

3. The third theoretical principle of *The Society of the Spectacle* is the concept of commodity, defined with Lukács as the "universal category of social being": "The spectacle corresponds to the historical moment at which the commodity completes its *colonization* of social life" (§42). Debord interprets commodity fetishism as the first social spectacularization, founded on the rise of exchange value at the expense of use value: in other words, on a surreptitious inversion between the authentic value of things and their apparent value. In the system of capitalist production, the object produced by human labor is idolized *not for what it is but for what it represents*; this is the paradigm of substituting the image for the thing and the copy for the original in which every process of alienation consists. The critique of commodities has a clearly dualistic foundation and lends a Manichean rigidity to Debord's interpretation: use value, which is natural, is expressed in the qualitative dimension of utility (the primacy of praxis) and corresponds to the "real" needs of human beings; exchange value, which is artificial, because it is produced socially and inflated by the market, is quantitative and fallacious. Everything produced by spectacle only replicates this original axiological inversion: "Exchange value could only have arisen as the proxy of use value, but the victory it eventually won with its own weapons created the preconditions for its establishment as an autonomous power. By activating for human use value and monopolizing that value's fulfillment, exchange value eventually gained the upper hand. The process of exchange became indistinguishable from any conceivable utility, thereby placing use value at its mercy. Starting out as the condottiere of use value, exchange value ended up waging a war that was entirely its own" (§46).

Debord's theoretical gesture, later adopted by Giorgio Agamben, is summed up by the Italian thinker as follows: "The 'becoming-image' of capital is nothing more than the commodity's last metamorphosis, in which exchange value has completely eclipsed use value and can now achieve the status of absolute and irresponsible sovereignty over life in its entirety, after having falsified the entire social production."[7]

Agamben: From Spectacle to Glory

It is enlightening to reread Debord through the interpretation Agamben offers of him throughout the *Homo Sacer* series. Inspired by Heideggerian philosophy, Agamben's reading sacrifices what remained of the debt that *The Society of the Spectacle* still owed to the Marxian and Lukácsian tradition—historicism, materialism, and especially faith in the proletariat as the historical subject of the revolution—to arrive at an even more exaggerated philosophical and political romanticism (and idealism). In order to grasp the reasons for this radicalization, it should be noted that in addition to the theory that explains the production of image through value and defines spectacle through the concept of commodity fetishism (reinterpreted through Benjamin),[8] Agamben inherits a principle from Debord: that of casting the subjugation of the society of spectacle as the effect of an omnipresent systemic and strategic plan. From this point of view, Debord's approach can be compared to that of thinkers inspired by the Frankfurt School or by Foucault, according to whom every ideological production is maneuvered occultly by instrumental reason and power. In the wings of the society of the spectacle there would be concealed a "machine"—a machine like the one in *Dialectic of Enlightenment*, which Adorno and Horkheimer attributed to the culture industry, on the basis of the continuity between totalitarianism and capitalism. In 1967 Debord, too, argued that liberal-democratic *doxa* was structured similarly to totalitarian propaganda: the *concentrated* spectacle rotates around the charismatic figure of the leader and disseminates a clear, complete ideology, orchestrated by the apparatuses of government that oversee the censorship and control of public opinion, while, in the *diffused* forms of spectacularity, public opinion, which only apparently circulates anarchically, is made to converge toward an impersonal and empty center by journalists, advertising, and communicators. This analogy becomes an actual equivalence thanks to the concept of *integrated spectacle*, which would be introduced in *Comments to the Society of the Spectacle* (1988). Debord's third paradigm, ideally represented by the media culture of France and Italy in the late 1980s, melds the Stalinist model with the American one:

> The integrated spectacle shows itself to be simultaneously concentrated and diffuse, and ever since the fruitful union of the two has learnt to employ both these qualities on a grander scale. Their former mode of application has changed considerably. As regards concentration, the controlling center has now become occult never to be occupied by a known leader, or clear ideology. And on the widespread side, the spectacle has never before put its mark to such a degree on almost the full range of socially produced behavior and objects.[9]

In contemporary democracies, the media and advertising only appear to be free from state control; in reality, they operate under the false mask of "consensus" and collaborate in the total colonization of the communicative sphere, giving rise to what Agamben, in *Means Without End* (1996), defines as "a global civil war" for "the control of appearance." The parts of Agamben that reinterpret Debord's prophecies in a Schmittian key, and in the light of the events following the fall of the Berlin Wall, are worth citing at length. In addition to forcefully reasserting the common identity of totalitarianism and democracy, which in ordinary thought are generally viewed as opposed to each other, and the "governmental" notion of power—the two topics that undergird his entire theoretical project—Agamben states openly what is at stake in a critique of social appearances and, more generally, in the relationship between aesthetics and politics. Appearances, he reminds us in the wake of Hannah Arendt, are the place of freedom, or, better yet (expressed in the language of Agamben), of pure "potentiality," the dimension in which human beings—who do not have a nature, an essence, or a specific destiny to realize—decide which "face" they will give to their communities:

> The task of politics is to return appearance itself to appearance, to cause appearance itself to appear. The face, truth, and exposition are today the objects of a global civil war, whose battlefield is social life in its entirety, whose storm troopers are the media, whose victims are all the peoples of the Earth. Politicians, the media establishment, and the advertising

industry have understood the insubstantial character of the face and of the community it opens up, and thus they transform it into a miserable secret that they must make sure to control at all costs. State power today is no longer founded on the monopoly of the legitimate use of violence—a monopoly that states share increasingly willingly with other nonsovereign organizations such as the United Nations and terrorist organizations; rather, it is founded above all on the control of appearance (of *doxa*). The fact that politics constitutes itself as an autonomous sphere goes hand in hand with the separation of the face in the world of spectacle—a world in which human communication is being separated from itself. Exposition thus transforms itself into a value that is accumulated in images and in the media, while a new class of bureaucrats jealously watches over its management.[10]

In *The Kingdom and the Glory* (2007) the theory of the spectacle is finally reformulated in historical and genealogical terms. The concept of glory allows Agamben to trace the origins of the government of *doxa* from a long-term perspective. In the Christian tradition of political theology and political economy, the function of the glorifying angelic hierarchies would be equivalent to that exercised by contemporary mediacrats and communicators, and the concept of *oikonomia* would illustrate the logic that bends the aesthetic dimension of appearance to that of economic administration. The totalitarian-capitalist interpretation on which *The Society of the Spectacle* was founded thus receives validation. However, its genealogy is made to stretch back well beyond the history of modern capitalism and the birth of the commodity-form, beyond which Debord did not dare to venture. Indeed, in Agamben's view the contemporary society of the spectacle has its origin in the concept of providence, which rules the world created by God, and on which the management of glorification depends.[11] In the ancestral temporality typical of Heidegger's philosophy, the alienation of the apparent "face," in which the political potential of human beings consists, ends up being lost in the mists of time immemorial. This makes its redemption impossible in any form that is not conceived in turn in a theological form: the inoperative wait for the messiah. And the myth of real life relinquishes any public and social dimension, to be embodied in the exemplarity of the individual—in the authenticity of private life, as the only genuinely political element able to resist the universal alienation. The last volume of *Homo Sacer*, *The Use of Bodies* (2014), opens accordingly with a panegyric of the exemplary life of "Guy," in which, between more or less intentional references to the Gospel and Rousseau's *Confessions*, all the Christian romantic motifs are joined together in one seamless convergence.

Debord's Iconoclasm

Let us take stock, then, of *The Society of the Spectacle*. By making the spectacle solely the product of the capitalist economy, maneuvered from above, Debord completely circumvents the anthropological foundations of a social aesthetics. He never asks whether society must rest on an imaginal dimension, whose *ordinary* reach must be established before launching into a condemnation of its *extraordinary* manifestations. The charm of romantic anticapitalism—which succeeds in combining the realism of the critique of political economy with the idealism of Plato, and the cynicism of demystification with the emotional appeal to transparency and authenticity of Rousseau—explains the success that his work still enjoys in contemporary critical theory: among his lapidary aphorisms can be found the most diverse and seemingly incompatible forms of radical revolt against the status quo. However, from the theoretical and practical points of view, the paradigm has ceased to be fruitful, as demonstrated by its inability to offer satisfying analyses of the social-aesthetic processes at work today. Neither the stark opposition between being and appearing nor the demonization of commodities and consumption nor a philosophy of history that replicates the Christian schema by nourishing itself on regret for a lost paradise and a messianic eschatology can explain our relationship with social appearances and contribute properly to their "critique."

The theory of totalitarian power especially leads Debord to overlook the spectacularity that is always implicit in the dynamics of visibility, communication, and recognition, which permeate everyday life. Although this spectacularity is not immune to strategic aims and to the constant risk of deviation (that "drift" we saw going back to the principle of eccentric positionality and to the logic of the separation and autonomization of the image, which the individual perceives as a "tragedy" but which, in reality, is an inescapable social law), it is never entirely controlled by a "government." In the images that every social interaction necessarily produces and that every act of communication necessarily causes to circulate in the public space, Debord sees only lies—fabrications constructed and maneuvered in secret to mask, betray, and alienate the *vie réelle* (real life). The spectacle is created by occult powers to deceive the gullible, passive masses: here we have the old thesis of *religio instrumentum regni*, religion as an instrument of government, readapted to the new capitalist "religion" of spectacularity.

Debord's polemic does not spare any invectives against the social danger of the gaze. In it can be discerned echoes of Lukács (the rise of a contemplative attitude at the expense of a praxis is seen as a symptom of the reified culture) and of Heidegger (in the "era of the image of the world," vision is said to prevail over the other senses, imposing its objectifying and representational conception on every aspect of life). Similarly, in Debord the society of the spectacle has substituted sight, the faculty of undue abstraction, mediated representation, and derealization, for touch—the sense, he says, through which a direct, unmediated relationship with things is conveyed. Watching means keeping oneself at a distance, accepting the world as if it were governed by laws that are natural and immutable, not created by historical human practices. It also means not participating in the concreteness of life: *contemplating so as to not act*. Accentuated by Debord's hyperbolic rhetoric, these simplifications end up working against the fruitfulness of his own phenomenological insights and prove to be equally inadequate to judge past and present. If history teaches us that the contemporary form of life is not the only one to have produced a high degree of spectacle, and thus invites us to try out an anthropological approach, comparing ancient and modern, Western and non-Western social aesthetics (as will be suggested at the beginning of part 3 of this book), it is also clear that the contemporary form of experience has instituted a relationship with images that is too intense and structural to accept an analysis that dismisses the eye in the name of a return to the primacy of the hand.[12]

Here we cross paths with the criticism that Jacques Rancière formulated against *The Society of the Spectacle* when he rejected its binary system of oppositions: to watch versus to know, appearance versus reality, and passivity versus activity. In Rancière's view, Debord's theory is "nondemocratic," because it is founded on an asymmetric division of roles and relationships of distribution and transmission of knowledge. More specifically, it would violate the principle of equality of intelligences, consequently lapsing into the ontological dualism of Plato and beyond, into the political elitism that necessarily follows from such a dualism. Debord's spectators are passive, unaware of their ignorance, and incapable of grasping the truth that lies hidden behind the veil of appearances. They are incapable of being anything other than stupid consumers:

> The situation of those who live in the society of the spectacle is thus identical to that of the shackled prisoners in Plato's cave. The cave is the place where images are taken for realities, ignorance for knowledge, and poverty for wealth. And the more the prisoners imagine themselves capable of constructing their individual and collective lives differently, the more they sink into the servitude of the cave. But this declaration of impotence rebounds on the science that it proclaims. To know the law of the spectacle comes down to knowing the way in which it endlessly reproduces the falsification that is identical to its reality.[13]

The perspective that I propose in this book intersects Rancière's at several points. However, there is one crucial aspect that distinguishes my path from his: what I criticize about Debord is primarily his *inability to adequately conceive of the specific "logic" of social appearances and their grounding in the intersubjective anthropological experience*. To make the critique of the spectacle truly effective, it is not so much a more edifying a priori conception of human abilities that is required but rather a more accurate and dispassionate analysis of the sensible dimension of shared life. Only a profound understanding of the social-aesthetic complex allows us to identify the locus and real workings of the "eccentric" mechanism that separates images from lived life. Moreover, by shifting the locus, we acquire the capacity to demystify the power of seduction that is exercised through the aesthetic dimension and to maximize its emancipatory potential, which in Debord's iconoclastic perspective is absolutely irretrievable.

I will return to these issues in part 3 of this book. In concluding this "critique of the critique" of spectacle by reflecting on the question of power, I will limit myself to one more remark. Instead of thinking about the problem solely *from above*, one should explain how and why the deluge of images that invades the social world is also produced *from below*, rising out of its human depths. In other words, what is needed for the slaves of Debord's cave is also a new presentation of the old problem of "voluntary servitude" formulated by Étienne de la Boétie: we need to understand why we love the spectacle that dominates us, and why human beings are unable to break the immaterial chains of appearances, despite their being so fragile and insubstantial. Deep down inside, human beings seem bound to these evanescent images; spectators seem to produce the spectacle on their own, at least to a certain extent, and even to drug or poison themselves with it.

The problem of manipulating appearances can no longer be framed in the unilateral way Debord and his followers view it—in terms of a "government of spectacle" or a "reign of glory" possessed with the means to bombard spectators with hypnotic phantasmagoria.[14] Undeniably, anyone interested in dominating others seeks to foster the production of spectacle, to control and direct it to her advantage; but this fostering and guiding action *always expresses itself in the immanent production of social images*. The docile material in which its props are sunk always lies in a sociability already saturated with appearances, a sociability so illusory and phantasmagorical that for centuries Christian moralism likened it to a vanity fair. (It is no coincidence that, like the neurotic symptom of a centuries-old repression, the expression resurfaces once more, in Debord's work: "What childish respect for images! This Vanity Fair is well suited to these plebeian spectators [*plèbe des vanités*].")[15] If this were not the case, the same complaints to be found in Debord would not also exist in Rousseau or Pascal. And yet, when these two writers were condemning the alienating inversion of being and appearing, the historical social form they had in mind was quite different from that of advanced capitalism.

As Siegfried Kracauer puts it, the magic of images takes hold of the masses from inside: it never drops in entirely unexpected and undesired; it is welcomed and produced by the social subjects themselves.[16] The key to interpreting this feedback loop between immanent production and instrumental direction for the purposes of domination might reside therefore in a concept of spectacle similar to the Freudian notion of compromise formation:[17] in it, *the action of power should be seen not solely as what exercises a repressive censure against the spontaneous demands of individuals but also as what contributes to actively producing them*. Instead of pursuing this line of thought, romantic anticapitalists continue to dally with the myth of a transparent society to which one might return once the universal alienation has been undone. Unable to accept mediation, representation, and artifice—the forms of alienation tied to the "eccentric" tendency that is implicit in the human condition—romantic anticapitalists yearn for an Edenic community always on the point of vaporizing into a New Age atmosphere, in which humanity exists in a world of integrity and presence to itself. This is a world where human beings show themselves in all their nudity without veils and masks, and instead of representing themselves in images, they communicate transparently and sincerely—it is a society that still resembles too closely the one fantasized by Rousseau: "They were not content to subsist on images."[18]

The fact is that no society can rid itself of images. Social appearances are inauthentic not only because, as in Plato's cave, someone or something projects them from behind our backs or above our heads but because a dose of spectacle—and therefore of *representation and fiction*—is built into the anthropological structure of any social exchange and nourishes any social body, even the groups smallest and closest to natural simplicity. To demonstrate his theory that social life is staged, Erving Goffman made the crucial move of not starting from an urban elite lifestyle. Instead, he began with the everyday life of a small island in the Shetlands—precisely the type of antimodern, precapitalist community that romantics like Rousseau would have praised in reaction to the alienating proliferation of social mediation and theatricality present in aristocratic courts and big cities. Before delving into the diagnosis of the "fatal disease" that supposedly augurs the end of humanity, let's take the path opened by Goffman and focus our attention on this unavoidable representational domain: *all forms* of social life are a spectacle. As a preliminary gesture to every critical inquiry, the analysis needs to be brought back to a neutral position. Let's do so by starting over with the fertile definition that begins Debord's diatribe: "The spectacle is not a collection of images; rather, it is a social relationship between people that is mediated by images."

9

AGAINST AESTHETIC VALUES

Aestheticism, Aestheticization, and Staging

Aesthetic Values, Moral Vices

Having examined and critiqued the main theoretical arguments and obstacles that stand in the way of properly framing a theory of social appearances—a path that will lead us to the threshold of a social aesthetics—it now behooves us to pause on the question of "aestheticism" and "aestheticization." Used often, and often glibly, in current discussions, these terms allude to the negativity that some conventional wisdom bears toward the social assertion of aesthetic values. These prejudices are traceable to two distinct thought traditions. The first has become synonymous with the name of the artistic and literary movement that recognizes Walter Pater and Oscar Wilde as its founders. "Aestheticism" negatively identifies individuals or groups who pursue "the aesthetic life"—a life dedicated to the cult of sensual pleasures and to seeking intense, sophisticated sensations and formal qualities. This is the vice afflicting those who are dedicated to superfluous beauty, who put futile things before necessary ones and their own selfish satisfaction over the common good. "Aestheticization," on the other hand, is not a subjective behavior; rather it is a social process of distortion and corruption that affects areas of life and knowledge considered, by definition, to be "nonaesthetic," such as politics, religion, or morals. When the aestheticization of politics or everyday life is denounced, what is being referred to is a transformation like the undue "becoming-image" that Guy Debord attributes to the phenomenon of commodities, since it stimulates the exchange value to absorb and pervert the use value. Consequently, as in Debord, the hidden precondition in the idea of aestheticization is the opposition between authentic and inauthentic, and then between integrity and alienation.

As different as the two concepts are, they share a polemical attitude to the aesthetic domain, which is made responsible for an axiological and, before that, ontological perversion. In the idea of *aestheticism*, the aesthetic sphere is viewed as something outside society. While promising individuals a concrete good—that is, an enhanced experience of the senses and their pleasure—it is said in fact to impoverish and empty them of authentic values: aesthetes live immersed in the illusion of appearances and are consequently estranged from reality. The concept of *aestheticization* always alludes to a separation between reality and fiction, but aesthetic value is also conceived of as socially invasive, as an excess or surplus that infiltrates the shared world until saturating it. Because of the pervasiveness of its effects, the aesthetic exerts an easily recognizable power. It creates a sort of second reality within reality, a curtain of seductive appearances, which ultimately comes between the subject and the world and, hence, creates forms of idolatry—the worship of appearances rather than of authentic values.

Despite being anachronistic, inspired as it is by a naive form of moralism, the accusation of aestheticism is still surprisingly widespread among social theorists. And not only, as one might jump to the conclusion, from those who subscribe to a materialistic interpretation of Marxism and therefore define aesthetic purposelessness as the contrary par excellence of economic necessity: as the Latin saying goes, *carmina non dant panem* (poetry won't feed you). In actuality, some of the greatest thinkers on the relationship between aesthetics and society include philosophers who interpret Marxism and historical materialism from an aesthetic perspective strongly influenced by German idealism and the romantic conception of art: Lukács, Adorno, Benjamin (from a certain point of view), Ernst Bloch, and Marcuse did not hesitate to give art and, more generally, aesthetic experiences a prominent role in social life. They recognized the great power of artistic works for explaining historical and sociological phenomena and, since art is sensible manifestation of truth, they put art on a comparable or even higher plane than philosophy. Their problem, if anything, was that they fenced Great Art off from its ideological degenerations or simulacra. However, outside the German tradition there have also been attempts to positively rethink the relationship between aesthetics and society in the light of Marx. In the case of Jacques Rancière, the connection is not based so much on the Hegelian "truth value" of art but on the relationship that the aesthetic dimension (understood in the broad sense as a form of collective perception, of *social aisthesis*) entertains with the structure of the social world and its system of inequalities. Far from being a secondary moment in the superstructure of collective life, the "partage du sensible (the distribution of the sensible)" is the founding moment of the community's symbolic and material order: it establishes the a priori forms of collective life, the global perception of social space, and the division of the activities, roles, and tasks given to each person; it sets up the "police," who have a gatekeeping function, to defend the boundaries of the visible and the invisible and decide what may or may not be said, listened to, circulated, and imitated in public.[1] According to Rancière, whether the aesthetic attitude is creative or receptive, it has a primary role socially and politically, because each act of political affirmation or negation passes through the collective senses and perception by calling into question *the way the shared world appears*. The very words *aestheticism* and *aestheticization* actually lose any meaning according to his reasoning, since *politics is always, by definition, an aesthetic matter*. As Slavoj Žižek polemically asserts against those who associate the political use of aesthetics with the propaganda of totalitarian regimes, Rancière has the merit of showing "*the aestheticization of politics*, the assertion of the aesthetic dimension as INHERENT in any radical emancipatory politics."[2] This issue will be discussed at length in the pages to come.

Still, if the enemies of aesthetic values do not lurk in the Marxist tradition, where are they to be found? The most explicit and fierce indictment against the aesthetic that has been formulated in the history of social theory occurs in a passage from *The Division of Labour in Society* (1893) by Emile Durkheim, whose influence on twentieth-century French sociology has been enduring:

Art . . . remains entirely resistant to anything resembling an obligation, since its domain is one where freedom reigns. It is a luxury and an ornament that it may well be fine to possess, but that one cannot be compelled to acquire: what is a superfluity cannot be imposed upon people. By contrast, morality is the indispensable minimum, that which is strictly necessary, the daily bread without which societies cannot live. Art corresponds to the need we have to widen those of our activities that lack purpose, for the pleasure of doing so, whilst morality constrains us to follow a path laid down, one which leads towards a definite goal. He who speaks of obligation speaks at the same time of constraint. Thus, although art can draw inspiration from moral ideas or is to be found intermingled with the evolution of strictly moral phenomena, it is not moral in itself. Observation might even establish perhaps that, *with individuals as with societies, from the moral viewpoint the excessive development of the aesthetic faculties is a grave symptom*.[3]

These ideas of Durkheim are emblematic in many respects, starting with the way he opposes morality to aesthetics, on the basis of an implicitly Kantian distinction that opposes the useful to the beautiful and the necessary to the superfluous. Art can be considered a luxury and an ornament only if it is thought of as an activity free and devoid of purpose, completely liberated from "real" human needs. These needs are not defined by Durkheim according to a strictly economic criterion: they do include moral needs and thus avoid the crude anthropological hierarchy that distinguishes between things useful for material survival and the secondary needs of the spirit. However, extending the sphere of the necessary to that of the moral ultimately aggravates the accusation brought against aesthetic practices. They are deemed guilty of promoting individualism and anomie, as shown by the surprising assertion that the intensive development of aesthetic faculties would be a grave symptom of moral decadence. Obviously, these reflections of Durkheim need to be historicized because they are imbued with his contemporary culture and with the identification between *aestheticism* and *aesthetics* in Decadentism that was spreading during his time. In the spectrum of the lascivious aesthete—a social parasite who isolates himself from the community to devote himself to his selfish aesthetic enjoyment—it is easy to recognize the figure of Des Esseintes, the hero of *A Rebours*. Yet Durkheim's distrust toward aesthetic values is so rooted that it returns in an even more developed theoretical form, in his lectures on moral education, in which the arts are assigned the bottom ranking in the scale of subjects worthy of being taught in schools: "There is genuine opposition between art and ethics. Art, we maintain, makes us live in an imaginary environment. By this very fact it detaches us from reality, from the concrete beings—individual and collective—that compose it. People say, do they not, that the real service that art performs is to make us forget life as it is and men as they are? Quite the opposite, the world of morals is precisely the world of the real."[4]

Bourdieu's Prejudice

The shadow cast by Durkheim's words, as I was suggesting, has had an enduring influence on the character of social thought and has strongly hindered French acceptance of Simmel, for example, whose sociological aesthetics is still suspected of aestheticism, even by his most important and enthusiastic interpreters, and it continues to project itself onto contemporary sociology. Indeed, all of Pierre Bourdieu's work can be interpreted through its filter, even though at first glance his sociology of culture would seem to be diametrically opposed to Durkheim's antiaesthetic prohibitions. While the latter located the aesthetic domain *outside* society, attributing it to the anomie of a subjective illusion, Bourdieu brings it back into the social world, showing that aesthetic activities are not simply individualist evasions but collective practices. These practices are characteristic of the higher classes and necessary to their power dynamics, because they serve to conquer and consolidate the elite's social hegemony. This is how aesthetics became a central topic of sociology. *Distinction* (1979), Bourdieu's masterpiece of sociology of aesthetics, examines primarily the parallelism between aesthetic practices and economic practices, which leads him to demonstrate the universal "utility" of aesthetic values and the substantial convergence between aesthetics and economics. Following a path all his own, Bourdieu arrives at very similar conclusions to those of Debord or Agamben, by demonstrating complete identification between capitalist economy and aesthetic values: the struggle for symbolic distinction shows that, in the realm of appearance, specific weapons are used to wage the same type of battle that ignites the market and that economic value finds its most faithful and industrious ally in aesthetic value.[5] The crucial difference is that while for Debord and Agamben the spectacle, *doxa*, and glory are *historical* productions of a specific social form (advanced capitalism for Debord and the era of theological economics for the most recent Agamben), in Bourdieu's view, the subordination of aesthetic values to economic ones is a wider principle that applies to every form of society, even though it develops into different forms and combinations depending on historical circumstances. The economy of aesthetics, which in Bourdieu's language takes the revelatory names of "economy of symbolic goods" and fight for "symbolic capital," is equally applicable to the villages of Kabylia studied in *Outline of a Theory of Practice* (1972) and to the urban lounges of the upper-middle class that provide the backdrop for *Distinction*.

In Bourdieu's theory, especially in its first phase, the aesthetic domain is therefore completely absorbed into the utilitarian-economic domain according to an overarching functionalistic framework, which creates a strict hierarchy between human needs and practices. Economic reasoning conditions and dominates the secondary spheres in order to pursue its own ends while making use of their language and values: "A class is defined as much by its being-perceived as by its being, by its consumption—which need not be conspicuous in order to be symbolic—as much as by its position in the relations of production (*even if it is true that the latter governs the former*)."[6] Behind every social phenomenon there hides a demonstrable utility. Without exception, then, every aesthetic practice can be interpreted as a mask of the strategic function that is its true end: to conquer positions of power in the social field. It is clear once again that this approach, whose purpose is to demystify what "appears" socially, must have profound consequences on the plane of knowledge that studies the phenomenal realm: the entire aesthetic experience has been diminished, traced back to strategies of power, for which it serves as a powerful but obliging instrument. Nothing from the realm of appearances exists as an end in itself or can simply possess its own rationale. In his last works Bourdieu seems to have softened this rigid, functionalistic framework, placing at the center of his anthropology a drive that is no longer simply economic and that is more complex than strategic material interest: the need for recognition. The need for recognition has a more constitutive relationship with social appearances, insofar as it prompts human beings to seek confirmation of the legitimacy of their existence in relationships with others, and therefore to want their "social image" to be valued and taken into account in the public sphere:

> In fact, he [the child] is continuously led to take the point of view of others on himself, to adopt their point of view so as to discover and evaluate in advance how he will be seen and defined by them. *His being is a being-perceived, condemned to be defined as it "really" is by the perception of others.*
>
> Such might be the anthropological root of the ambiguity of symbolic capital—glory, honour, credit, reputation, fame—the principle of an egoistic quest for satisfactions of *amour propre* which is, at the same time, a fascinated pursuit of the approval of others: "The greatest baseness of man is the pursuit of glory. But it is also the greatest mark of his excellence; for whatever possessions he may have on earth, whatever health and essential comfort, he is not satisfied if he has not the esteem of men."[7]

In his later work, Bourdieu refers explicitly to French moralists, in particular to Pascal, and ends up adopting the modern, negative anthropology of vanity and glory. This greater opening toward the meaning of *esse est percipi* and the mechanism of the social *libido*, as well as toward the issues of the body and the imagination, leads him to place more attention on the specificity of the aesthetic logic of the social experience. Nevertheless, this shift is not sufficient to uproot the basic economic framework: Bourdieu's model remains in tension between two different anthropological models.

This is how the eighteenth-century paradigm on which Durkheim rested his criticism of aesthetic values was transcended although not wholly abandoned. What remains of the Kantian notion of aesthetics—its essential bond with freedom—merges in Bourdieu's work with his fundamental insights about Thorstein Veblen's *Theory of the Leisure Class* (1899) and Norbert Elias's theory of civilization, engendering an original idea. For Bourdieu, too, therefore, as for Kant and Durkheim, aesthetics is a *free activity*, but not in the sense that it is devoid of purpose, disinterested, useless, abstracted from the social world. Quite the contrary: aesthetics is free only in relation to its social conditions of possibility, as a privilege that rests on social inequality, because only superior social groups, who have eliminated the material concerns of life, can possess the leisure and free time needed to dedicate themselves to aesthetic activities. At the same time, aesthetic practices are necessary activities, without which the dominant class would be unable to pursue and capitalize on the symbols of its social recognition. The aesthetic remains a "Sunday" privilege—the day when the work of the social takes place predominantly on the plane of what Agamben would define as *glory*, meaning the celebration of the providential economic plane: aesthetic practices serve not only to establish the prestige of the dominant class but, more broadly, to legitimize and celebrate the symbolic and material order of society as a whole.

Bourdieu recognized the central role that aesthetics plays in sociology and social theory and hence opened the way toward a social aesthetics. Once the reductionist and functionalist aspects of his thought had been amended, he continued to be one of the chief moving forces in leading the way to the social-aesthetic approach I am proposing in this book. And yet, his attitude toward aesthetic values remained imbued with Durkheimian prejudices. This taboo is evident in the aversion Bourdieu betrays toward any type of formalism and toward the principles of pure art. Sensitivity to formal values, which he identifies with aesthetic values tout court, is condemned in *Distinction* as the domain where social truth is denied: "Here the sociologist finds himself in the area par excellence *of the denial of the social*."[8] Form exists and can be appreciated only in relation to other forms, in an oppositional-distinctive relationship: it lives in a symbolic world of structural cross-references that is void of content and, for this reason, alien and distant from reality. Reality, according to Bourdieu, would instead remain linked to other living content, such as emotions and ethical interests: "Everything takes place as if the emphasis on form could only be achieved by means of a neutralization of any kind of affective or ethical interest in the object of representation which accompanies (without any necessary cause-effect relations) mastery of the means of grasping the distinctive properties which this particular form takes on in its relations with other forms."[9] Once again, *the aesthetic coincides with aestheticism*, with abstraction from life, with the derealization of the social world. Not surprisingly, a still perfectly visible trace of Durkheim's moral prohibition can be found in many other passages, including the following: "The aestheticism which makes the artistic intention the basis of the 'art of living' implies a sort of moral agnosticism, the perfect antithesis of the ethical disposition which subordinates art to the values of the art of living."[10]

Before concluding this initial discussion on *Distinction*, however, it must be acknowledged that its interpretation of aestheticism is much more nuanced than Durkheim's. Durkheim goes no further than to condemn the immoralism of the phenomenon—its estrangement from collective values and the context of social solidarity. Bourdieu, on the other hand, from this perspective thinking along the lines of Simmel and, more than anyone, of Nietzsche, grasps perfectly the snobbish, aristocratic side of the aesthetic attitude: the *pathos of distance* and the discriminatory violence of taste can make aesthetic judgment an eminently elitist issue, intended for the elect few, and in this sense a practice of social distinction. In Bourdieu's notion of aesthetics, aestheticism is not simply the positive pursuit of sophisticated pleasures and the tendency toward *illusio*; it is above all *distancing*: a *gesture of negativity* and *radical separation*. Aesthetes are horrified by vulgarity and feel distaste for those who feel and judge differently. Whoever says, "I like" also says, "I don't like"; he or she socially discriminates, separates, and hierarchizes. As we will see further on, the secret of the connection between aesthetics and the social lies hidden in the solidarity between taste and distaste.

Aesthetic Capitalism

Some of the problems raised by the critique of aestheticism are also to be found in the other tradition, referred to as "aestheticization," best represented by the current in contemporary theory that occupies itself with "commodity aesthetics," "aesthetic economics," or "aesthetic capitalism."[11] All its exponents come together on a few common points: (1) they view the progressive and increasingly relentless predominance of aesthetic values as a typically contemporary phenomenon, owing to the expansion of commodity fetishism into all areas of life; (2) they link the end of the traditional distinction between high and low art to capitalistic commodification, too, in connection with the increasingly massive production of commercial art, which contributes to legitimizing the status quo by giving it an aura of pleasantness; (3) they see the multiplication of consumers' aesthetic needs as a form of alienation, which reveals an anthropological vulnerability that the new capitalism sinks its hooks into even more firmly in order to strengthen its dominion. On this basis, the critique of aesthetic capitalism views itself as a natural continuation of Frankfurt critical theory,[12] from which it salvages a few well-known basic concepts: in addition to the principle of commodity fetishism and the culture industry, a key notion is that of *the aestheticization of politics* (*Ästhetisierung der Politik*), which Benjamin formulated with regard to fascism in "The Work of Art in the Age of Its Technological Reproducibility" (1936). Today critics understand it as a principle of intelligibility for all areas of life that have been colonized by capitalism. This is what Benjamin wrote:

> Fascism attempts to organize the newly proletarianized masses while leaving intact the property relations which they strive to abolish. It sees its salvation in granting expression to the masses—but on no account granting them rights. The masses have a right to the changed property relations; fascism seeks to give them expression in keeping these relations unchanged. *The logical outcome of fascism is an aestheticizing of political life*. With D'Annunzio, decadence made its entry into political life; with Marinetti, Futurism; and with Hitler, the Bohemian tradition of Schwabing. *All efforts to aestheticize politics culminate in one point. That one point is war.*[13]

In Benjamin's view, fascist aestheticizing culminated in war (the event that allows total technological mobilization without changing property relations) and reached its ideal expression in D'Annunzianism and Futurist art. In the complaint of the critics of aesthetic capitalism, the target is the culture industry. Based on the by now familiar equivalence between capitalist ideology and totalitarian propaganda,[14] by controlling the media the culture industry would achieve the same aims as fascist dictatorship: to justify the status quo by allowing the masses to express themselves aesthetically; to enjoy themselves while being politically uncommitted; and to satisfy their false needs without calling into question the inequitable structure of social relations. Just as the Futurists gave an aura of glamour to war by proclaiming its beauty, contemporary mass media has done the same for entertainment and the seduction of the masses.

What characterizes this explanation of capitalist aestheticization, like Debord's idea of the spectacle, is that aesthetic value is conceived at the same time as an *added value* and as an *alienating dimension*: something that social life in its authentic, uncorrupted form would not contemplate; something that is inoculated in the social body like a harmful artificial additive; a "poison" and a "drug" causing a fatal separation between reality and fiction that also encourages the alienation of individuals from reality. (The implicit assumption of this way of thinking is always that of *religio instrumentum regni*, as in Debord, and of spectacle as the secularized equivalent of religion: just as the ancient Roman emperors used the spectacle of gladiator fights, the crypto-totalitarian government of commodities uses staging as a weapon of mass distraction.) In Gernot Böhme's explanation, which is the most sophisticated and adheres most closely to the peculiar logic of aesthetic processes, the Marxian criticism of commodity fetishism, founded on the rise of exchange value at the expense of use value, is supplemented with an important amendment: a third value, that of "staging" or "show" (*Inszenierungswert*), is introduced into the dichotomy between use value and exchange value. Initially produced as an offshoot of exchange value, in advanced capitalism staging value is said to have established itself as an independent, dominant value. In a market where the supply of goods exceeds demand and competition is increasingly unrestrained, commodities must be aestheticized, that is, made more attractive and desirable through specific cosmetic actions on their sensible appearance. This process of image enhancement through "aesthetic labor" gradually breaks free from the ancillary function it performs for exchange value, becoming independent and reflecting back on use value: the sensible form of the commodities is ultimately sought for the pleasure it provides and ends up stimulating the consumer to seek aesthetic value as an end in itself. What the aesthetic economy produces in this way cannot be defined as "functional" in the strictly utilitarian sense, but it does serve to enhance life through the pleasure of the senses. Individuals become progressively enslaved to the insatiability of their desire, according to the distinction that Böhme picks up from Bataille and Kojève between *finite needs* (which come to an end the instant they are fulfilled) and *infinite desires* (which grow exponentially along with their satisfaction).

Thus even Böhme's theory, which is more aesthetically aware than those of his colleagues, does not manage to avoid the romantic impasse. It presupposes that there is a natural dimension of value, that of finite needs anchored to the true usefulness of things, whose solid and healthy natural grounding would crumble if threatened by the potentially unlimited dynamic of aesthetic desire—a desire that creates something like an unstoppable "speculative bubble": "Equipment, radiance and conspicuousness have no natural limits. On the contrary, every upward step demands a yet higher one. And since growth is an essential feature of capitalism, at a certain step of development marked by the fundamental satisfaction of the needs of a population, capitalist production has to bet on desires if it is to develop further. In this way the economy becomes the aesthetic economy."[15] This explanation is not that different from Rousseau's in *Discourse on Inequality*, which is founded on a strict distinction between finite natural needs and infinite artificial needs. It also recalls the criticisms against the chrematistics of classical and Christian inspiration: the aestheticized image, like money, allows needs to be unpegged from the real and to invest in imagining and predicting the future, giving rise to the typically modern condition of "speculation" as a lack of foundation. *The critique of aestheticization ultimately converges with the critique of economics in condemning capitalism as an ever-increasing production of fiction and alienation from reality.*[16] Here we encounter the first significant element of convergence between economics and aesthetics, which will be the focus of the next chapter.

The theory of *staging value* can be compared with Jean Baudrillard's theory of *sign-value*, developed in the 1970s. The latter focuses on the relationship between aesthetic appearances and consumer goods, not so much to explain the production of aesthetic values starting from the competition of commodities on the market as to provide an account of the function of consumer goods in the symbolic order of society, as *status symbols*. In addition to their immediate practical usefulness, commodities are recognized as having a supplementary value, which, subject to the social positioning demands of the consumer, acts as a signal within a hierarchical system of structural links. The consequence in this case, too, is *derealization*, the loss of reality, the ontological "emptying" of the world. In this case, too, the proximity with Debord's thought is striking: along with a critique of the spectacle, Baudrillard's theory of *simulacra* shares the idea that contemporary society is distinguished by the triumph of appearance over being—and by a similar, implicit moral condemnation of the unsatisfactory nature of the "image," as a substitute that lacks the substance or quality of the original.

It should be noted that Baudrillard's *sign-value*, like Böhme's *Inszenierungswert*, can be defined as an aesthetic value, because it is made to appear and be perceived in the social space. However, as in Bourdieu's concepts of distinction and form, which descend via Veblen from this same approach, its "aestheticity" is limited by the fact that the sign counts only as an arbitrary reference inside the oppositional structure—as difference and not as a true status "symbol." The quintessential property of the symbol, as we know from the arts, is its irreducible substance—the positive, sensible density of the signifier. Conversely, the sign-as-difference only has a negative function: it refers to nothing but its own distinctive function and emptiness within the system of oppositions. Although symbols are never interchangeable—at most, they weave those strong analogical ties between them that have inspired poets and writers associated with symbolism, such as Baudelaire, Rimbaud, or Proust—one sign is as good as the next, because they only depend on a convention. The example of Proust is particularly interesting because his symbolic interpretation of aesthetic value influences his sociological sense for distinctive dynamics, shining a perfect spotlight on the principle that—as we shall see in the next chapters—lies at the core of social aesthetics: aesthetic value produces economic value, and vice versa. The social prestige of the Guermantes, for example, does not reside purely in their wealth but also in the auratic sensuality of their name, especially in the evocative "orange syllable," whose incantatory effects Proust analyzes with a sophisticated philosophical poetics of the proper name.[17] Advertising notoriously exploits a similar synthesis. In a nutshell, those who follow a strict structuralist approach reduce the sensible consistency down to a sort of degree zero, but the sensible consistency is an essential and irreducible part of the aesthetic experience of the subject and of what will be defined, in the third part of this book, as *aesthetic power*.

The limits of all these "pathological" approaches, which condemn social aesthetics as a purely exogenous and harmful phenomenon, become evident particularly through their paradoxical consequences: the instant aestheticization is conceived as a disease of contemporary society, the possibility of understanding its processes and dynamics with the appropriate tools is shut down. In reality, there is little point in saying that capitalism has arrived at the stage of pure appearance without questioning the nature of appearance itself, along with the specifically anthropological and aesthetic reasons behind its empire. It serves little to condemn a world in which images and simulacra have supposedly taken the place of "true" things and imposed their rule over all spheres of everyday life, unless we clarify the anthropological mechanisms that were shown in part 1 of this book to underlie representation and the general aesthetic mediation of social relations. And even without calling into question the emphasis that often accompanies the idea of an agency or an effectiveness of images, so dear to many scholars of the arts and visual culture (Bredekamp, Freedberg, Mitchell, and Warburg himself), it is evident that no critique of aesthetic capitalism can give an account of aestheticization without questioning the specific power of action and seduction that the sensible reality exerts. That which acts by seducing must be attractive, stimulate taste, and excite desire. Why else would we allow ourselves to be conquered by immaterial realities, by harmless appearances?

Rather than attempt a thorough analysis, by examining social appearances according to their own principles and equipped with the appropriate aesthetic tools, the critic of aestheticization moralizes. Philosophers such as Wolfgang Fritz Haug have compared the consumer's relationship to commodities with voyeurism in the era of sexual repression: buyers now contemplate goods passively instead of enjoying them in an active way. The pleasure that the naive consumer–aesthete derives from the sophisticated design of an everyday tool, such as a lamp or a computer, is illusory, because he or she is unaware of being the victim of a swindle, of being defrauded by those who traffic in appearances instead of in "truly useful" things. With the same mix of puritanism and romanticism, the exponents of aesthetic anticapitalism invite us to rid ourselves of the images imposed by marketing so that we can return to an economy of authenticity and use value. However, since it is precisely the image—the sensible form of things—that the aesthetic consumer enjoys, these solutions are obviously absurd. For this reason, the only critical current of aesthetic capitalism capable of offering an original contribution to what Debord has written is an approach, like Böhme's, that anchors itself in a generalized phenomenological aesthetics: an aesthetics that is attentive to the qualitative factor, based on concepts such as aesthetic labor, staging, aura, and atmosphere.[18] Although Böhme's work is not entirely immune from a vestigial yearning for the immediate and the original, it is one of the most interesting approaches to a nonreductionist understanding of social-aesthetic phenomena.

Continuing in this direction, our inquiry develops in the conviction that, like the economic dimension, social appearance has its own mode of being, its own logic, its own specific hold on the human psyche and corporeality, which is the only explanation for its effectiveness and powers. Most importantly, aesthetics and economics should never be viewed as independent or mutually exclusive spheres. To understand the importance of this theoretical step, I will embark on a final critical excursus, through the history of the opposition between aesthetics and economics.

10
TWO BAPTISMS AND A DIVORCE

Homo Economicus *Versus* Homo Aestheticus

Two Profane Sciences

The conflict between economics and aesthetics can be traced back to the historical circumstances in which these two forms of knowledge originated, in relatively recent times, and became established as independent and distinct fields. The birth of modern aesthetics, we are often reminded, dates to the mid-eighteenth century: the new discipline was initially baptized and gained ground in the period between Alexander Gottlieb Baumgarten's *Aesthetica* (1750) and Kant's *Critique of Judgment* (1790), in the form of a theory of sensible knowledge and the judgment of taste. It evolved into the philosophy of art during the first half of the nineteenth century, through the work of Schelling, the romantics, and Hegel. It was this romantic concept of aesthetics that ultimately prevailed in the nineteenth and twentieth centuries, accompanied by the sacralization of "Great Art." Only during the last few decades has it been challenged under the form, on the one hand, of a reassertion and reevaluation of the gnoseological and ontological dimension of aesthetics and, on the other, of an extension of its domain of competence to forms of sensible experience other than the fine arts: popular or minor arts, the nonhuman aesthetics of animals or natural landscapes, nonartistic entities like atmospheres, emotions, lifestyles, everyday experiences, and so forth.[1]

Although this history is well known, rarely is it noted that the modern disciplinary foundation of aesthetics coincides with that of political economy, the other typically eighteenth-century discipline that guided the nascent social sciences during the period between Adam Smith, Adam Ferguson, and Marx. *Political economy and aesthetics*, the most original and innovative fields of knowledge produced by the Age of Enlightenment, *were basically sister disciplines*: they shared the same historical and cultural influences, the same epistemological paradigm and, as we will see, they also shared the object of their investigation.

In an essay composed in 1931, titled "The Two Worldly Sciences: Aesthetics and Economics," Benedetto Croce remarked on an affinity that escaped those who noted superficially the distance separating the two fields of knowledge. Aesthetics and economics are both earthly, antiascetic "sciences," which are united by their common interest in the senses (originally in the singular, "the sense") and by their hedonistic attitude—the tendency to recognize a legitimate purpose in the pursuit of pleasure. Croce sees this reassessment of the sensible reality as a modern conquest over medieval moralism and its sense of transcendence, a conquest that would coincide with the assertion of worldly immanence, the value of life in itself, and the dignity of the human body: "This was in fact a 'redemption of the flesh,' as the phrase goes, of mere life as such, of earthly love in all its guises. . . . [Without these two sciences] the circle of the immanentist conception of reality could never have been closed."[2] However, what he writes after this is even more interesting. From the antidualistic and antimetaphysical spirit that unites aesthetics and economics, Croce deduces the anti-Platonic program of a new evaluation of the sensible, understood as much in its cognitive function as in its practical implications, which extend to the legal and political spheres:

> The term the "senses" however had two connected but distinguishable meanings; on the one hand it referred to those cognitive activities which are not logical or ratiocinative but sensuous or intuitive, on the other to that part of practical life which is not in itself moral or dictated by duty but simply desired because it is loved, desired, useful or pleasant. Consequently, the theoretical justification of the senses produced on the

one hand, by its science of aesthetic or pure intuitive apprehension, a "logic of the senses," or "poetic logic," and on the other a "hedonistics," a "logic of utility," economics in the widest sense.[3]

Contrary to the cliché that portrays Croce as a blind supporter of an idealistic aesthetics, here he seems to subscribe to a Baumgartenian idea of aesthetics as a general science of sensibility, which would lead him beyond the dichotomy between the beautiful and the useful toward a reassessment of aesthetic insight as an everyday activity.[4] Drawing inspiration from these two points, one might expand the idea of the "sisterhood" between aesthetics and economics by arguing that before the historical division of labor was created between the spheres, these two "profane" sciences also shared a common *logic of the senses*. Given that there is no justification for a radical separation between the two spheres of sensibility—because the senses and the emotions involved in the two forms of experience are constituted and function in the same way—*could poetic logic or utilitarian logic not spring from a sort of common source, a sort of archi-logic of the senses?* This insight is also confirmed historically, it seems to me, by the work of the great eighteenth-century thinkers who practiced both these disciplines, on the threshold of the parallel births of aesthetics and political economy. Montesquieu published on taste as well as on its laws; Rousseau wrote a discourse on arts and another on political economy; Adam Smith, who was a professor of rhetoric and literature at the beginning of his career, also authored *The Wealth of Nations*; Cesare Beccaria occupied the second chair of economics in Italy and composed a treatise on stylistics. This casual back-and-forth between the fields of aesthetics and economics, which would be unthinkable for a researcher of today, is not simply a sign of "eclecticism," a practice made infeasible by current scientific standards for the division of intellectual labor: specialists in aesthetics only work on aesthetics; economists only work on economics. Rather, it is a sign of the pioneer enthusiasm with which the most brilliant minds of the Enlightenment age explored—from an immanent, antidualistic perspective—the diverse yet still related territories that made up the new continent of the sensible world, along with the various forms that legitimated the pleasure of the senses.

While interest in the sensible reality testifies to an affinity, the relationship between aesthetics and economics also seems bound inextricably to a structural, and mutual, hostility. Like sisters who resemble each other too closely and try to distinguish themselves in every way possible, at the critical moment when the two disciplines had to differentiate themselves, each constituted itself as the negation of the other. As I have recalled on several occasions, the first defined its object as the *useful* (economic goods are those that the human subject relates to from the perspective of self-interest, material enjoyment, functionality, and a specific practical end), while the second, at least from Kant's third *Critique* on, defined its object as the *useless*, from the perspective of disinterest—that is, the nonnecessary—and as purposeless pleasantness (the aesthetic object, by definition, is devoid of any purpose). This definition based on the opposition between respective sensible objects was mirrored in a parallel division of the field. Economics gave itself the area of material *necessity*, subject to the laws of the market and money: the domain of the "system of needs" and of an idea of civil society in which the concept of "civilization" is understood as something with little or nothing to do with artistic or spiritual matters. Aesthetics marked off its territory as the opposite and complementary realm of *purposelessness*, contemplation, illusion, and the "free play" of the faculties, to use the well-known expression from Kant's *Critique of Judgment*.[5]

To sum up, the history of political economy and modern aesthetics should be interpreted along the lines of Plutarch's biographies: as parallel lives. The followers of the two most distant and antagonistic disciplines in the system of knowledge often jeer at the limits of their opposing field. From one side, their opponents are accused of aestheticism (that is, of failing to recognize the prosaic and economic side of reality); from the other, they are accused of economicism (that is, of reducing everything that is free and purposeless to a functionalist explanation). In reality these disciplines conceal a shared history and structure. Both are the offspring of a new, eighteenth-century epistemological foundation that first legitimized the entrance of the senses into the system of knowledge, then asserted their importance in both cognitive and practical terms, and, finally, created a transcendental division between the useful and the beautiful, the necessary and the frivolous, the self-interested and the disinterested. This division, which still persists, whose validity few people openly dispute, has encouraged the phenomena of the lifeworld to be polarized within the confines of two hostile, if not enemy, camps. In this schema, the threads of experience, which are interwoven into a confused fabric in the lived reality of the *Lebenswelt*, are purified, separated, and wound onto two mirror-image spindles, both of which are equally limiting and abstract: pure aesthetic illusion and brute material utility. The relations of reciprocity are artificially severed: the useful versus the purposeless, function versus form, economic enjoyment versus aesthetic contemplation, money versus art, economic capital versus symbolic capital. The force that this system of oppositions still exerts on scientific concepts and everyday life is massive. To lay the foundations for a new paradigm we will have to make an effort to go beyond these oppositions, specifically by defining the common *logic of the senses*, or *sensible logic*, in which both economics and aesthetics have their roots. Deleuze's *Logic of Sense*, which joins forces with social aesthetics in explicitly rejecting dualism and its ontology of surface, and Derrida's reading of Condillac can serve as precious allies for pursuing this deconstructive work. The short notes that Giorgio Agamben has written on the topic of taste, in a little-known article from his youth, are also interesting, because they explicitly engage with the topic.

Like Croce, Agamben notes an "unexpected affinity" between aesthetics and political economy, on the basis of the relationship between knowledge and pleasure. Aesthetics, knowledge of the "excessive signifier," or of the beautiful as a "je-ne-sais-quoi," is a "knowledge that does not know," that is incapable of entirely accounting for the knowledge it nevertheless senses that it possesses. Political economy embodies instead an oxymoron that is complementary to the first, of a "pleasure that does not enjoy." The reason for this, according to Agamben's definition (which seems influenced by both the romantic idea of usefulness and the Weberian idea of capitalist rationality as lay asceticism), is that political economy would place the accumulation of resources before immediate satisfaction and exchange value before use value. To reconcile this split between knowledge and enjoyment, Agamben proposes that taste be restored to its ancient conciliatory role, by reconceptualizing the concept of taste as a "knowledge that knows" and a "pleasure that enjoys":

> Mallarmé's observation, according to which aesthetics and political economy are the only paths open to research of the mind, is thus more than a superficial analogy. Aesthetics and political economy, *Homo aestheticus* and *Homo economicus*, are in a certain sense the two halves (a knowledge

that is not known and a pleasure that is not enjoyed) that taste struggled to hold together for the last time in the experience of a knowledge that enjoys and a pleasure that knows, before their explosion and liberation helped set in motion those tremendous transformations that essentially characterize modern society.[6]

Continuing down the trail of taste, but going further back than Agamben, whose critique of capitalism never liberated itself from the romantic and antimodern temptations (as his rejection of exchange value and accumulation without enjoyment shows), social aesthetics aspires to rethink the relations between aesthetics and economics by reconceiving their common relationship to the sensible, and by breaking down the oppositions between art and money, image and commodity, art for art's sake and art for consumption.

Bourgeois Life and Aesthetic Life

As this reconstruction makes evident, the distinction between aesthetics and economics dates to the formation of a knowledge that began to be established during Kant's time and later triumphed in our current disciplinary system. However, what further contributed to polarizing the issue was the huge transformation in Europe that straddled the French Revolution and was tied to the crisis and ending of the Ancien Régime. According to many observers, including, to begin with, artists such as Goethe, Proust, Thomas Mann, Tomasi di Lampedusa, Fitzgerald, and Visconti, the crucial aspect was the way the advent of the Third Estate was accompanied on the sociocultural plane by the perception of a gap between the prosaic "economic" lifestyle of the rising middle class and the luxurious "aesthetic" lifestyle of the declining aristocracy. The conflict between the group on the rise and the group in decline dragged out all through the death-throes of the old order, from the rumblings of the French Revolution to World War I. Indeed, throughout this period not only did the process of economic self-assertion, still referred to simplistically as the "triumph of the middle class," clash with a vigorous and effective resistance on the part of the nobility, but when it came to lifestyle and controlling the symbolic resources, the aristocracy showed itself, at least initially, to be aesthetically superior. In his acclaimed book on "the persistence of the Old Regime," the historian Arno Mayer has provided a picture of this historical drama. In it, he repeatedly insists on the role played by social appearances:

> Although relegated to the margin of the republican polity, the French aristocracy maintained its social and cultural preeminence. *As if to compensate for its absolute political fall and relative economic decline, it became more self-consciously mannered and proud-minded than any other European nobility.* Old highborn families learned to valorize their renowned names and ancestries. Some thirty grand aristocrats married American heiresses during the Belle Époque, while many others forged family alliances with indigenous fortunes, including Jewish ones. But this marriage strategy *worked only because the aristocracy as a whole continued to seduce the bourgeoisie with what were so many inflated illusions and appearances.* Rather than standing out as decadent, corrupt, idle, and vain, the French nobility dazzled Paris and foreign notables with its charm, elegance, and finesse.[7]

Adorno suggested that the matter of Proustian snobbery should be interpreted along the same lines. As he saw it, snobbery was at the heart of the *Recherche*'s social problem; it would explain why Proust represented the aristocracy in a phantasmagoric, almost surreal fashion in "passages scattered throughout his work that lead unsympathetic readers to complain about his snobbery, passages that challenge the stupid notion of a mediocre Progress, which asks why one should be interested in an aristocracy that by Proust's day had already been deprived of its actual function and that is not at all statistically representative."[8] The *Nachleben* of aristocratic prestige, which survived through its sensible image, like a ghost well beyond the legal death of its "body," was also masterfully recounted in *The Leopard*. Think of that famous scene involving Angelica and Tancredi, the scions of the new generation who have swept away the old regime: enchanted by the apparition of the fascinating vestiges of a world that has all but vanished, they explore the abandoned rooms of the Donnafugata palace.

Out of this constellation of factors there arose two phenomena that were decisive in the history of social aesthetics during the nineteenth and twentieth centuries. The first is the one named by Adorno—that is, *snobbery*:

a characteristically social-aesthetic phenomenon because it is mimetic. Every form of *mimesis*, not excluding the social form, has always had to do with representing specific sensible appearances and with copying them. It is characterized by a dual tropism. On the one hand, a snob is someone who imitates upwardly, so to speak: he is the bourgeois gentleman, like Molière's Monsieur Jourdain who tries to copy the image of the upper class, whom he contemplates from afar, in the hope of becoming like it. On the other hand, snobbery describes the movement of someone who seeks to stand out from the crowd, by which the nobility asserts and signals its irreducible difference by creating a distancing aura for itself: *noli me tangere*. The dictionaries of all European languages, which define *snobbery* in both ways, testify to the fact that these movements are identical in their social significance. This is well illustrated by the image of the social ladder that Hippolyte Taine uses to summarize the work of Thackeray, who was the first to analyze and "baptize" the phenomenon: "The snob is a child of aristocratic societies: perched on his step of the long ladder, he respects the man on the step above him, and despises the man on the step below, without inquiring what they are worth, solely on account of their position; in his innermost heart he finds it natural to kiss the boots of the first, and to kick the second."[9] In reality, it is the same mimesis, simply looked at from its two dialectical poles, from opposing sides of the social ladder, in other words, as *mimetic snobbery* and *distinctive snobbery*: in *In Search of Lost Time*, it opposes a few minor snobs to the Duchess of Guermantes; or, in *The Leopard*, the character of don Calogero, Angelica's father, to the Prince of Salina. The reason the concept is of interest is because, in addition to describing a social custom, it lends itself to serving as an analytical tool in all hierarchical forms that guarantee a certain social mobility. The forms of distinction analyzed by Bourdieu in the France of the 1970s, for example, are snobbish in the strict sense of the word: through the fight for social appearances, they seek to restore and reproduce quarterings of symbolic nobility in a society where—officially—status differences no longer exist in the eyes of the law.

The second cultural phenomenon that can be associated with the persistence of the Ancien Régime was the prevalence of the axiological opposition between *bourgeois life* and *aesthetic life*: the tendency to conceive of an irreconcilable contrast between the misery characteristic of life in modern society, which is ruled by economic rationality, and the intensity of the artist's life (or of anyone who claims to create an authentic experience from aesthetic values, from the art critic to the dandy), which always connotes an aristocratic air but more in an intellectual sense than a social one, as a "nobility of the spirit." The consciousness of this split triumphed in the great romantic antithesis between prose of the world and poetry as escape from the world (or, in the most political version of the same paradigm, as rebellion against the world). This antithesis would give rise in its turn to the nineteenth-century ideal of an identification between art and life—an ideal that extended from the myth of the bohemian to the decadent myth of *art for art's sake*, all the way to the aesthetic militancy of the twentieth-century avant-garde movements.

But the conflict extended well beyond the world of art. In the work of many critics of capitalism who are indebted to the romantic tradition, one has the impression that the critical impulse originally rises out of a sense of repulsion toward the middle-class form of life, a sentiment that often prevails over their disdain for inequalities and social injustices and that leads them to indulge in snobbish aristocratic posturing. This repulsion is evident in all of Guy Debord's films and autobiographical works. It is even more clearly perceivable in the equivalence between politics and poetry that runs through Giorgio Agamben's thought. When he identifies the poet as a salvific figure for humanity, someone who through the cult of the revelatory and world-making word opposes in exemplary fashion the instrumental rationality of the merchant, Agamben is putting forward an anticapitalistic version of Heideggerianism; but he is also going back to one of the most powerful myths of German literature, which we will examine in the following pages. But the fact that it is, indeed, a myth leads us go beyond his now dated oppositions. In one of the most important books on social criticism published in the last few decades, Luc Boltanski and Eve Chiapello show that the "new spirit of capitalism" has by now absorbed and neutralized "artistic critique": not only has it succeeded in satisfying the demands for authenticity, creativity, and aesthetic intensification that were called for by the youth protest movements of the 1960s and 1970s, it has even made them the driving force behind the new "creative economy."[10] This is a further demonstration that the romantic paradigm is definitively running dry. *Homo aestheticus* is not necessarily the enemy of *homo economicus*: he might just as well be his traveling companion or *Doppelgänger*.

Wilhelm Meister's Dilemma

The opposition between *Homo economicus* and *Homo aestheticus*, whose various origins we have briefly reconstructed, had its legend created in Goethe's story of Wilhelm Meister, the young merchant who decides to abandon his father's trade so that he can follow his theatrical vocation. The conflict experienced by Wilhelm Meister has a strongly allegorical meaning for modern consciousness, something that Goethe sought to highlight in several ways. The first version of the novel, which the author left unfinished (1777–85), is referred to as *Sendung* (*The Calling*). In it, Wilhelm tells his friend and rival, Werner (who in the symbolic system of the novel personifies the values of economic life), that he feels divided between two female figures that compete for possession of his soul, like the masks in a sacred play from the Middle Ages. One character personifies the muse of tragic poetry (*die Muse der tragischen Dichtkunst*) and the other is an allegory of commerce and industry (*das Gewerbe*):

> I still recall a poem, which must be around somewhere, where the Muse of Tragic Poetry and another female figure, in which I had personified Commerce, argued right boldly with one another for my worthy self. . . . With what horror I had depicted the old matron with her skirt tucked into her belt, her keys at her side, her glasses on her nose, always busy, always in motion, quarrelsome and frugal, petty and grouchy! How miserable I described the condition of him who bowed beneath her rod and earned a servile living in the sweat of his brow! And how different the other appeared! What a vision for tormented hearts! Splendidly crafted! To be viewed in her character and conduct as a daughter of freedom. Sense of self gave her dignity without pride; her dress became her, covering every part of her without distortion, and the ample folds of the material repeated, like a thousandfold echo, the charming movements of this divine person. What a contrast! And you can readily guess to which side my heart turned.[11]

The figure represented by Goethe in the guise of a surly, bespectacled administrator justifies more than ever the use of a word that is fashionable today: *oikonomia*. The contrast with art is reinforced in Werner's diatribe. In order to praise the superiority of *Homo economicus*, he embarks on a long eulogy of the intrinsic rationality and "beauty" of double-entry bookkeeping.[12]

In the second version of the novel, *Apprenticeship*, published in 1776, which became the model of the German *Bildungsroman*, Wilhelm explains to Werner the reasons why he chose to rebel against his fate as a businessman. The letter contains the ideological core of the opposition between art and economy and clearly elucidates its social implications. His reasons may sound dated today, since they are tied in with the particular role the theater played in eighteenth-century aristocratic culture, as a mirror of the courtly *Geselligkeit* (sociability) and a preparatory genre for introducing individuals into social life. According to Wilhelm Meister, the theater would be the only form of *Bildung* to guarantee individuals a harmonious and complete development of their personality, precisely thanks to its aesthetic cachet. The mastery of appearances involved in acting educates the individual in a harmonious and nondualistic self-presentation that gives equal attention to gestures and speech, body and soul, interiority and exteriority. Most importantly, with words destined to resonate throughout the tradition of twentieth-century German thought, Goethe claims that the actor's profession has an ethical-social value and purpose, an idea that through Plessner, Arendt, and Habermas later thematized the normative function of the *Öffentlichkeit* (public sphere).[13] Rather than making the human being an isolated individual, the theater aims to produce a truly "public person" (*eine öffentliche Person*), a mask capable of performing multiple roles on the world stage and of having a political influence in the public sphere, through speech, gestures, and expressive and rhetorical abilities:

> I have an irresistible desire to attain the harmonious development (*Ausbildung*) of my personality such as was denied me by my birth. . . . I have, for example, improved my voice and my speech and can truly say that in society I make a favorable impression. But every day my desire to be a public person [*eine öffentliche Person*] becomes more and more irrepressible, with the result that I am always trying to please and to be effective in wider circles. . . . You can see that as far as I am concerned, all this is to be found only in the theater; only there can I really move and

develop as I would wish to. On the stage a cultured human being can appear in the full splendor of his person, just as in the upper classes of society. There, mind and body keep step in all one does, and there I will be able simultaneously to *be* and to *appear* better then anywhere else.[14]

In another critical passage, Wilhelm explains to his friend that in Germany the only people who must leave the environment where they grew up are those that come from the middle class: they are forced to seek on "stage," a surrogate of the representative public sphere, the *Bildung* that aristocrats enjoy from birth as part of their form of life. The aesthetic scene is the only place where the son of a merchant can master the skills in appearing that noblemen acquire in the public space of the court and the army, thanks to their public functions of representation and display, and to the cult of manners and ceremonies: in other words, thanks to an atavistic familiarity with the game of social appearances:

> The middle class can acquire merit and, if driven to extremes, develop the mind; but in so doing it loses its personality, however it presents itself. A nobleman who consorts with distinguished persons is obliged to behave in a distinguished manner, which, since all doors are open to it, becomes a manner that is free and unconstrained, so that, whether at court or in the army, his currency is his person and the figure he cuts. As a result, he has good reasons to regard the way he appears as a matter of importance, and to show that he does. A certain formal grace in ordinary affair, coupled with a certain relaxed elegance in serious and important matter, becomes him well. He is a public person, and the more cultivated his movements, the richer his voice, and the more controlled and measured his whole personality, the more accomplished he becomes.[15]

Members of the nobility, Wilhelm concludes bitterly, exist by appearing, while members of the middle class must be content with only being; and however they seek to appear is ridiculous and insignificant.

The various solutions with which Goethe sought to resolve Wilhelm Meister's conflict, by gradually altering the plot in later versions of the novel, lead toward a growing reconciliation with the prose of the world. This direction runs parallel to the evolution from *Sturm und Drang* to classicism taken by Goethe's poetics. The three different endings of the story herald some of the principal forms that the opposition between bourgeois life and aesthetic life would assume during the centuries to come. First, the romantic, bohemian path of radical rejection in *The Calling*: Wilhelm becomes an artist and joins a company of acrobats. Second, the snobbish path of *mésalliance*, in *The Apprenticeship*: Wilhelm leaves the theater and receives his aesthetic education from the Masonic Society of the Tower, which leads him to marry the aristocratic Natalie. This ending prompted a caustic witticism from Novalis, who dubbed it "Wilhelm Meister's apprenticeship, or, the pilgrimage toward the diploma of nobility." Finally, in the third and final version of the story, *The Journeyman's Years, or the Renunciants* (1821–29), we are given the painful but necessary *Entsagung*—the definitive renunciation of the youthful illusion of freedom and the universality of aesthetics, in the name of adult thinking based on pragmatism and social utility. Wilhelm abandons both bohemianism and snobbery in favor of the most middle-class of professions: medicine. This decision is described by the literary critic Franco Moretti as a gesture of surrender to economic thinking: "Gone is the conflict between the useful and the beautiful that had been the key to the previous novel about Wilhelm Meister, the *Apprenticeship* of 1796; in the 'Pedagogical Province' of the *Wanderjahre* conflict has given way to functional subordination; having 'chosen to be useful.'"[16] In reality, diverging slightly from Moretti's view, the social usefulness that Goethe defends in the last version seems to be quite different from an economic one. Instrumental reasoning does not put individuals in mutual competition and enslave them to the imperative of capitalist reification and optimization; rather, to borrow a Hegelian category that comes from the same period as Goethe's work, it is *ethicity* (*Sittlichkeit*) that assigns the individual a specific role in a community held together by solidarity and the social division of labor. By choosing to be useful to society, Wilhelm sacrifices his individual aspirations to the collective good. One might very well argue that *Sittlichkeit* is the embodiment of the middle-class ethos. However, while it might be true that Meister's final episode sanctions the end of aesthetic rebellion, the defeat of *Homo aestheticus* does not coincide with the victory of *Homo economicus*, since it begins the attempt to transcend the romantic antinomy in a new form of normativity.

The Culture of Appearances and the Discrete Charm of the Aristocracy

A final excursus will help us situate more precisely the problem that Goethe expressed in the form of a modern myth. In Norbert Elias's reflections on the court society, which can be read as a "socioanalysis" of Wilhelm Meister's complex, the German sociologist focused on the rupture that was created in the sensibility and practices of the ancient noble elite when the bourgeois model of life first made its entrance. By introducing a stark separation between public and private and an ethos centered on economic rationalization instead of visibility and recognition—that is, the pursuit of a positive image in other people's opinion—the middle-class mentality lost much of the aesthetic savoir faire that had shaped the mores of the aristocratic court. Social taste was actually at the center of the Ancien Régime's aristocratic culture. Its practices were always explicitly and showily aesthetic because they were meant to publicly represent rank: ceremonial, formalized, stylized down to every detail, directed toward staging and ostentation. For centuries, from the late Middle Ages to the end of the eighteenth century, in its two most characteristic environments—the monarch's court and the worldly urban society known as *le monde*—the European elite cultivated the art of social appearances and accumulated a wealth of aesthetic expertise. This is how Elias sums up the meaning of this historical rupture in social aesthetics:

> For those making up the *bonne compagnie* of the *Ancien Régime*, the tasteful arrangement of house and park, the more elegant or more intimate decoration of rooms according to fashion and social convention, or the refined cultivation of relations between men and women, were not only amusements enjoyed by individuals but vital necessities for social life. . . . Almost everything that shaped court society in the seventeenth and eighteenth centuries, whether it be dance, the nuances of greeting, the forms of conviviality, the pictures decorating the houses, the gesture of courtship or the *lever* of a lady, all this moved more and more into the sphere of private life. It thereby ceased to be at the centre of the tendencies shaping society.[17]

In light of this analysis, one might be tempted to view an interest in social appearances as a matter for the sociology of elites, as have researchers like Veblen, Elias, and Bourdieu, who were interested in this social aesthetic from the perspective of their research into the habits and values of the dominant classes. This temptation is more than understandable. The culture of appearances in the old European regime and in the segment of the American leisure class that reproduces it has for a long time been the prerogative of a group of *rentiers*, people of independent means, who were interested in promoting it to satisfy their needs for rank. This is still partly the case today. The old and new forms of nobility are invested in aesthetic taste and try to ensure their hegemony over the legitimate criteria for its practice because they know that in order to preserve, justify, and, from a certain point of view, even create their position of power they have to "look like nobles." For a member of the higher classes, and even more for a parvenu like the Great Gatsby, maintaining an elegant and expensive lifestyle may turn out to be just as imperative as the bourgeois need to balance the books at month's end—and the laws of prestige can be as rigid as those of the double-entry bookkeeping praised by Goethe's Werner. Hippolyte Taine loved to illustrate this point with his well-known anecdote about the Duke of Richelieu, who took the purse of money his grandson had returned him, still full, and threw it out the window, accusing the boy of not knowing how to live nobly.[18] Elias's great insight was that there existed an economy of appearance, a "court rationale," that possessed a logic every bit as ruthless as that of the economy. The tradition of savoir vivre manuals, which flourished during the Italian Renaissance and the French Classical period, should be interpreted from this perspective: Castiglione's *Courtier*, Della Casa's *Galateo*, Guazzo's *Civil Conversation*, Nicolas Faret's *The Honest Man, or, The Art to Please in Court*, Antoine Gombaud's *Conversations*. The aim of these texts is to articulate the rules of appearing in public and to offer something to the elites that comes closest to the idea of a social aesthetics understood in its normative dimension.

With the concept of distinction, Bourdieu extended this insight to all forms of social aristocracy, not just to those with official titles. The class factor was made conclusive by a point continually stressed by Bourdieu, that to acquire an education in taste and aesthetic skills demands appropriate means and environments, such as the possibility to travel, visit museums, and own and collect works of art: to conquer these conditions of privilege requires that one first eliminate any concerns tied to survival; one must possess material resources and free time. The first character to argue this was, once again, Wilhelm Meister, when he admits that he envies the loftiness and freedom of the noble life, which he equates with an unburdening from the toil and struggle to which members of the middle-class fall victim. A free relationship with forms is the luxury of those who do not become "deformed" by need and by the division of labor. "Thrice happy and praiseworthy are those whose high birth elevates them above the lower classes of humanity. . . . What comfort and ease an inherited income provides!"[19]

Economic ease is undoubtedly an important condition for living an aesthetic life; but it is not a necessary one. We need to be careful not to confuse *the plane of the hegemony and sociology of power*, according to which the upper classes strategically use their aesthetic expertise to impose their taste as the dominant one, with the social-anthropological plane, which shows how aesthetic practices have a role in constructing the identity and forms of life of *all social subjects*. The control of one's image, the public expression and formation of the self, the tendency to stylize gestures and behaviors are features open to everyone and potentially shared by all classes, groups, and individuals—all the more so today, thanks to the growing democratization of lifestyles and aesthetic reflexivity, shown by the contemporary sociology of consumption and culture. Bourdieu, who was prompted by the oppositional thinking of structuralism to focus his attention primarily on the upper strata of society, those who produce the distinctive "difference," tends to dismiss the existence of the working-class aesthetic with the general concept of "popular taste." In actuality, this is an antiaesthetic concept: as a criterion that lacks an autonomous logic of the senses, it tends to dissipate into praise for the functional and a sensation of closeness to nature (the "truly useful" object independent of the form, a tasty, nutritious meal prepared in a nonsophisticated way, and so on). Immersed in their material pursuits, the dominated classes are supposedly less concerned with their image and the way they are perceived socially. However, had he developed his recurring argument on *"the relative autonomy of the logic of symbolic representations* with respect to the material determinants of socio-economic condition,"[20] Bourdieu would have had no difficulty in recognizing that everyone, no matter what his or her position in the social field, possesses an interest and an expertise in the field of appearing: the entrepreneur as much as the factory worker, the farmer as much as the business owner, the manager as much as the secretary. Even keeping to the paradigm of distinction, it is evident that the culture of appearances is not concentrated solely at the top of the social pyramid: the obsession for decorum typical of the lower-middle class, for example, can rival that of the court aristocracy, considering the bourgeoisie's pursuit of "luster," "brilliance," and a costume that transforms it (to use the words of Siegfried Kracauer, who gave us a first bleak phenomenology of it).[21]

In other words, although the elites are most certainly motivated to assert their hegemony over the aesthetic sphere, to impose their lifestyle as the most prestigious one, and to devalue that of other social groups, *taste is not exclusively a matter of distinction. Social aesthetics is a general social phenomenon that is rooted in the anthropology of appearance, self-display, and reflexivity,* as we have seen in the first part of this book. The time has come to present a plan of social aesthetics and to delve into some of its general structures.

PART III
TOWARD A SOCIAL AESTHETICS

On the Sensible Logic of Society

11
THE OPENING

Aesthetic Foundations of the Common World

From the Pathology to the Physiology of the Social

As the extended analysis in the second part of this book made clear, a social aesthetics shares many themes and issues with theories of "aesthetic capitalism" and with the variously formulated romantic critiques of social appearances. However, unlike them, it disputes the underlying premises of their "pathological" approach. Until now I have primarily reconstructed the philosophical arguments of this debate and criticized the notion of alienation and the Platonic metaphysics of the two worlds, which surreptitiously form the foundation of this thought tradition. Let us now recall a few historical aspects as well.

Social aestheticization can hardly be considered a phenomenon specific and exclusive to modernity, its totalitarian political forms, and its late-capitalist economic structure. A quick glance at history and cultural anthropology suggests the opposite: other forms of civilization have produced social phenomena that, while certainly not equivalent, are in some ways comparable to those we witness in our contemporary form of life. Among Western societies with the highest degree of aestheticism, classical Greece comes first to mind. This was a culture devoted openly to the cult of beautiful appearances and to the prestige of its elites, a culture that extolled the aesthetic potential of politics, created spectacular institutions such as the theater and the Olympic Games, celebrated glorious action performed in public (*kléos*), entrusted the celebration of its heroes to poetry and the other arts, and even had a unique concept for expressing the values of the beautiful and the good.[1] The exemplarity of the Greek model is so strong yet so ambiguous that it has been a beacon for the propaganda of totalitarian regimes—in the cinema of Leni Riefenstahl, for instance. It has played a similar role for a tradition of thought that has intransigently opposed totalitarian manipulation and defended a democratic idea of the relationship between aesthetics and politics—as expressed in Hannah Arendt's work, for example.

Another example of precapitalist aestheticism can be traced to the Western courts of the early modern era, which we discussed earlier when looking into the "elitist" propensity of aesthetic culture. One need only think about the importance of ceremonies and clothing in the everyday life of aristocrats, and the spread of manuals on *civilité* and good manners starting in the Renaissance: this was a literature expressly dedicated to the art of presenting oneself, behaving and reacting in front of others. Then there was the daily spectacle of the *lever et coucher du Roi* (rising and retiring of the King) and other nonmaterial constraints that obliged courtiers to always represent an image in public that was worthy of their rank.[2] And to those who might object that both ancient Greece and the courts of the Ancien Régime are nothing more than close relatives of contemporary Western culture—and therefore that their example simply confirms the genealogy and the unity of a given cultural tradition—it should be noted that research that does not focus on the history of the West seems to suggest the same sort of findings. The Japanese civilization, for example, attained a high aesthetic cachet long before learning about capitalism.

According to a recent interpretation, Japan underwent a specific "process of civilization" in which the arts and the formalization of behaviors played a decisive role, independently from the influence that Western models may have exercised on its development.[3] This aestheticization was not exclusively an elitist phenomenon. A tradition of outside observers, especially from France (including Kojève, in his famous notes on "Japanese snobbery," and Barthes, in his *Empire of Signs*), has suggested the existence of a mass form of aestheticism, which they say has permeated all Japanese environments and social classes.[4] Because of its sociological impressionism, along with the tendency to essentialize centuries of culture in a single identity, effective over a long duration, an interpretation of this sort needs to be handled with care; still, it was also encouraged by the readings of "inside" authors such as Jun'ichirō Tanizaki and Kuki Shūzō.[5] Finally, even the current of contemporary thought known as "everyday aesthetics" explicitly appeals to general categories like Japanese aesthetics to define the peculiar sensibility that consists in cultivating the beauty of everyday activities and in stylizing gestures and rituals, such as tea drinking, flower arranging, and hanging up the laundry in the sun.[6] Some of these practices, for example, the art of displaying and wrapping (*furoshiki*), recall phenomena that are typical of capitalist aestheticization, such as packaging, and deserve to be studied from a comparative perspective—while respecting the differences between their respective sociocultural grammars, of course.[7]

This interest in the use of the social-aesthetic chiasmus in non-European parts of the world could be developed further through examples taken from ethnographies of other cultural areas, such as New Guinea or Amazonia.[8] However, as far as the aims of this chapter are concerned, the point should already be clear: when expanding the perspective back in history and beyond Western confines one cannot help but wonder not only to what extent social aestheticization can be considered a specifically Western and modern phenomenon but also at what point it should be considered a "pathology." The fact that the cult of sensory and formal values has left its mark on such diverse aspects and periods of human culture suggests social aesthetics should be viewed instead as a dimension shared by a variety of forms of human life, one that presents significant variations but also significant constants. The lifestyle that we will talk about in the last part of this book, exemplified by the art and poetics of Andy Warhol, is undoubtedly modeled on the urban consumerist media experience of the last two centuries in the West; but the bases for a loose comparative development can be found in the anthropological foundations of social aesthetics. What I will sketch out in these chapters is, in the first place, a social aesthetics of modernity and late modernity. But my observations also contain a formal, minimal a priori approach that can be adapted to a large variety of forms according to the characteristics of specific contexts.

To signal how remote this approach is from pathological approaches, another point must be clarified: it concerns the definition of appearance as deceitful illusion and that of aesthetic value as a toxic alteration. Close readings of Rousseau, Debord, and the aesthetic anticapitalist tradition show that this way of defining the problem underlies both a Platonizing, dualistic metaphysics and the notion of alienation as a fall from a condition of fullness. Now, instead of thinking of aesthetic value as a pathogenic agent that corrupts something natural and innocent, it should be thought of as a given value, or more precisely, as an inevitable precondition for social exchange, the "sensible a priori" of the social. Aesthetic value is always liable to be transformed artificially, to be "worked on" aesthetically, and to undergo processes of "stylization"; under certain conditions, it can be enlarged and stylized to the point of prevailing over other spheres of reality—and can certainly also be artfully cultivated by anyone who can control it. This approach safeguards the possibility of offering a critique. However, whereas the romantic critic thinks in terms of drastic oppositions, social aesthetics eschews the use of a dualism and thinks in terms of aesthetic *mediation*, along the lines of the theory of representations that was laid out in part 1. It invites us to think in terms of a dialectical understanding of contexts and their specific lifestyles rather than in terms of absolute innocence and irreversible corruption.

Above all, what serves to found a new social theory is an approach that respects the specific *sensible logic* of the social, without reducing it to some other logic such as economic utility and viewing the latter as more essential and instrumentalizing it. The logic of the social arises out of the logic of the senses and is therefore properly sensible and sensory. The phrase "the sensible logic" is thus to be understood as referring to both. But it might be helpful to spell out exactly what I mean by "logic." As the Italian philosopher Remo Bodei pointed out, we shouldn't be intimidated by the seriousness surrounding the term and think that logic is associated only with strictly rational phenomena: the root of *logos* and *leghein* is humble and unassuming, the same as that of "legume," and they allude to the work of the harvester, who gathers together and puts in order what has been harvested. In the same way, logic can be thought of as the movement that joins together a series of phenomena that follow specific, determinate principles: nothing stops us from thinking about a logic of the passions, about a logic of delirium, like the one Bodei examines, and, thus, also about a logic of the "sensible."[9] The sole viable approach to understanding a social-aesthetic phenomenon, whether of today or in the past, is therefore by tackling it in accord with its own principles: by calling into question the senses, sensible qualities, and forms; by examining taste; by bringing out the arsenal of conceptual and analytic tools that the philosophies of perception and art put at our disposal. Only in the light of a nonreductionist and immanent understanding will it also be possible to write a chapter critiquing particular forms of contemporary social aestheticization.

Most importantly, contrary to the tendency of the pathological approach, aesthetics and economics should never be viewed as separate, independent, or mutually exclusive spheres. In the everyday effectiveness of our social experience, the dynamics of economic exchanges merge with the dynamics of material appearing and perceiving, and material needs are intertwined with nonmaterial ones: aesthetic sensations and economic utilities are at play together, and they form each other through a constant process of reciprocal influence. Human reality should not be thought of as a homogeneous field that is reducible solely to the capitalist systemic law of utility: it is a diversified territory that is under tension, in which forces act alongside one another, with no need to establish which is the "ultimately" fundamental, original, or determining sphere. Social aesthetics does not claim in any way to replace political economy as the ultimate metaphysics of social reality. It subscribes fully to the *Wechselwirkung*—the "interplay" of material and ideal factors—so that neither the former nor the latter can be considered the exclusive cause of social phenomena: an idea that Simmel considered an inalienable methodological principle in his interpretation of the real. As he wrote in his programmatic preface to *The Philosophy of Money*: "Every interpretation of an ideal structure by means of an economic structure must lead to the demand that the latter in turn be understood from more ideal depths, while for these depths themselves the general economic basis has to be sought, and so on indefinitely."[10]

We pick up our path, then, where Simmel opened it up and where we ourselves embarked on it in part 1: with *aesthesiology*. We will examine the function and social value of the senses. If sensible appearance is the medium through which social exchange necessarily takes place and is constituted, then the senses, which are the vehicle and condition of possibility for this appearance, must be the starting point of social aesthetics.

The Senses, Aesthetic A Prioris of Society

Aisthesis is the point of departure for any analysis of the social. Starting from this simple but crucial insight, in a short "Excursus on the Sociology of Sense Impressions" (1907), later worked into his book *Sociology* (1908),[11] Simmel first sketched out the groundbreaking project of a *social aesthesiology*: an investigation into the role that the senses play in constituting and shaping social relations, not only by allowing individuals to reciprocally connect with one another and to interact but also by influencing the nature of their relations from the ground up. In mediating the interaction, the senses give it a particular "aesthetic impression." The senses are not neutral channels designed to drop away once the contact is created. Like all media, they shape their content by infusing it with specific sensible qualities: this is what Simmel defines, using an explicitly aesthetic lexicon, as the "coloring" (*Färbung*), "temperature" (*Temperatur*), or "accentuation" (*Betonung*) of a relationship. This is its specific sensorial and emotional totality (for example, the sparkle of society events, the coldness of a hello or goodbye, the greyness or "blue" of a depressing atmosphere, the warmth of intimate relations, and so forth) and its "style"—its specific formal constitution, the way the elements of an interaction create a unity and enter into play with one another. Thanks to this twofold capacity to connect and influence—to transfer content and at the same time to form and qualify it—the senses can be considered *the aesthetic a prioris of society*.[12] Twenty years after Simmel, this idea reemerged in the anthropology of Helmuth Plessner, who founded a philosophical aesthesiology.[13]

The definition of the a priori role of *aisthesis* (which can, in turn, be considered a form of the "somaticization of the a priori," given that human beings are sentient subjects because they have a body, and it is this body that puts them into relationship with the world and others) is thus the first, indispensable step in a social aesthetics. Indeed, unlike theories of social aestheticism and capitalist aestheticization, which conceive of the aesthetic cachet as something inoculated from the outside, my theory of social appearances starts with the presupposition that every social relation, *the social relationship in and of itself, is already and will always be connaturally aesthetic*. Therefore, when the qualitative aspects of a particular relationship are transmuted, through an intensification or stylization of relations, for example, these changes do not fall under the category of alienation or perversion but under the category of *development, transformation,* or *"aesthetic labor"*—Gernot Böhme's expression that we will use from now on, although without giving it any specific negative connotation.[14] This aesthetic labor, exemplified in the activity of the artist, shapes sensible appearances to give them a different particular aspect. However, these processes are not always obviously intentional and personal, as if someone "artfully" maneuvered them; they also take place through the anonymous dynamics of social processes, such as ritualization, imitation, or distinction.[15] One of the principles that guides the sensible logic of the social (and distances the social-aesthetic explanation from that of "governmental" manipulation from behind the wings) *is the immanent stylization of appearances*: an (often) impersonal and unconscious "taking-form" that accompanies and sustains the forms of stylization experienced and handled more consciously by social subjects.

Modernity as an Aesthetic Environment: The Court, the Metropolis, the Media

The approach taken by Simmel (who placed his excursus in the chapter in *Sociology* that examines the spatial organization of society) is of special interest to us because it evokes the "primary scene" of social aesthetics: the physical copresence of people in the same space. Individuals gathered in a shared milieu must necessarily sense each other, even without being conscious of it, because their bodies communicate, and they perceive each other through sensations that may also be subliminal: the elementary forms of *being-with-others* and *conflict* have their bases in this reciprocal *aisthesis*. Starting from this insight, Simmel lists and analyzes how each sense organ contributes specifically to social relations, and then comments on their philosophical significance. As usual, his reflections are balanced between two approaches: phenomenological and sociological. For this reason, they need to be considered alongside the observations in his essay "The Metropolis and Mental Life" (1903), which can be read as a sociohistorical complement to aesthesiology, and which picks up on some of the fundamental ideas in the third part of his *Philosophy of Money* (1900).[16]

In addition to the scale of interactions between individuals, the sensible a priori also acts on an environmental scale. According to Simmel—who inaugurated the line of research that would later be reworked by his inheritors Siegfried Kracauer and Walter Benjamin, and later still by cultural studies—perception has always had a strong contextual dimension: social sensibility varies not only depending on the differing physiological characteristics of the sense organs but also according to the characteristics of environments, which are shaped by cultural values, by institutions, by the different techniques used to educate and mold the body, and by the level of technological development. One of his examples has circulated widely: the function and social significance of sight and hearing are not the same in a village and in a big city, where it is possible, for example, to have the typically modern experience of frequently watching the people who travel with us on public transport without ever speaking to them. All the same, one must resist the temptation to read these pages romantically, as yet another nostalgic criticism of the past aimed at the depersonalization and anonymity of modern social relations. Simmel always viewed modernity with a dialectical, ambivalent gaze: the same phenomena that can, on the one hand, become autonomous and subjugate the social actors can constitute, on the other hand, a means of emancipation, the conditions for the birth and development of new freedoms.[17] To preserve the spirit of his method I will recall an ironic remark made by Hans Blumenberg: the fact that city dwellers no longer talk to one another does not necessarily mean that they had something meaningful to say to one another in the past—conformism, social control, and the weight of tradition can make social relations in a village just as unbearable as modern urban solitude. From this and other analyses of the same type, Simmel concludes that in the context of urban experience, sensibility tips sharply toward the organ of sight, which becomes *the hegemonic sense of modern experience*. Big cities turn into a sort of stage for phenomena that are visually dominant, such as fashion, advertising, and conspicuous consumption.

This genealogy must be integrated with what we have already noted about the relationship between social aesthetics and the civilization process: the "court form" also contributed to molding the modern sensorium into a stage for mutual observation and an intensely aesthetic milieu. There is a close continuity, both historically and morphologically, between the social models of court and city: both Werner Sombart and Norbert Elias have stressed their relationship, showing that these two closed spaces of spectacle fostered the development of social dynamics with a strong aesthetic imprint. They also inspired key phenomena in the lifestyle of the modern era: the sophistication of manners, consumption and luxury, hedonism and fashion. This is a fundamental point for countering reductive explanations that go back to the critique of aesthetic capitalism, because it allows the issue of Western aestheticization to be unhitched from an exclusive connection with the twentieth-century capitalist economy and its genealogy to be pushed back by several centuries. The production of aesthetic values does not depend solely on commodity fetishism, that is, on the need to increase the exchange value of things to the detriment of their use value; rather it is rooted in social dynamics of consumption and representation typical of life in cities and renaissance courts.[18]

Furthermore, as shown by Erich Auerbach in his study on the catchphrase that named the seventeenth-century French theater public, *la court et la ville*, courtly and urban fashionable elites ("les mondains") composed two complementary stages in the formation of the modern concept of "the public"—which was originally theatrical and then cultural and political in the broad sense.[19] Both played a crucial role in forging the new *critical* aspect of the modern aesthetic public sphere, whose courtly origin Reinhart Koselleck has also championed and traced, extending it into the history of modern public opinion and the French Revolution. This was the inner forum that the absolutist state had preserved, and through which the "eye" of moral political judgment would be progressively exercised until it was ready to become the "voice" of public conscience and turn against power. The inner forum extended itself and was naturally amplified in places of urban sociability where enlightenment criticism was cultivated,[20] where discussions and debates took place but also leisure, consumption, and sensual pleasure. Salons and clubs served this role par excellence, and their sensory, aesthetic cachet is recalled by the name of the periodical that was the symbol of the Italian Enlightenment: *Il Caffè* (*The Coffeehouse*, 1764–66).

To complete this "social history of *aisthesis*," which paraphrasing Kant, we might also define as the "transcendental socioaesthetics of modernity," the peculiar spatial reconfiguration that took place in courts and modern cities must be allied with the restructuring of time relations. New, characteristically modern forms of time are marked by the acceleration of experience, an intensified perception of contingency and change (both perfectly encapsulated in the essentially modern phenomenon of fashion), in the uncertainty of the future, and especially in the delays and planning involved with managing of money. Hence, the genealogy of the modern sensorium should start from the issue of how contingency, the unpredictability of the future, and acceleration are handled. The issue of distance, which in spatial terms takes the form of a "reserve" and protection from contact and shock, in temporal terms becomes a technique for delaying, for planning and deferring, for speculating on the future. This line of thought should be traced with the help of other guides, too: Niklas Luhmann, Hans Blumenberg, and Harmut Rosa.

This is how aesthesiology, understood as an anthropological and formal domain, acquired the historical and sociological dimension typical of modernity, the new milieu that is the environmental condition of modern experience: *a new "sensorium" takes shape, one destined to transform and characterize the new forms of consciousness, experience, and lifestyles in a specific way.*[21] Thus, according to Simmel's diagnosis, among the characteristics specific to modern social aesthetics there are the primacy of visibility and a less informative acoustic experience—based on the replacement of speech by noise, the triumph of shock (a theme generally attributed to Benjamin but actually authored by Simmel, his Berlin teacher), a new equilibrium between the senses, the intensification of the life of the nerves with the consequent dialectic between hyperaesthesia and anaesthesia, and the rise of a new form of aesthetic individualism. Modern individuals respond to the proliferation of the sensory stimuli that shape them by accentuating the aesthetic inclination of their nature, attempting to fulfill themselves by expressing originality and difference. However, given that more than a century separates us from these pioneering ideas, it behooves us to update them in the spirit rather than in the letter and to modernize his theory in light of recent advances in cultural sociology and media and sensory studies.[22] Simmel's project can be brought forward by examining how our contemporary sensorium has been profoundly modified by technological, media, and artistic innovations such as television, cinema, design, the internet, and social media. Under these new conditions, a new form of "aesthetic experience" takes shape that is extremely intense and pervasive, affecting all social fields but in particular the middle-class lifestyle—and it has nothing to do with the idealistic and romantic experience of the autonomy of art. Far from defining itself as a foreign sphere that is distant from the lifeworld, the aesthetic dimension reengages itself with social reality, or rather, it demonstrates that it had never really emancipated itself from the social reality. *Aisthesis* acts as a primary actor of the "social fabric" and merges with communication, with the dynamics of power and economics, with processes of value creation and exchange.[23]

To call on yet another apt metaphor from Blumenberg, our contemporary socioaesthetic can be conceived of using the figure of the metropolis as a modern version of the Platonic cave, which recalls the aesthetic experience that takes place in a movie theater: a closed, confined environment with a massively concentrated space and accelerated time, where individuals undergoing intense perceptual and affective stimuli watch the "film of social life" while immersed in a collectively shared, intense sensory illusion.[24] Unlike what Guy Debord would argue along with Plato and Rousseau, this experience does not arise out of some tragic alienation or fatal separation between being and appearing; it is not a nightmare that one must escape from thanks to philosophical enlightenment or political revolution but rather is reminiscent in some ways of daydreams.[25] As Simmel sees it, the high degree of sensoriality, emotionality, fiction, mimesis, and imagination involved in the modern urban experience is a powerful resource for individualism and the modern desire for autonomy, expressiveness, and emancipation. Similarly, for his pupils Benjamin, Kracauer, and Bloch, a promise of happiness can be found by browsing real or virtual store windows or in the phantasmagoria of commodities and fashion.

A historical point of view is helpful for illustrating this dialectical reflection. Starting as early as the nineteenth century, big cities such as Paris and, later, New York became places of hard-won freedom and dreams of improvement, where it was possible to make a new life for oneself, where a poor adventurer could try his luck and a commoner could rise in status, where a young rebel, homosexual, or woman suffocated by her family and life in the provinces could imagine themselves differently and reinvent themselves from head to toe. In short, urban anonymity and illusion can offer the opportunity for freedom and creative self-reinvention.[26] Once again, we need to be wary of analyses seeped in social romanticism, which quickly slide toward condemning a process intended as a coherent whole. The growing degree of aestheticism and artifice in modernity is not necessarily a sign of decadence, and, contrary to what Plato, Rousseau, and Debord thought, it may be precisely inside theaters and thanks to movies that viewers can find stimuli and models to emancipate themselves.

"Aesthetic Ecstasy" and the Social Sensorium

In the first chapter, I described how the senses serve as "bridges" to connect people, filling up the space that separates them and creating passageways between them. From now on, we will also consider the senses to be "doors": thresholds that allow exchange and, to a certain extent, a mingling between inside and outside, subjectivity and objectivity. Sensoriality is the opening through which the "ecstatic" condition comes into being, because of which human beings are always opened and exposed outside themselves; it also causes the outside environment to circulate, to flow inside them, until it "mixes up" with their psychic world, as it were, making it almost pointless to distinguish substantially between "in" and "out." At most, as in Plessner, we can talk about "limits" or "boundaries" between inside and outside; but the existence of these shifting boundaries must not be confused with a dualism, as if interiority was spiritual in nature and exteriority only corporeal, and as if the *I* did not comprise pieces of the external world brought into its interiority through the senses and, conversely, the external world pieces of objectivized psychic entities. This is no mere play on words, then: human beings are ecstatic inasmuch as they are aesthetic, inasmuch as they are open to the world and involved in the world through the senses. And since in this world human beings live together with others, this aesthetic exposure automatically takes on a dimension that is intersubjective and, consequently, social and political.

Inspired liberally by Hannah Arendt, who read the existential ontology of Heidegger from a similar angle,[27] I will call the opening in which the experience of shared life develops *Öffentlichkeit*—the public sphere or *publicity*. Inside this sphere, in addition to "communicating" with their fellows, exchanging signals, ideas, and information, social beings are profoundly involved in their sensorium, which influences their bonds, their emotional life, and their inner states. The senses are not limited to connecting individuals. Their medial function must be understood in the double sense of the word *medium*, which can indicate both a means of transmission and a *milieu*, an environment, or better yet, an atmosphere in which things are included and with which they are permeated. The environment in which human sensoriality and sensibility are exercised designates not only a physical or cultural "place" but also a kind of sensory *ambience* that can be perceived and sensed in its turn. We can think of it as a connective tissue that is created by the interweaving of sensibilities but that is greater than their sum. Sensations, qualities, and sensible forms circulate continuously in this atmosphere. Society is inseparable from its *milieu*, which at the same time *connects and contains it*, like the space for which Newton coined the pregnant expression *Sensorium Dei*: we could call this social medium a *Sensorium Societatis*.

The overused metaphor of the "social body" leads spontaneously to this conclusion: for a collective entity to preserve its unity, it must be able to mediate the internal relationship between its parts through a common sensible organ and a "coenesthesia," the general feeling of inhabiting one's body that arises from multiple stimuli from various bodily organs. This is what was argued, for example, by Jean-Marie Guyau (1854–88), who was a contemporary of Durkheim but, unlike him, a fierce supporter of the irreplaceable sociological function of the aesthetic experience and art. Guyau's conception is decidedly romantic and therefore at odds with the premises of social aesthetics that were set out in part 1 and that will be developed in this part of the book. His notion is worth recalling, though, because it provides a useful critical starting point for reconceiving the aesthetic dimension of the social.

According to Guyau, in order to exist and preserve itself, every society needs a form of sensory solidarity that makes the community vibrate in unison in a single *aisthesis*, a common perception. Guyau defines this aesthetic vibration as *sympathy* and demonstrates its effectiveness based on the earliest and most primitive of all societies—the individual conscience: "The cells of the body that form a society of living beings need to vibrate in sympathy and solidarity to produce a general consciousness, or *coenesthesia*. Individual consciousness itself is thus already social, and everything that resounds in our entire body, in our entire consciousness, takes on a social aspect." He continues: "We say *me*, but we could just as easily say *us*. The pleasant becomes beautiful to the extent that it incorporates more solidarity and sociability among the parts of our being and all the elements of our consciousness, to the extent that it can be attributed more to the *us* that resides in the *me*."[28] The bases for every "us"—according to Guyau—are to be found in this aesthetic medium, reminiscent of the ancient Stoic and Renaissance concept of the *pneuma*, in which the harmonic consonance founded on the common sensibility is produced between diverse parts. The aesthetic medium is also the condition for consensus, which is primarily a *con-sensum*, a sensing and perceiving together (the opposite is true, of course, for the disagreement represented by dis-sent, which also has an aesthetic basis). This is why the aesthetic experience, no matter what form it takes, has an intrinsic capacity to *make society*. Art solidifies bonds founded on the most concrete aspect of human beings—their sensible bodies.

Guyau's theory resonates with other romantic aesthetics: the oldest fragment of the system of German Idealism, Wagner, William Morris, the Arts and Crafts movement. The recurring idea in all these versions is that the *medium of the collective bond is to be found in the aesthetic realm*, which has the ability to "make people feel together," to create a "we," and to keep community ties alive. Romantics think that the realization of a political community depends deeply on the arts and on all forms of sensible experience: myths, fables, festivals, plays and musicals, the construction of environments, architecture, cathedrals, even furnishings, such as house fittings, wall hangings, and upholstery. The problem is that the romantic perspective places too much faith in immediacy: there is always a direct passage from the *me* to the *us* and from the *us* to the *me*. Guyau's vision is an aesthetic version of Rousseau's general will: he conceives of aesthetics as the transparent medium to form a *Gemeinschaft* (community) and not a *Gesellschaft* (society), to promote an organic community based on a single homogeneous spiritual identity and not a modern society founded on *aesthetic mediation*, which implies reflexivity, representation, and the preservation of that healthy distance between individuals that allows the free expression of differences.[29]

Now, one of the presuppositions of my social aesthetics project is that the aesthetic model of communal romanticism (which still exercises a great fascination on opposing currents of contemporary thought)[30] has become irrecuperable, not only and not so much because it seems to be vitiated by a totalitarian temptation—as argued by those who immediately associate the total work of art with a certain interpretation of Nazism and Fascism. The reason behind this inadequacy is mainly a theoretical one. The romantic aesthetic flattens the relationship between aesthetics and society into an empathetic, fusional vision of the social bond as an immediate coenesthesia, and thus effectively equates *Gesellschaft* with *Gemeinschaft*. Conversely, social aesthetics grants a specificity and autonomy to the social as well: it asserts the ability of the senses to connect people but without identifying and flattening divergences in the name of a single, shared "spirit." This allows social aesthetics to protect a space of détente in relations, a distance in which dissimilar forms of *aisthesis* can arise, freely proliferate, and live next to one another.

There are at least three characteristics that distinguish my social aesthetics from romantic political aesthetics. First of all, the way the social sensorium should be conceived is without the idea of a necessary and constant copresence in the same space and at the same time, so that it works instead through distance, mediation, and representation. Unlike the sensorial community of Rousseau's "people" in the festivities described in his letter to d'Alembert, or the "public" of Bayreuth, society can exist between people who never meet face to face but who are nevertheless in a reciprocal relationship through media entities: because, even when separated by space and time, they share the same images, listen to the same music, or, more indirectly, they are users of the same media, connected to the same social network; they watch the same television shows, listen to the same radio stations, and consume the same products.[31]

Contrary to another romantic commonplace, the aesthetic media that promote a social bond can be synthetic and artificial, futurist and modern. Every form of romantic thought harbors suspicion toward artifice and believes in the opposition between natural authenticity and cultural sophistication, but in reality this opposition is never clear, and Plessner's quip that whatever is human is "artificial by nature" carries the day. In other words, to create a society aesthetically there is no need to chase after origins, to conceive of culture as myth or as a profound expression of the spirit of a *Volk*, to be nostalgic for handicrafts and guilds, or even to oppose the machines of the industrial revolution to organic and phytomorphic forms. The aesthetic mediation can take place by virtue of representational conventions and absolutely modern expressive means: technological, industrial, and digital.

Finally, another fundamental point that puts social aesthetics at a distance from the romantic aesthetic of community is that there is a form of communicative alienation inherent in these notions: not all sensory stimuli, not all aesthetic messages reach the receiver intact; there is always the possibility of a deviation.[32] Furthermore, in Plessner's terms, there is a strong component of *eccentricity*: a game of masks that overlap one another and multiply without having to presuppose an established identity. The theory of aesthetic mediation, in other words, should represent the irrevocable backdrop against which to understand these observations on milieu. It is a theory of representations that is strictly foreign to every temptation of immediacy and Rousseauian transparency. Just as the medium of transmission always stands with its opacity and reflective dispersive power between the poles of communication, the medium as milieu is not an organic totality without fractures, tears, and vanishing points. To pick up again on the Newtonian metaphor, the social sensorium cannot be perfect and omnipresent like the *Sensorium Dei*:[33] it is imperfect, gaping, open to the outside, in the two senses of leakage and contamination; and it is intermittent and discontinuous, cut through by distance and absence. The sensible connection that it makes possible is full of silent intervals and poorly perceived signals.

The Aesthetic Public Sphere

Now, to arrive at an accurate idea of the properties of the public sphere as it is understood here clearly we cannot turn primarily to the tradition personified by Habermas, which views it as the privileged space for the exchange and construction of rational arguments. The fundamentally aesthetic nature of the sensorium prompts us to pick up instead on an alternative thread in the history of thought, which runs from Vico to Gadamer to Arendt, and which holds that, prior to any common *reason*, human beings are bound together by a *sensus communis* (a concept that is nonetheless not free of romantic temptations and that therefore must be understood in terms of aesthetic mediation).[34] The *Öffentlichkeit* is thus conceived as an aesthetic public sphere: as the realm of appearance and mutual sensing in which individuals relate to one another through sensible forms and in which these forms are not only transmitted and perceived but also created, reproduced, transformed, manipulated, interpreted, discussed, and finally criticized. The public sphere is the aesthetic laboratory of the shared world. Also thanks to this rootedness in *aisthesis* and appearance it is able to become a space for deliberation and conflict, in which one exercises the aesthetic political faculty—the faculty we call "critical." The fact that perception reveals a shared dimension is a condition of possibility—indeed, a prerequisite—for dissension. To criticize means to formulate judgments, and judging presupposes taste, in the highest and most noble sense of the word, as an estimative faculty. Hannah Arendt, once again, has written some crucial passages on this topic:

> In aesthetic no less than in political judgments, a decision is made, and although this decision is always determined by a certain subjectivity, by the simple fact that each person occupies a place of his own from which he looks upon and judges the world, it also derives from the fact that the world itself is an objective datum, something common to all its inhabitants. The activity of taste decides how this world, independent of its utility and our vital interests in it, is to look and sound, what men will see and what they will hear in it. Taste judges the world in its appearance and in its worldliness; its interest in the world is purely "disinterested," and that means that neither the life interests of the individual nor the moral interests of the self are involved here. For judgments of taste, the world is the primary thing, not man, neither man's life nor his self.[35]

Even so, Arendt is overly indebted to the way Kant defines the aesthetic attitude and the judgment of the aesthetic attitude versus that of the economic attitude, as if each "interest" of individuals and groups had to be completely neutralized and excluded from the public sphere in order for politics—true love for the shared world—to exist. From this point of view, her concept can be balanced through Rancière's. Starting from a similar aesthetic idea of the political ("I call the distribution of the sensible the system of self-evident facts of sense perception that simultaneously discloses the existence of something in common and the delimitations that define the respective parts and positions within it"),[36] Rancière insists on the key importance of the notion of interest. The world he has in mind is one cut violently across by social inequalities and class conflicts. Following Marx, Rancière argues that the interest of the completely excluded part (the proletariat, the common people, the pariahs, the migrants, everyone who is left not only empty-handed but also imperceptible) is what calls into question the distribution of the sensible. Only the "division" that is completely excluded from the "divvying up" has the capability to claim that its particular interest coincides with the general interest. And it is this division, with its interest, that assumes an aesthetic form in criticism. Think, for example, of the political role that a demonstration plays in challenging the established order: even before providing a place for particular concrete demands, it is the locus where new political subjects "demonstrate themselves," become perceptible in the shared world, demand visibility and voice, and appropriate the public space. A phenomenon of this type is certainly aestheticized and "spectacular" but in an emancipatory sense, which is opposite to the meaning Debord gives the term.

Nevertheless, from the viewpoint of social aesthetics, the connection between interest and criticism is also justified on the basis of a more idiosyncratic, absolutely nonuniversalistic conception of taste: the dynamics of sympathy and antipathy that subliminally determine what will be defined in this book as a social sensibility—in which taste has a much less noble political role than that described by Arendt, since it is more similar to an immediate sensory reaction than to a true judgment. We will see this in greater detail in the next two chapters. To conclude this excursus, it must be remembered that the modern concept of critique can be historically connected to two different cultural matrixes: political discussion in the public sphere, but also discussions on art and literature, which represent a source of the modern idea of social critique that is less widely known but just as important historically. This second tradition argues that by critiquing works of art and culture one intervenes politically in reality, and that in aesthetic conflicts what is at stake is something much more important than mere idiosyncrasy or individual entertainment: as Adorno used to say, *de gustibus est disputandum* (we *must* dispute about taste). The conflict between aesthetic values is for this reason the privileged activity of the public sphere.

There will be no more discussion on the relationship between aesthetics and politics in the following chapters. My intent is to reinterpret a series of key issues in social philosophy, including that of recognition and the origins of social value, from the new aesthetic perspective that has been opened up with aesthesiology.

12
AISTHESIS

Senses and Social Sensibility

Sensory Interactions

The first and perhaps most important of sensory social relations is the one created through the gaze. Not surprisingly, it has been the focus of modern social theoreticians and philosophers of intersubjectivity. One of the most famous and trenchant analyses, in addition to Rousseau's in *Discourse on Inequality* and *Emile*,[1] is that of Sartre. "We are 'Us' only in the eyes of Others, and it is in terms of the Others' look that we assume ourselves as 'Us.'"[2] Simmel also liked to recall how "looking in each other's eyes" is the original bond between human beings, and he stressed that this sensory relationship is distinguished by its symmetrical, perfect *Wechselwirkung* (reciprocity): "The eye unveils to the other the soul that seeks to unveil the other. While this occurs obviously only in immediate eye-to-eye contact, it is here that the most complete mutuality in the whole realm of human relations is produced."[3] The image still preserves a touch of romanticism in alluding to the mutual revealing of inner lives that is said to be encouraged by the play of the eyes. In reality, there is no need to evoke the idea of a soul to observe how the gaze is the form of social interaction par excellence.

The mutual glance expresses, in the first place, a positive social understanding: it is the sign used by accomplices of all sorts, not only by lovers, like Elias Canetti and Anna Mahler,[4] but also by partners in games and swindles, by team mates during a sports match, and by card sharks. A glance can also easily unmask a clandestine closeness: the gaze reveals the existence of a bond because the gaze itself is what binds. Many positive social passions, such as admiration or emulation, find their fondest metaphors in the gaze. Conversely, various aspects of conflict are expressed in the play of eyes: the test of strength that consists in not lowering one's eyes first in front of a rival is well known; and we all are aware of eye-rolling movements of contempt, which fall from high with their unbearable weight, or the "sideways" glances of symbolic hostility: "envy" derives from *invidere*, and originally meant to look at someone askew, to cast an "evil eye" on them.[5] The visual games of indifference are not to be neglected either. The art of "looking through" someone, as if the person being seen did not exist and was physically invisible, is a subtle form of social disacknowledgment (of which a rich literary phenomenology can be read in Proust's *In Search of Lost Time*, or in Ralph Ellison's *Invisible Man*: in Proust, "looking through" identifies the behaviors of snobs; in Ellison, that of racists).[6] The anonymous, distracted glance that we cast on whoever is sitting next to us in a theater or on public transit is a sign of a minimal social interaction that is nevertheless indispensable for peaceful coexistence in the public space, which Goffman has defined as "civil inattention": we use it to signal to strangers that we have taken note of their presence and that we want to avoid any gesture or behavior that might be detrimental to their space or personal tranquility.[7]

Although the eye has dominated theories on social sensibility for the reasons just cited, partly due to the "public" and sharable nature of its perceptions, the ability to weave social relations is in no way exclusive to sight. *All the senses* have this property: hearing, which makes the exchange of verbal language possible (deafness is said to alienate people from the shared world even more dramatically than blindness); touch, with which we communicate our proximity to others, through a handshake, a caress, a hug (obviously, tactile bonds also involve modes of conflict, starting with the possibility of "getting one's hands on somebody"). The same is true of the more subjective and idiosyncratic senses, such as taste and smell, which appear to be less charged with meaning for intersubjectivity. A mother and an infant who exchange kisses and engage in breastfeedings together and lovers during sexual intercourse "taste" each other, establishing the closest social relation possible through the mouth and the palate. A long-standing literary and psychiatric phenomenology has described smell as a metaphor of the most enthralling physical bonds—exemplified, once again, by the love between mother and infant and by erotic love. Some of Baudelaire's most beautiful poems allude to this connection:

> So a lover from beloved flesh
> plucks subtle flowers of memory . . .
> In bed her heavy resilient hair
> —a living censer, like a sachet—
> released its animal perfume,
> and from discarded underclothes
> still fervent with her sacred body's
> form, there rose a scent of fur.[8]

Now, in a precious aside in *The Sociology of the Senses*, developing a Kantian theme, Simmel points out that every perception (and therefore every social perception too) can be analyzed along two distinct and complementary perspectives.[9] From a subjective point of view, sense impressions present themselves as "my" sensations and provoke reactions of pleasure or displeasure inside me, accompanied by the feeling of a state of mind, a mood, a rise or drop in vital energy. In this case, perception matters because of its capacity to subjectively arouse pleasant or unpleasant feelings—*because of its aesthetic value*, not its knowledge value. From the objective point of view, however, sense impressions are directed outside me, toward the external world; they serve as a means of information for me about the nature of things and people, as a means for recognizing them by "characterizing them."

From this "double intentionality" one can draw an important conclusion regarding social *aisthesis*. While the two aspects are easily separable in nonhuman objects (it's easy for me to distinguish between the heady sensations aroused in me by the perfume of a rose and the objective characteristics of the flower), to come to know another person through knowledge that is completely purified of sensible impressions would seem in principle to be much more difficult. Our relationships with others are closely dependent on what we perceive about them—their appearance, their voice, their scent, and the atmosphere that seems to accompany them. In short, our knowledge of others depends on what Simmel defines as the "reaction of feeling to the sensible image of a person" (*sinnliches Bild*):

> Our sense impressions of a person allow the emotional value, on the one hand, the usefulness for an instinctive or sought-after knowledge of that person, on the other, to become jointly effective and for all practical purposes actually inextricable in the foundation of our relationship to the person. To a very different extent, of course, the construction being done by both, the sound of the voice and the content of what is said, the appearance and its psychological interpretation, the attraction or repulsion of the environment and the instinctive sizing-up of the other based on that person's mental coloration and sometimes also on the other's level of culture—in very different measures and mixes both of these developments of sense impression construct our relationship to the other.[10]

We can deduce a few principles from this crucial passage that will serve as a guiding thread for our social-aesthetic inquiry:

    1. Every social *aisthesis* is a mixture of objectivity (information about the perceived person) and subjectivity (reactions of pleasure or displeasure inevitably tied to the individual sensibility, emotions, and judgments of taste that are more or less subliminal), and the balance between the two varies in degrees and modes according to the specific combinations and characteristics of the senses involved. Sight and hearing tend primarily toward objectivity and have a high informational content: this makes it easier to share their perceptions (for this reason, too, they have often been described as the "public" senses) and exploit their political and moral potential.[11] Taste and smell, and probably touch, too, have more subjective associations, and they show a more individualistic, idiosyncratic, and potentially antisocial inclination.

    2. Given that social perception is always accompanied by pleasant or unpleasant sensations, the knowledge people have of each other is necessarily charged with emotionality and affectivity. The key to intelligibility of a social sensibility, that is, the role that sensibility plays in the nonrational dynamics of evaluation, distancing, and social hierarchization, lies concealed in the sensory, nonreflexive reaction that inclines us toward or away from the other person, originating in a movement of sympathy or antipathy.

3. *Aisthesis* is the a priori through which all the cognitive and practical dimensions of interaction pass. Their differentiation into separate spheres is shaped and conditioned beforehand by the aesthetic, fundamental dimension. This explains, among other things, why the arts that make it possible to influence social perception (all forms of publicity, staging, advertising, rhetoric, and erotic seduction, which we will connect to the concept of "prestige") hold so much weight in social and political dynamics. Rhetoric, for example, whether verbal or visual, is much more than a simple communication technique. It is a veritable art of social stylization: an art that acts on social mechanisms through the capacity to shape appearances and control the sensible logic that governs the laws of human attraction, the social production of value, and belief formation.

Nasal Questions

This examination of the sensory bases of social interactions ushers in a novel "aesthetic" approach to the philosophical question of recognition—that is, the idea that consciousness of self depends on the opinion and esteem of others and that human beings need respect, consideration, regard, attention, love, and other forms of symbolic appraisal from those with whom they share social interactions: How is our original "opening" toward others and our attitude in judging them and assigning them a value and status influenced by the inclinations of our senses? This approach has remained methodologically remote from philosophers like Axel Honneth or Paul Ricoeur, who have examined the topic in ethical and political terms (recognition as the respect we owe others) or, at the most, in cognitive terms (recognition as identification, as *Erkennen*).[12] The few studies that treat the sensory aspects of the phenomenon confine themselves generally to the sense of sight and consider the notion of visibility to be synonymous with that of recognition, in both the empirical and the normative senses.[13] We will come back to the role the eye plays in processes of social esteem. Here we will focus mainly on the senses of smell and taste, which, as we will see, can be taken as a single thing. The originality of the social aesthetic approach is best revealed in analyzing the "lower senses" and, in particular, the "chemical" ones.[14]

The most intriguing sense is that of smell. Despised by the philosophical tradition, which tends to view it as inferior, animal, not properly human because of its overly close bond with corporeality and its apparently meager informational content,[15] the olfactory sense is of great sociological interest precisely because it leans so strongly toward the subjective side of intentionality. This imbalance is what explains the strength of olfactory reactions and their tendency to be transformed into subliminal inclinations. While this phenomenon applies to all the senses, in smell it acquires a singular intensity, in the form of more forceful reactions of approval and disgust. Taste and smell serve as the "gatekeepers" to the environmental odors and substances that enter our bodies, and they play a vital role in avoiding danger and keeping distance.[16] Transposed into the realm of intersubjective interactions, these characteristics are reflected in turn in the approaching-distancing process that forms the basis of spatialization and social hierarchy. For this reason, the olfactory sense will serve as a guide to social aesthesiology.

Kant explains the negative, reactive violence typical of the sense of smell in his *Anthropology from a Pragmatic Point of View*: "Filth seems to arouse nausea not so much through what is repugnant to the eyes and tongue as through the stench that we presume it has. For taking something in through smell (in the lungs) is even more intimate than taking something in through the absorptive vessels of the mouth or throat."[17] Simmel picked up on Kant's analysis, bending it toward a sociological perspective. Unlike the senses that relate to the object through the mediation of representation (sight and hearing), smell inhales the emanations of the object and consumes them within itself. A sense of intimacy is created in the individual along with a feeling of fusion with the perceived object, which has no equivalent in the other senses, with the exception of taste. If associated with unpleasant feelings, this sensation of proximity and fusion can translate into an abrupt distancing: "it is obvious that this must lead to a discrimination (*Auswahl*) and a distancing (*Distanznehmen*) with a heightened sensitivity toward olfactory impressions altogether, which to some extent forms *one of the sensory bases for the social reserve of the modern individual.*"[18] Simmel alludes to the specifically *modern* form of the social aesthesiology of body odors: the "reserve" that in the pages of *The Philosophy of Money* and the essay on the metropolis represents the defense strategy typical of urban life. The idea has a more general philosophical value, however, in that it allows us to conceive of *smell as the sense of spatialization*, which regulates the dialectic between proximity and distance from deep inside.

The other socially relevant characteristic of the olfactory sense is its *lack of freedom*. The eyes are said to be free because they can decide not to look, to turn elsewhere, to withdraw behind the protective darkness of the eyelids. They have the privilege of possessing natural shutters and, similar in this respect to the palate, they can expel the object by withdrawing their perceptual availability (narrowing the eyes or pretending not to see are powerful expressive symbols of contempt). Of all the senses, sight seems to be the most free because it has the capacity to cut out and *choose its object* from inside the environment: it is the most extroverted, as if it came out of its den to venture into the public space, explore and probe the world, capture its images on the basis of the qualities that attract, and satisfy its taste.[19] In short, the freedom of the gaze demonstrates a propensity for an objectivizing and elective relationship. Glances scan and scrutinize before filling up with approval or disdain, and, maybe for this reason, the gaze has always been considered by philosophy to be the privileged vector in the rise of social passions, such as shame, embarrassment, honor, and glory, which form the medium for recognition and the granting of esteem.

A certain margin of freedom also seems to belong to the other senses, with the exception of smell. While hands or external devices can be used to avoid touching something dangerous and to stop up the ears, and the mouth can be closed, reject food, and spit it out, the nose is totally defenseless before the inhaled object and has no way to block its perceptions: if we plug our nose, we are forced to breathe through our mouth, which is notoriously ineffective at preventing nausea. This aspect too was discussed by Kant in his *Anthropology from a Pragmatic Point of View*, in which smell is defined as the *antisocial sense*: "*Smell* is taste at a distance, so to speak, and others are forced to share the pleasure of it, whether they want to or not. *And thus smell is contrary to freedom and less sociable* than taste, where among many dishes or bottles a guest can choose one according to his liking, without others being forced to share the pleasure of it."[20]

The uncontrollability of the olfactory sense is accompanied by the special synthesizing power of smells—their capacity to evoke the totality of an environment and a sensory atmosphere—which Baudelaire, Proust, and Walter Benjamin celebrated in their reflections on involuntary memory. In this case, too, smell is the vector of a distance-closeness relationship, which, since it occurs in time instead of space, takes the form of the presence-absence dialectic.[21] But the same *synecdochic function applies in the negative*. The "stink" of others—the sweat of the person next to us on the bus, or the unusual aroma of foreign foods that floats out from our neighbor's kitchen onto our landings and invades the privacy of our homes—forces us to share the world with people who are unfamiliar to us, whom we perceive as strangers and perhaps as threatening because they appear different from our looks and lifestyles. Simmel, a Jewish professor who was sidelined from German academia, recalls phrases like the "smells of Jews" and "Blacks," as well as "the sweat of workers," and concludes with a brilliant observation that *"the social question is not only an ethical one, but also a nasal question (eine Nasenfrage)."*[22] Nonetheless, despite his acuity, his analysis stops at a descriptive level, stating only that bad odor is the dominant sensation of social disgust: a recurring motif in condemnations of degraded environments and in racist and discriminatory insults. To go beyond description requires an examination of the history of stigmatizations produced by smells and the particular modes of their social construction.[23] This idea, to which I will return at the end of this chapter, is echoed in the autobiographical pages that George Orwell wrote about the "olfactory secret" of class distinction:

> That was what we were taught—*the lower classes smell*. And here, obviously, you are at an impassable barrier. For no feeling of like or dislike is quite so fundamental as a physical feeling. Race-hatred, religious hatred, differences of education, of temperament, of intellect, even differences of moral code, can be got over; but physical repulsion cannot. . . . It may not greatly matter if the average middle-class person is brought up to believe that the working classes are ignorant, lazy, drunken, boorish and dishonest; it is when he is brought up to believe that they are dirty that the harm is done.[24]

The question of a "politics of smell" has returned in contemporary normative philosophy but mostly in a form of bland humanism: for example, references to olfactory disgust appear in Martha Nussbaum's works, which condemn the way discrimination works against certain social groups, such as homosexuals and people of color.[25] The question deserves to be addressed with a much more radical approach. Rereading Nietzsche from this angle, we might hypothesize that politics consists in an olfactory relationship, since disgust at the odor of others is nothing but the sensory translation of the original, irrational friend–enemy distinction. Nietzsche, who said he had a special "nose" for other people, turned the metaphor of a bad odor—"Bad Air!, Bad Air!"—into the aesthetic a priori of intolerance. Condensed in intolerance toward the smell of others is a rejection of what is most individualizing, singular, and irremovable about them: their material body: "My instinct for cleanliness is characterized by a perfectly uncanny sensitivity so that the proximity or—what am I saying?—the inmost parts, the 'entrails' of every soul are physiologically perceived by me—smelled."[26]

If Nietzsche got it right in pointing out that almost nothing separates olfactory disgust from political conflict—whose true nature is a sensory "hand-to-hand" combat—his aristocratic conception represents the opposite of the democratic one espoused, for instance, by Rancière, who would raise the social-aesthetic question from the point of view of the excluded, those accused of "stinking," rather than from the perspective of those who exclude them. The consequences of the two approaches are nevertheless very similar for a critique of the rational enlightenment foundation of politics. The hypothesis of a civil conversation à la Habermas and Honneth, arranged out of the respect that derives from mutual rational and moral recognition, must come to terms with the preexisting aesthetic mediation that is inclined toward the idiosyncrasy of sensory exclusion, by neutralizing or sublimating it. How can respectful and egalitarian discussion take place with someone who has already been "prejudged" by the senses and rejected beforehand from the legitimate sphere of *aisthesis*?

As the sensory organ in which the mechanism of social esteem is made manifest in all its primal violence, the sense of smell plays a role similar to the role taste plays in Bourdieu's *Distinction*: a role that is simultaneously synecdochic–metonymic (the sense that represents the totality of the senses) and metaphoric ("It stinks!" as the principle of every social distancing). A new analogy between smell and taste is conceptually justified by the notion of *Oralsinn* (oral sense) that was introduced by psychiatric phenomenology and certainly deserves to be developed. Before continuing in this direction, though, we must explore the "atmospheric" nature of perception.

Air, Atmospheres, and Oralsinn

"That we smell the atmosphere (*Atmosphäre*) of somebody," writes Simmel, "is a most intimate perception of that person; that person penetrates, so to speak, in the form of air, into our most inner senses."[27] The image is interesting both because of its reference to air, the external element that can penetrate into the perceiving individual and fuse with him or her, and because of the return of the concept of atmosphere, which came up in the preceding chapter in connection with the social sensorium. The notion, which cannot be reduced to a simple metaphor, experienced a wave of popularity in the intellectual lexicon of the early twentieth century (especially in film theory and German-language psychiatry between 1900 and 1930),[28] and is undergoing a remarkable revival in contemporary philosophy.[29] Given that atmospheric theory fits in well with that of the social sensorium, I will attempt to update it by purifying it of its romantic aspects, akin to the phenomenology and philosophy of life—aspects that may point to the search for an original and immediate dimension of sensibility. The following remarks must be interpreted, as always, in light of the concept of aesthetic mediation and an "eccentric" idea of the sensorium.

In Simmel's vision the atmosphere is an envelope that surrounds the individual as the manifestation of his or her sensible image: the *sinnliches Bild*. Simmel also talks about nonpersonal atmospheres, which emanate from physical spaces and social circles: there are the atmospheres of alpine countryside, factories, and rough neighborhoods. In all these examples the presupposition is apparently that personal or impersonal atmospheres are sensible entities, quasi-things or quasi-places, possessing ontological independence and spatial autonomy (one goes in and out of them) as well as a capacity of emanation and capture (one gets caught in their sphere). Furthermore, every atmosphere is synesthetic. Simmel talks about *Bild* through metonymy, in virtue of the particular social significance of sight, but we can conceptualize the image as the product of multiple sensible perceptions, which transcend the visual dimension and meld together in a single overarching impression: the voice, for example, and the sounds and noises that a person produces intentionally and unintentionally (the sound of footsteps, sneezing, coughing); tactile elements like the prickliness of a beard or the fluffiness of a dress fabric, or even the simple sense of the tangibility of the body in space; not to mention smells, which include the natural odor of the body but also the artificial scent of perfumes, elegantly defined by Simmel as an "olfactory adornment." The comparison demonstrates that atmospheres are not natural entities—they are not auratic properties of the things themselves; they are artificially produced and influenced by human hands or by cultural *dispositifs*, such as architecture and design. Indeed, Peter Sloterdijk shows that the *air* is always *conditioned*, and that atmospheres are political entities: they can be designed in a multisensory fashion in order to govern and induce particular behaviors.[30]

Moreover, the example of perfume perfectly illustrates the "radiant" nature of atmosphere.[31] The propensity *to spread by emanation-irradiation-propagation* is an essential characteristic of the sensible sphere, which seems to possess a force of its own, far greater than the mere ability to transmit or connect that one normally associates with the senses, and that in Simmel's work is compared to a form of *social radioactivity*: "The perfume enhances the person's sphere as the sparkle of gold and diamond; one situated near it basks in it and is thus, to some extent, caught in the sphere of the personality. Like clothing, it covers the personality with something that should still work at the same time as its own radiance."[32]

To illustrate his idea of atmospheres, Simmel often compares the perception of people with that of places, unwittingly echoing a motif central to Proust's *In Search of Lost Time*, which dates from the same period. Just as for places, the sensory atmosphere of a person is at the same time a *medium*, the element of synthesis that connects the two poles—objective and subjective—of perception and a *milieu* in which they are contained and joined. The person who perceives, then, is not external to the perceived object, as a subject is from the object, but is entangled with it, caught in its atmosphere and impregnated with its unique "air." As Proust shows admirably in the description of the gaggle of young girls in flower who appear on the beach in Balbec or in the long passages on the atmosphere that surrounds Odette and envelopes her home, her clothes, and all her habits within a single harmony, the atmosphere goes well beyond the physical body of the individual with whom we come into contact, encompassing his or her entire "world."[33]

After Simmel, thought on atmospheres became a major topic in the phenomenologically inspired literature of psychiatry. The French psychiatrist Eugène Minkowski dedicated an entire chapter of his book *Vers une cosmologie* (*Towards a Cosmology*, 1936) to it, in which he analyzes the atmospheric nature of the smells that imbue themselves in things and people by diffusing in the air, thereby crossing over the boundaries between inside and outside, material and spiritual. "Smell," writes Minkowski, "reveals the existence of the atmosphere. It is the atmosphere endowed with its fundamental quality."[34] The German psychiatrist Hubertus Tellenbach, in his *Geschmack und Atmosphäre* (*Taste and Atmosphere*, 1968), introduced the crucial concept of *Oralsinn*, an "oral sense" that combines the functions of taste and smell.[35] For the individual, this sensory organ represents the point of penetration and fusion with the atmospheric element: unlike the objectivizing senses, which appropriate the external reality by means of representations, the senses that are traditionally considered inferior "englobe" fragments of this same reality, eating and breathing them, giving the impression of fusing them with the subject's inner world.[36] The conclusion that Tellenbach arrives at is philosophically provocative: at the source of our relationship with the world, as demonstrated by the experience of newborns, there is no clear distinction between subjectivity and objectivity, between consciousness and reality, but a "state of global affection." We are thus led to the concept that is the complement of atmosphere: that of *Stimmung*.

Sympathy, or the Aesthetics of Recognition

In daily life we perceive others in a holistic vision, which fuses all the various sensorial layers into a single impression charged with emotional factors and value judgments. We might define this as "atmospheric impression," as suggested by Léon Daudet, the medical writer and politician who championed Proust and in 1928 published a book full of profound insights titled *Mélancholia*. One of the problems discussed by Daudet is that of synthetic perception, which he defines as "impression d'ambiance." According to this theory, when we meet people, especially on the first encounter, what strikes us is the atmosphere that surrounds them: "We make an overall impression of them, which translates into a series of physical observations, summed up in a feeling of sympathy or antipathy. Only later, when remembering or meeting them a second time, do the elements of a portrait appear."[37] The atmospheric impression is doubly synthetic: from the objective point of view, it roots the various perceptions in a single sense impression, the overall appearance of the person; from the subjective point of view, it unifies the different dimensions—cognitive, aesthetic, and moral—which we are used to viewing as distinct, in a single affective state. We see people, their "air" strikes us positively or negatively, and we immediately react, sometimes openly at other times subliminally, with "I like them" or "I don't like them." This private innermost mixture of perception and taste is the principle of what I will define as *social physiognomy*, which basically follows impressionistic criteria. Of course, first impressions with their consequent immediate inclinations are adjusted and change even radically over the course of subsequent exchanges; but a nonimpressionistic attitude toward others is only possible at the cost of the wearying abstraction demanded by a reflective mediation.

The most appropriate philosophical concept for delving into the sensible logic that influences reciprocal relations of evaluation and recognition is that of *Stimmung*. Similar to the notion of "qualitative experience" that John Dewey theorized around 1930,[38] *Stimmung* is an aesthetic "experience," something that transforms perceiving subjects, making them different from what they were. And, as Dewey suggests, it is a "holistic" experience. When we perceive someone, when we breathe their atmosphere, the experience takes on a form inside us that makes it impossible to distinguish clearly between the cognitive dimension (what we know of them thanks to our perception), the emotional dimension (the sensations and feelings stimulated by the perception), and the practical dimension (the different relationships that can be established with this person). These three levels are fused into a single, predominantly sensible state characterized by a specific emotional tone that "colors" the experience with a qualitative individualization—referred to throughout Simmel's work as *Färbung*. (As understood by the philosophies of romanticism and German idealism, the synthesizing, unifying, and mediating function seems to be specific to the aesthetic dimension.) In this holistic sphere, the primitive intersubjective relation is always *preconditioned by an inclination that disposes us toward the other* in an endless multiplicity of given nuances: attraction, admiration, uneasiness, disgust, confidence, mistrust, love, sympathy, antipathy. Whether it is possible for a neutral and therefore colorless *Stimmung* to occur in a state of indifference remains to be determined.

It is actually *Stimmung* that lies at the origins of our "opening" to the world, just as Heidegger always pointed out, for that matter, reminding us that *being-in-the-world*, ec-static, in other words, constitutively external or "outside oneself," is always qualified by a specific emotional tonality.[39] Taking Heidegger's analytics in a specifically social direction, we must add that this is valid in the same way for the particular relationship to the *Umwelt* known as *Mitsein*, or *being-with-others*: although characterized by a large plurality of possible emotions, this "existential" finds a sort of primary structure, of which all the other emotions can be considered derivations or complications, in *the sympathy-antipathy pair, in other words, in the sensible inclination that attracts us to others or repels us from them.*

In brief, this examination of the atmospheric nature of social perception leads us to view "sympathy" as an original aspect of recognition, akin to the phenomenon that Axel Honneth speaks about in his book on reification: sympathy is "an elementary recognition," always charged with affective and qualitative elements. It reveals our participation or involvement in the existence of others, placing us in an affective disposition in relation to them.[40] Yet unlike Honneth's recognition–empathy, which addresses the generic humanity of the other ("we existentially experience the fact that every man is an *alter ego*," he argues)[41] and which claims universality, the model of recognition that can be drawn from *Stimmung* and *sympathy* addresses the individual personality of the other and distinguishes itself by its irreducibly idiosyncratic meaning: "I like them" or "I don't like them." So, if empathy is an emotional recognition that arises on the basis of what is common between me and the other—the experience that we share or that I am able to conceive of through the imagination—then sympathy is a fusion of emotional singularities. This is specifically due its aesthetic nature, which makes each encounter with others determined by the uniqueness of the circumstances of sensory perception and by the affective singularity of the individualities involved: the singularity of the other's sensory appearance, the singularity of my sensory reaction, the singularity of the sensory context in which the sense impression arises.[42] This is the gist of the provocative statement Joseph Brodsky made in his Nobel Prize acceptance speech: *"Aesthetics is the mother of ethics."* According to the poet, the categories of "good" and "bad" are first and foremost aesthetic ones: "The tender babe who cries and rejects the stranger or who, on the contrary, reaches out to him, does so instinctively, making an aesthetic choice, not a moral one."[43]

This aesthetic foundation of ethics, in which the universalist dimension is mediated on the basis of what Simmel would define as "qualitative individualism," clearly poses many problems at the normative level. Indeed, we can reflect on the consequences that the discovery of this aesthetic aspect of recognition—*sympathy*—has on moral recognition proper, in particular on the aspiration to treat others in an egalitarian and disinterested fashion. In what way, and against which forms of resistance, can the normative injunction to treat others with justice be asserted? What is this justice, and how does it relate to the *injustice* of that original qualitative inclination, the "coloring" that always gives rise to preferences and makes us discriminate against others according to the feelings they inevitably arouse in us—of pleasure and displeasure, sympathy and antipathy, like and dislike? From a Kantian perspective, would this justice consist in an equality of treatment and consideration, namely, in the affirmation of universal respect focused on the humanity of the other in the form of his or her rational capacity, an affirmation that must struggle against the sensible inclination by repressing it? Or does justice consist in cultivating an original sympathy, which can be universalized through progressive corrections and decentralizations—according to the teachings of the Scottish school of moral sentiment, especially those of Adam Smith? As can be guessed from its premises, social aesthetics proceeds in the second direction, toward the study of the dynamics of social sympathy and their possible moral and political stylization. But it does so by giving an original twist to this tradition, reinterpreting it in the light of the theory of reflexivity and spectoriality presented in the first part of this book—and thus tackling the moral problems raised by the aesthetics of recognition using the weapons of reflexive distancing. On the path of inquiry that I intend to follow, in other words, the way out is made possible thanks to our "spectator": not the external, social one that the Scottish thinkers and symbolic interactionists refer to but, rather, even before that, the *internal spectator*, who never coincides with what we are and feel in actuality, and who "shatters" our perceptions and expressions by mediating them. This is the only way the dynamics of *aisthesis* can be understood critically and be stripped of the subliminal influence they exert through aesthetic "biases." These questions are beyond the scope of this book, however, and will be addressed in future studies. In the following chapter, I dig deeper into the anthropological mechanisms of social aesthetics, especially into the role of taste and the dynamics of value and power.

13
SOCIAL TASTE AND THE WILL TO PLEASE

Simmel and Bourdieu

A comparison with Bourdieu's model of social distinction is invaluable for clarifying my theory of social sensibility, whose bases derive from Simmel.[1] While Bourdieu shares with Simmel the insight that what is at stake in aesthetics profoundly influences matters of recognition and social esteem, he fails to fully exploit the potential of this idea because he relegates it essentially to the sociology of elites. In the model used in *Distinction*, only the dominant classes practice discrimination and aesthetic distancing, by making it an instrument of their class domination. They can do so because they have the economic resources and free time (*scholè*) necessary to cultivate taste and acquire competence in the "realm of pure forms." As we have seen, Bourdieu tends to reduce the logic of aesthetic interaction to his understanding of material preconditions, hence, to the logic of class interest, so that his ultimate explanation remains an economic one. The perspective opened up by Simmel, on the other hand, is much broader because it rests on a foundation of philosophical anthropology, which has a more universal scope. While this wider perspective aids in understanding the strategy of the leisure class of his time, for example, in his analysis of the distinctive function of fashion,[2] in principle it addresses all the forms of interaction that take place in the social-aesthetic realm: the practices of all classes, all groups, and all individuals, including the least wealthy and educated, all of whom can be recognized as having an aesthetic competence and a social sensibility as complex and sophisticated as that of the elites. Social taste and sensibility are part of the essential "sensible baggage" with which every human being acts and lives in society (and, as we have recalled several times, it should be viewed as anything but a secondary factor: on the contrary, it is a primordial aspect with the power to fatally precondition and prejudice all our social relations). Admittedly, this leaves open the question of legitimate taste, in other words, of aesthetic hegemony (most of the time, to paraphrase Marx, the tastes of the dominant class are the dominant tastes), yet what matters in this broadening of perspective is that the aesthetic dimension becomes an ingredient and a decisive factor in any search for recognition and power.

Bourdieu's theory can be enriched by another of Simmel's insights, which proves to be invaluable: *social value is inherently aesthetic in nature*. This is a consequence of the social-aesthetic origin of recognition, a consequence that will be discussed in the following paragraphs. Nevertheless, it must be emphasized that Bourdieu's approach allows us to correct Simmel's with regard to at least two vital aspects, both of which are implicit in the theory of *habitus* formulated in the *Sens pratique* (1980)—which, not surprisingly, is closer to an anthropological approach.[3] First, thanks to its insistence on incorporation, Bourdieu's materialism attenuates Simmel's formalism, which surreptitiously threatens to lean toward idealism. We know that it is the issue of the *body*, in all its materiality, in all its energy and inertia, that is ultimately concealed behind sense and perception. Simmel has an ambiguous attitude toward this problem: sometimes he refers to it explicitly or indirectly (material bodies are glimpsed behind his numerous allusions to the "sensory copresence" of individuals in space), but he never engages deeply with the issue of the body. Consequently, the reader sometimes gets the impression that in his theory there are senses without flesh and appearances without bodily substrates.[4] Second, and even more importantly, Bourdieu's approach helps to correct the phenomenological style of Simmel's philosophy, which sometimes places too much reliance on the spontaneity of the senses. Bourdieu constantly reminds us that *aisthesis* and taste are also socially constructed and determined by patterns of perception, appreciation, and action that incorporate the structures of the social world (categories, values, systems of classification and power). For this reason, according to Bourdieu, our appreciative judgments are proper class or group strategies, molded by relations of power and aimed at social reproduction. What pleases or repels us is often what society has taught us to find pleasant or disgusting through the conscious and, more often, unconscious training of our sensory habits. This is why we must always be wary of *inclinations* that are mobilized in the experience of social *aisthesis*, as suggested by the orchestra metaphor that often resurfaces in Bourdieu's work: behind the sensations of agreement or disagreement that are implicit in all *Stimmung* (a word that alludes to an idea of harmonious convergence),[5] there often hides an impersonal "direction" that coordinates the members of the orchestra and has previously ensured that their instruments are in tune. Any theory of social aesthetics must take this constructivist reservation into account, following the methodological principle of *Wechselwirkung* in the analysis of social sensibility, too: one must consider the continuous interaction between subject and milieu, and therefore the way the habitat influences the *habitus*, the social sensorium, the individual sensorium, and vice versa.

Social Libido

As we have seen, the reactions of pleasure and displeasure that we experience when perceiving people necessarily involve an evaluative aspect: I like him, I don't like her, she's appealing, he's unappealing—these are all initial judgments of value that emerge from the physiognomic game inherent in social sensibility. When we come in contact with the air of other people, when we "sense" them acting inside us, we form a particular *aesthetic disposition* toward them. As Joseph Brodsky pointed out in his Nobel prize speech, cited in the previous chapter, this disposition is also *ethical* in character, inasmuch as it judges and evaluates people, with the implication that pleasing = good, displeasing = bad. It also announces a future practical attitude. The sensation of spontaneity with which this inclination is experienced conforms with the individual's socially constructed aspect, which is rooted in the *habitus*. With smell, this reaction is very impulsive, making it a sense that blatantly reveals the deeply irrational dynamic of social taste. Even so, this happens with all the senses in varying degrees of mediation, because of their subjective intentionality. The fact that every sensory impression is *mine*, that it brings pleasant or unpleasant sensations into *my* body and *my* psyche, necessarily involves an act of affirmation and negation on my part—the taking of a stance, the expression of an idiosyncratic *aesthetic-ethical taste*.[6]

The senses evaluate; the senses "esteem-ate." By virtue of being grounded in the body and in sensibility, life is therefore a continual creating and receiving of values. Perhaps no one has shown this with more vehemence than Nietzsche. According to the explanation given in *On the Genealogy of Morality*, the process of evaluation originates in the human psychology and physiology of pleasure. Every sensory perception is accompanied by a qualitative transformation of the individual's "vital sentiment" and, through appreciation or disgust, becomes the founding act of an external order. Taste not only discriminates between the objects that come under its sway, it also establishes classifications and hierarchies between them. Every apparently harmless "I like" or "I don't like" involves the propensity for ranking and for the subjective subjugation of the external reality, which Nietzsche defines as the pathos of distance. By means of our taste, we also define an order that creates power relations. The strong will seek to impose their taste as the dominant taste, by bending that of others and encouraging the making of a common sense according to the law of their own sensibility. This is the foundation of what we have defined as *aesthetic hegemony*: the fact that the tastes of the dominant groups are the dominant tastes. Bourdieu's sociology of distinction is based on these unexpressed Nietzschean assumptions, which surreptitiously inspire and inform it.

The way Simmel addressed the question of social sensibility was strongly influenced in its turn by Nietzsche. Simmel's interpretation not only emphasizes the theme of "distance" and the discriminating attitude of the senses, it also develops in an anthropological direction that explores the way mechanisms of social taste give rise to forms of seductive sociability. As much as human beings are interested in judging and classifying others in order to dominate them, the fact is that what they want even more is *to actively please them*. This desire to be appreciated and valued by others would seem to be a universal motivation. Let us not forget that Simmel is a contemporary of Freud: in his eyes, too, the world of human beings is permeated by a sort of universal libido that regulates the laws of attraction and desire. However, Simmel's pursuit of pleasure does not rise from the depths of sexuality as does Freud's (Simmel does not recognize any clear separation between depth and surface and therefore cannot even conceive of the psychoanalytical dimension of the unconscious) but rather resides in the phenomenal world of social sympathy. It is a desire for approval or, even more "superficially," a desire to capture attention, to pursue an admiring or interested glance. Although this impulse has a genetic and phenomenological association with what Simmel defines in his writings as "eroticism," it is actually closer to *vanity* than *eros*.[7]

This *social libido* does not have the pulsional body of urges as its direct protagonist; instead, it is mediated by the sensible entity of the social image or figure, which includes physical appearance but also reputation, honor, and so forth. Most importantly, the social libido is not involved in or subject to any symptoms or repression and is not encapsulated in an archaic timeless sphere: it is "superficial" (we need only think back to the phenomenology of vanity presented in chapter 6), constantly exposed to everyone's gaze, and ephemeral. To highlight where this concept is positioned, ideally in the intersection between Nietzsche and Freud, we will call it the *will to please*. It is also worth noting that because this theme is linked, as we shall see, to the concept of *Geselligkeit* (sociability), which is based in turn on the practices of the "salons," it might very well seem to be the most dated in Simmel's view. In actuality, it has proved to be a prophetic insight that is especially valuable for rethinking contemporary lifestyles. By now, the experience of social networks in particular has made it familiar, by resurrecting it in new forms of media sociability, perfectly illustrated in the success enjoyed by digital conversation practices (messaging and online chat rooms) as well as in the feedback between self-presentation (images and posts published by the individual) and aesthetic audience evaluation (via "likes" and comments).

Because of the pronounced aesthetic component of the social libido, vanity, or the will to please, has a kinship with "play." In this ludic, lighthearted, entirely "worldly" sphere lies the essential difference from the tragic social anthropology that Bourdieu would set out in his *Pascalian Meditations*, whose last chapter is devoted to the need for recognition as profound tragic motivations in the "social game." Bourdieu's explanation as to why human beings need to please and seduce one another is still close to that of the Augustinian moralists (significantly, his inspiration comes from commenting on Pascal's *Pensées*), founded on the idea of denied transcendence, of a world abandoned by God and grace. Simmel, on the contrary, describes an anthropology of absolute immanence, one that is radically antidualistic and not tragic (with the exception of the final, pessimistic phase of his thought, which is not in question here). For this reason, his vision of society is "worldly" in the double sense of the term that we have already recalled: the earthly "worldliness" in which humankind lives deprived of transcendent values and indulges in the practice of playful and casual sociability—the life of "society."[8] The "lightness" of Simmel's notion of society is made explicit in his reflections on the essence of sociability and coquetry, which he views as similar, precisely on the basis of their social-aesthetic nature: "in the sociology of the sexes, eroticism has elaborated a form of play: coquetry, which finds in sociability its lightest, most playful, and yet its widest realization."[9] The "art of flirtation" is the game of seduction, which is never consummated and, indeed, bases its attraction on the mode of "maybe" (the perpetual oscillation between yes and no, which feeds the allure of uncertainty, making seduction similar to gambling) and on the eternal procrastination of the sexual "decision."[10] The relationship between the admirer and the coquette is an exemplary illustration of the wider phenomenon of sociability—the art of being with others and pleasing them. It weaves intersubjectivity into a fabric of relationships that are infused with seduction and yet devoid of any overriding sexual end.[11]

It must be recalled that in Rousseau's analysis from his two *Discourses*, which is surprisingly similar to the one Simmel would sketch out—in much more critical tones, though, still inspired by Platonic-Augustinian dualism and the condemnation of alienation—he also spoke of an obsession to please others ("désir de plaire"). This desire would constitute the primary motive of socialized individuals and, in the customs of fashionable society, would take expression in a specific sophisticated "art de plaire" (art of pleasing) that can be taught and translated into principles.[12] Rousseau also recognizes a strong similarity between the dynamics of vanity introduced in the romantic relationship between the sexes and the dynamics that are enacted in sociability: in both cases the desire to be loved and taken into account, *amour-propre* or *vanité*, leads to universal competition and the fight for distinction: "To be loved, one has to make oneself lovable. To be preferred, one has to make oneself more lovable than another, more lovable than every other."[13] As Rousseau thus argues in the *Discourse on the Arts and Sciences*, the process of civilization consists in an aesthetic refinement of customs, a process founded on the growth of the principle of seduction, to the point of paroxysm. His diagnosis would be echoed in the genealogies of Elias and Sombart on the association between appearances, politesse, the arts, gallantry, luxury, and wealth in modern capitalism. The material progress of society has gone hand in hand with the hedonism and aestheticization of forms of sociability. In other words, modernity corresponds to an intensification of social-aesthetic practices and values.

Simmel's notion of sociability involves another insight that deserves to be salvaged by social aesthetics, an insight founded, as always, on the methodological principle of reciprocal interaction: the dynamic of social seduction is a *mutual libidinal exchange*. To please others and to capture their admiring or desiring gaze, which gratifies and fulfills me, I must in my turn provide them with pleasure. And vice versa: to please others, I inevitably end up giving pleasure to myself. The term *pleasure* contains this implicit reference to reciprocity, which seems to replicate in non-sexual social terms a reference to *copula erotica* (erotic bond) (this similarity also becomes explicit in the phenomenon of flirtation). Thus—reads the first passage of the excursus on the psychology of jewelry and adornment—an initial goodness or desire to be a joy for the other, to please the other, is immediately compensated by the value that "flows back" on us: "Interwoven with the desire of the person to please associates are the opposite tendencies in the interplay of which the relationship between individuals generally takes place: a goodness is in it, a desire to be a joy to the other, but also the other desire: that this joy and 'favor' would flow back as recognition and esteem, our personality be reckoned as an asset." However, as Simmel stresses in one of the jabs in which his thought comes closest to that of Bourdieu, the mechanism of reciprocity is reversed automatically in that of power: "this need increases so far that it entirely contradicts that initial selflessness of the desire to please: even by this kindness one wants to distinguish oneself before others, wants to be the object of an attention that will not fall to the lot of others—to the point of being envied. Here the kindness becomes a means of the will to power."[14]

Simmel repeatedly uses the Hegelian name, *Anerkennung* (recognition), but his concept is distinguished from the Hegelian version by its strong aesthetic cachet—the fact that Simmel introduces it reflecting on the social meaning of ornamentation is highly significant—and, instead of leading immediately to ethical or political values, it unfolds according to the logic of the senses and the normativity of taste. Simmel's desire for recognition is not, as in Hegel's and Honneth's, like a desire for love, respect, or social consideration—all qualities that involve the deep inner moral sphere of the individual. It is something much more "sensible," tied to appearances and the social image. Those who seek recognition, in other words, do not want to be respected for their potentially universal moral dignity or to be considered for their specific contribution to the political community; they want to please like an aesthetic object, they want to be appreciated by the other's taste for their individual sensible qualities and social attractiveness. Unlike the Hegelian process, moreover, this elementary move has no universal normative dimension and falls onto the path of "desire for distinction," a strategic derivative of the will to power.[15] This mixture of the desire to please—and thus dependence on others, with the desire for superiority—gives rise to the flagrant contradiction that is typical of all models that see the quest for recognition as a form of the pursuit of distinction, like those of Hobbes and Bourdieu: "there arises thereby in some souls the strange contradiction that, with regard to those people over whom they stand with their being and activity, they nevertheless find it necessary to build up their self-esteem in their consciousness precisely in order to keep them subordinate." We have already commented on the reasons for this ambivalence of vanity, which in Simmel's version (unlike in the thought of Hobbes or Bourdieu) receives a form of compensation, since the egotistical aspect in the quest for distinction and superiority is "corrected," as it were, by the involuntary altruism of bringing pleasure to others. Now, this libidinal exchange implicit in the anthropology of pleasure—to obtain gratification you must give it to others—seems to be an essential characteristic of all sensible values. It explains not only the profound similarities that bind the *aesthetic exchange to those of the erotic and the economic* (the three spheres in which values associated with desire, pleasure, sensibility, and corporeality count for something), it also illuminates some of the reasons for what I have defined elsewhere as the "voluntary servitude" proper to the aesthetic dimension. What I mean by this is the love we bear for appearances, which we allow to dominate us so easily. The forms of power that pass through the aesthetic dimension take their foundation from the individual's active complicity, from his or her social libido and will to please.

To conclude, it should be noted how Simmel addresses the problem of recognition: he remains within the philosophical paradigm of the seventeenth and eighteenth centuries, by linking it to the phenomena of the individualistic pursuit of power and distinction, pleasure and sympathy, as do Hobbes, Rousseau, Hume, Smith, and so on. He passes immediately from the eighteenth-century anthropology of the passions to that of Nietzsche, thereby bypassing the normative turn of Kant and Hegel. His fundamental difference with Honneth lies in this anti-Kantian and anti-Hegelian approach. And it is precisely this aspect that I find interesting to reclaim in order to provide a philosophical understanding of social-aesthetic phenomena that fits the needs of our society and our times.[16]

14
AESTHETIC LABOR AND SOCIAL DESIGN

The Value of Appearances

Adornment as a Paradigm of Aesthetic Value

What human beings seek in the quest for recognition is above all a sensible value. We want to please and, before that, to be perceived: to receive attention and attract the eye, which increases the individual's social value through the mechanism of imitation and envy. Referring to a phrase that circulates in contemporary culture, we can associate this aesthetic theory of social value with an economy of attention,[1] in which value is produced precisely by its ability to attract attention and looks—to *"cause a sensation."* In this strategy of struggle for perceptibility, adornment plays a fundamental role, thanks to the sensual attention that it arouses. The latter immediately gives value to the subject, while at the same time conflating the Simmelian dialectic of the will to please, to be for oneself and to be for others: "The radiations of adornment, *the sensual attention that it provokes*, create such an enhancement for the personality or even an intensification of its sphere *that it is, as it were, greater when it is adorned.*"[2] Adornment intensifies the sensible image of the personality, which is diffused in its atmosphere. Among all adornments, jewels are endowed with a special power of social magnification, for the most elementary reason: not only are they superfluous (hence functionless) and expensive (hence distinctive), they shine—they are "brilliant." In turn, they illuminate the wearer and create a halo effect that illustrates, literally, *the law of the irradiation of the sensible*.[3] Brilliance is one of the most overused metaphors of social recognition that exist, for that matter: the brilliant person is the one who is most noticed and most remembered.

Simmel's notion of adornment can be compared with the definition that Thorstein Veblen gave to luxury a few years earlier in his *Theory of the Leisure Class* (1899). Luxury, according to the American economist, is *conspicuous consumption*: "spectacular" waste, intended to be exhibited in the public space and perceived as a grandiose appearance meant to attract attention, inspire admiration and envy. Luxury, in other words, is not simply and strictly an economic phenomenon; rather, it is a communicative, rhetorical, and hence social-aesthetic phenomenon: its essence is its appearance, its displayed image, which is indeed intended to be "consumed" but in ways that are very different from those foreseen by the paradigm of individualist and purely material hedonism. In Veblen's view, luxury is a staging that is inconceivable away from the representational sensorium of modern society. On this staging, the relationship between subject and object transcends the economic concept of utility, or rather reinterprets it with a curious twist. The object is not used strictly for the purpose for which it is apparently conceived (individual consumption of the luxury good); instead it is spectacularized to become a status symbol. This representational deviation is illustrated by the emblematic case of the idle servant who "does not serve" but whose job is to signify the wealth and leisure of a master who can afford to keep the servant idle. Another example is the trophy wife, who is exhibited in society as a representational apparatus instead of performing her functions as a wife, in the darkness of intimacy. Like Trimalcione's banquet in Petronius, like the parties given by Jimmy Gatz—who redeems the humility of his origins by magnifying himself through his phantasmagoric consumption and transforms himself into the Great Gatsby—Veblen's luxury is made to be seen, admired, talked about, so that its image can be communicated and propagated in the public space. This is why those who seek easy visibility and social recognition, such as snobs, social climbers, and parvenus, yearn so strongly for it.

There exists an emblematic literary illustration for what we have just discussed. It is a passage from Proust written slightly after the reflections of Simmel and Veblen, in the third volume of *In Search of Lost Time*, known as the Stagebox of the Princess de Guermantes. Proust describes an evening at the opera that condenses the entire aesthetic representation of high society, concentrated in the finely wrought *ekphrasis* of the social-aesthetic value of luxury adornment:

> At once plume and blossom, like certain subaqueous growths, a great white flower, downy as the wing of a bird, fell from the brow of the Princess along one of her cheeks, the curve of which it followed with a pliancy, coquettish, amorous, alive, and seemed almost to enfold it like a rosy egg in the softness of a halcyon's nest. Over her hair, reaching in front to her eyebrows and caught back lower down at the level of her throat, was spread a net upon which those little white shells which are gathered on some shore of the South Seas alternated with pearls, a marine mosaic barely emerging from the waves and at every moment plunged back again into a darkness in the depths of which even then a human presence was revealed by the ubiquitous flashing of the Princess's eyes....
> "That's the Princesse de Guermantes," said my neighbour to the gentleman beside her, taking care to begin the word "Princesse" with a string of P's, to shew that a title like that was absurd. "She hasn't been sparing with her pearls. I'm sure, if I had as many as that, I wouldn't make such a display of them; it doesn't look at all well, not to my mind (*je ne trouve pas que cela ait l'air comme il faut*).[4]

Marcel's neighbor is grossly deceived in judging the propriety of the staging: the pearls have, literally, *the air that they must have*. They are indispensable to the princess's social image; they are an essential part of her public figure, and for this reason they must be flaunted and squandered in all their garish abundance. Their prime reason for being lies precisely in their precious value and the lack of economy in their display: according to the teachings of Marcel Mauss and Georges Bataille, to properly bear witness to sovereignty and grandeur, consumption should be superfluous, excessive, and have the proportions of a spectacular sacrifice. Indeed, the value of the thing possessed is not as property but as an object of public perception, so that *to have* is transformed into *to be*; possession becomes an image as it fuses with the individual's public appearance. This *transformation of having into being* is one of the most important principles of social aesthetics. Complementary to the economic value of the pearls, and inseparable from it, is their *aesthetic* value—the set of sensible qualities that they possess and, chief among these, their *orient*.[5] It produces an aura around the princess, a sort of atmospheric halo that magnifies her perceptibility and "irradiates" like radioactive substances into the environment to create a sensation.

In general, the study of luxury should always be looked at from a dual perspective, by integrating an analysis of economic aspects and foundations, in any case indispensable, with an analysis of aesthetic aspects and foundations. This complicity is demonstrated exemplarily in what I will define as *prestige value*, which introduces an aesthetic and representational factor into the definition of the social hierarchy. *Prestige is actually status represented through the senses*—it is status in image, social value in sensible form. In addition to its economic bases and components, prestige must be understood through its qualitative consistency, its sensible perceptibility, its formal arrangement, and, last but not least, its appeal. As we shall see further on, the allure of status and the particular attraction of prestige are in reality one of the domain's greatest "sorrowful mysteries."

At this point, another brief comparison between my social-aesthetic approach and that of Bourdieu might be helpful. If social value is created by means of *aisthesis*, then social value itself must have sensible qualities; or, more precisely, *it must be a sensible value by itself*. Precious objects offer the best example of this, jewels and sumptuous clothes in particular and, even earlier, precious substances, which, not surprisingly, seem to have a particular relationship with the representation of social value in many cultures, even those that are distant from each other. Gold, diamonds, ebony, ivory, pearls, rubies, emeralds: after comparing the precious objects that different cultures have used to embody and represent status, the archaeologist Grahame Clark comes to the conclusion that their value is created by the specific organoleptic and *aesthetic qualities* of precious stones (the shine and transparency of the diamond, the luminosity of the pearl, the sanguine color of the ruby) along with their economic and social qualities (scarcity, difficulty in acquiring them, and so on). Precious stones speak a language of the senses, the same language as art, which provokes sensory experiences and gives pleasure to those who admire and own them.[6] A similar argument should be made with regard to the *formal*

Aesthetic Labor and Social Design 179

properties of objects, imparted to them by craftpeople through their technical skill. This art of transforming sensible appearances is what I will call "aesthetic labor": the way a gem is worked, its mounting, the design and embroidery of a dress, the style of a work of art. These attributes lend a material and objective aspect to aesthetic value that is irreducible to the game of social distinction: the social-aesthetic value is what effectively attracts and enduringly retains the viewer's gaze.

Once again, Bourdieu seems to have glimpsed the right trail. In his research he shows that strategies of social distinction are articulated with privilege through the possession of artistic objects and familiarity with the arts. Yet he oversimplifies the problem due to his reductive attitude toward the aesthetic sphere: in his view, when this sphere is reduced to its economic reasoning, it lacks any autonomy or specific logic. Moreover, as we saw in the second part of this book, his structuralist conception of value leads him to see pure *positional values* in objects and aesthetic practices, independent of the objects' *sensible and formal qualities and meanings*.[7] Conversely, for me, social value itself has a social-aesthetic origin and effectiveness. As adornment, objects of art attract attention and desire precisely because of their sensible qualities and forms. As we will see, the aesthetic labor on the sensible image of social subjects is subject to the same law.

A truly exemplary case of this idea is van Dyck's art. The Flemish painter was celebrated for his ability to represent social status, and in particular for his famous "treatment of hands," whereby he endowed his models with an additional painted finger bone to increase their distinction in the viewers' eyes.[8] This added finger bone, which creates an illusion of nobility, perfectly embodies the definition of prestige as status represented through the senses, or the representation of status in the public sphere—in a nutshell, "the image of status in publicity." What is obtained through the labor of appearances is an aesthetic *surplus value*, which interacts profoundly with the creation of social and economic values. Appearance is not limited to "aestheticizing" the economic and hierarchical relations of power, as theories of aesthetic capitalism would have it: appearance contributes actively to creating them, making them exist in the collective perception and sensing.

In general, the art of van Dyck, like that of Andy Warhol, which I will discuss at the end of this book, illustrates perfectly the profound complicity between different spheres of sensory pleasure that underlie the dynamics of social aesthetics. The *value* of something precious cannot be determined without accepting the idea that *economics* and *aesthetics* do not simply interact; they are fused in a single combined action. Not only is economics (the useful) not alone in creating aesthetic value (the functionalist explanation) but aesthetic value (that which is attractive and pleasing) mutually creates social value (to make oneself desired and thus generate a different kind of utility).

Exhibition and Display

When interpreted against the backdrop of a more general sensible logic, then, the analysis of adornment lays the foundations for a more general theory of aesthetic value. Simmel's analysis of adornment can be linked up with some of his other insights on value in *The Philosophy of Money* and even more in a short but illuminating essay on the Berlin trade exhibition, "Berliner Gewerbe-Ausstellung" (1896).[9] In this article Simmel reflects on the "exhibition form" (*Ausstellung*) and prophetically defines the emergence of a new sensible value in modernity, which he calls, using a felicitous expression, the "shop-window quality of things" (*Die Schaufenster-Qualität der Dinge*). This value, the *display value*, is a vital link in the chain between aesthetics and economics.

Here is Simmel's explanation. The production of goods in the regime of free competition and the predominance of supply over demand ensure that objects tend to show a seductive aspect that overshadows their utility. In order to attract the interest of the buyer, a further appeal must be added to the object's use value, through the way the product is arranged and presented. Simmel defines this characteristic as "putting into form," an "aesthetic *superadditum*" that takes place through the arrangement and display. The ability to give a more pleasing visual appearance to things that are useful, a talent typical of Eastern and Roman cultures, here stems from the struggle to win over the buyer. Anything inherently lacking in grace is made graceful: "The exhibition with its emphasis on amusement attempts a new synthesis between the principles of external stimulus and the practical functions of objects, and thereby takes this aesthetic superadditum to its highest level. The banal attempt to put things in their best light, as in the cries of the street traders, is transformed in the interesting attempt to confer a new aesthetic significance from displaying objects together—something already happening in the relationship between advertising and poster art."[10]

This analysis can be juxtaposed with the one offered by Gernot Böhme,[11] but with the crucial difference that the concept of "added" sensible value—which combines with the economic value to reinforce it—in Simmel's idea is joined with a notion of social exchange that is already mediated a priori by *aisthesis*. There is no clear difference in nature between the use value and the display value that echoes the substance versus appearance dichotomy in the Platonic ontology; nor is there a similar distinction between "natural" needs (primary utility) and induced (aesthetic) needs. Both spheres are "sister" divisions of the primary realm of sensory pleasure: aesthetics and economics.[12] Simmel's analysis of the origins of display value thus avoids lapsing into a unilateral critique of alienation, but it amounts to the still critical but more immanent analysis, open to dialectical developments, of a specific stylization and modern intensification of sensory values in which the preconditions are already contained in the aesthetic nature of social relations. Although modernity has certainly intensified and exasperated the aesthetic aspect of display, there does exist a current of anthropological continuity that links the forms of publicity and advertising characteristic of industrial capitalism with those used by common people to enhance the value of their merchandise. For example, the cries of street vendors, the display of goods in a market—and, indirectly, all the simplest everyday practices of decoration, adornment, and self-presentation.

Simmel then concludes by showing how the form of the display transforms the value of the individual objects in an exhibition, according to a dialectic that is similar to those of social competition: an object can be depreciated by a neighboring one that possesses better qualities, but it can also stand out to its own advantage; a leveling and uniformity prevail due to an environment of the same; however, a principle of individualization is also established. On the one hand, the whole is the summation of the exhibition; on the other, the whole is the single object. The sensory effect on the viewer, who is subjected to a disordered hodge-podge of sensory stimuli, is amplified by the whole. According to Simmel's analysis, the viewer reacts in line with the typical dynamics of modern life: hyperexcitation or blasé indifference (there is thus a profound similarity and reciprocity between the urban sensory form and the exhibition form introduced by industry, capitalism, and art exhibitions). The experience of visitors to the exhibition is marked by superficial attention, by the distracted glance of the *flâneur*, which glides over things.

Display is an excellent example of how the "form" with which the human hand transforms things—in this case by displaying them, mounting them, putting them in the best possible light—contributes substantially to creating their value and is intimately connected in modernity with the dynamics of artistic competition. Thus, for example, the painter Fernand Léger would argue at the beginning of the 1920s that the war waged by art dealers through the arrangements in their window displays had become the hidden model of artistic competition: "The front window spectacle has become a major preoccupation of the dealer's business. Unbridled competition lies there: the desire that animates our streets is that of being seen more than one's neighbor."[13] The artist and the window dresser had become the biggest competitors in the production of aesthetic value—a competition that in Léger's view triggered a crisis in the status of artists. After emancipating themselves from dealers, thanks to their ability to technically produce aesthetic value, artists saw this advantage threatened by the rivalry of display value: hence the race for visibility at all costs and the progressive spectacularization of the art world.[14]

In addition to the activities of the *window dresser* and the phenomena of *publicity* and *advertising*, prophetically mentioned by Simmel, an eyewitness to the first advertising posters, this form of aesthetic value creation via display has been crystallized in an exemplary way in one of the most representative professions of today's creative economy: that of the exhibition "curator," an increasingly important figure on the artistic and media scene. The primary function of the curator is clearly a socio-ontological one: that of institutional "framing," which consists in transfiguring the object, endowing it with the status of "work of art," by the very decision to exclude it from the everyday world and display it in a gallery.[15] But the curator is also the expert who lends an aesthetic surplus value to any object through the staging of its parts, the space, and the exhibition mode (it does not matter if the object in question already possesses an aesthetic value, as in the case of artworks), by putting one thing next to another but also by knowing how to enhance it through proper lighting, the choice of times and places, the right background, a suitably contrasting color, and so forth. Although there do exist artist–curators whose personalities eclipse the works they are exhibiting, a good curator is distinguished ideally by his or her ability to be invisible and act as a pure medium in creating objective value. However, the display value produced by the exhibition form is not in reality a transparent value, like the glass pane of the cases that ideally convey it. It adds real character to the exhibition itself. Because of its individualizing power and subliminal opaque nature, therefore, the form of exhibition can be compared with the equally value-enhancing form of style.

Style

Style is the sensible representation of character: it is the form that embraces the different contents of an entity, giving them an appearance that is unitary and coherent, an identity, and, above all, the *quid* that allows it to be characterized. Every identity, whether personal or collective, is a moral unity, and this unity, which exists in the psychic interiority of individuals or groups, manifests itself in the world, which exists instead in an intersubjective-objective mode, in the exteriority of the public sphere, by taking on an appearance. This sensible aspect has certain formal qualities that endow it with a unique personality: these formal qualities recall the reference to "mark" in the etymology of "character" (in classical Latin, the word meant a branded or impressed letter made by a seal that was a distinctive sign)[16] as well as the concepts of "firma" (designer label) and "marca" (brand), which dominate the Italian language of marketing and fashion.[17]

It has often been observed that the ability to express the character of a social whole is exemplified in the style of a historical epoch, whose various elements resemble one another, preserving the common traits of a family look. This stylization effect actually shows itself in every social group, each of which, without exception, is expressed in a specific style. There exist immediately recognizable styles of social stratum and class; of gender, profession, generation; of intellectual, artistic, and sports associations. Paradoxically, among the most stylized social groups we find those that one would expect to be more insulated from what they perceive as the temptations of aestheticism because of their calling, such as religious orders and social protesters, because there is no more eloquent way to express one's "difference" than to show it through immediately perceptible signs, qualities, and forms.[18] Each category has its morphological characteristics, its patterns and models, chromatic symbols and blazons, gestures, stances, and, obviously, customs, understood as much in the sense of an acquired bodily and gestural *habitus* as in that of costumes, in the sense of clothes, which constitute the most elementary signals of a collective membership. A painter such as Frans Hals, portraitist of the Dutch guilds, or a photographer such as August Sander, had the ability to harness the representational resources of social physiognomy, emphasizing the aesthetic effects that in themselves give social subjects the appearance of artworks.

Style not only unifies internally, it also distinguishes externally. Through style, a set of appearances acquire cohesion, they agglomerate and "form" a sensible identity that separates it from other identities and defines its position, or difference, in relation to other individual forms. This double movement of identification and distinction influences communicative pragmatics and thus has a substantial effect on perception and memory. One of the most important communicative functions of style lies in the *ability to impress*, to imprint itself on the membrane of our sensibility. As Simmel rightly remarks, "There are some kinds of conduct, some ways of speaking and some works of art *that impress us in such a way that we are wont to call them stylized*—while others strike us as evincing no such consistency of form across greatly heterogeneous contents."[19] Style allows an identity to be recognized and, even before that, to get noticed, by attracting attention and making itself memorable: the more style a character has, the more "effective" it is from the communicative point of view. Not surprisingly, one of the first rules of advertising art—even more important than that of simplifying content and forms—is precisely stylization. Stylization can be applied to a product or a brand but also to an individual, such as a candidate for a competition or political party: Mitterrand, for instance, whose innovative presidential campaign of 1984 was the first in France to be fully orchestrated by an advertising agency,[20] and more recently Obama, whose youthful, direct, elegant style was encapsulated in the "Hope" poster by Shepard Fairey during the election campaign.

Stylization is also at the basis of the concept of the "coordinated image" or "corporate identity" employed by marketing and branding. The concept is of great interest to scholars of aesthetics, as it leads us to reflect on the relationship that a collective entity (and not only a commercial business but also a public organization or a group of political activists) maintains with its sensible and visual form.[21] But there is more to this. The sensible form, *the style*, is not simply an added appearance, a decoration that aestheticizes a preexisting entity; rather it is what *creates the unity of the group*, enabling it to be represented in the public space and therefore to exist in a social form, fostering the identification of its members through common symbols. Once again, it is clear how aesthetics is the medium and condition for the possibility of the social.

The Division of Appearances

These considerations on the inherently "advertising" nature of style, which makes things more striking and memorable, also apply outside the advertising realm, where it is openly acknowledged as a professional practice. All seductive practices, from erotic to commercial ones, make use of advertising techniques. And, as we shall see, even prestige and glamour, the special forms of stylization that transfigure and produce status, work in the same way.

Indeed, besides its capacity to generate identity and differentiate, style is also classificatory and status-creating; it is the latter, fundamental attribute that completes its socially constructive constitutive function. To demonstrate this, simply call to mind a phenomenon known to experts in aesthetics, the correspondence between expressive styles and social status; but reverse the meaning normally given to it from the perspective of the sociology of art. We are used to thinking that the division of styles in the various artistic forms and genres corresponds to the real structure of the society: for example, the distinction between *sermo humilis* and *sermo nobilis* and between comic and tragic in rhetoric and literature; the rigid conventions in the history of Western painting that separate the state portrait, the official political portrait of the court, from the kinds of scenes in popular genres; or, to give two examples from music and architecture, the different leitmotifs in Wagner's tetralogy that distinguish the noble gods from the Nibelung and the five orders of architecture (Tuscan, Doric, Ionic, Corinthian, and composite), which during the Ancien Régime differentiated homes according the rank of their inhabitants. In other words, styles and forms reflect the preexisting, actual divisions in social strata, classes, genders, professions, and so forth. This is undoubtedly true and is in itself an indication of the flexibility of aesthetic forms, which seem to have the gift of adapting themselves to social content by virtue of a deep affinity. From this perspective, the complicity between aesthetic form and social content is explained semiotically, thanks to the "readiness" of the sign to take on an expressive and communicative function.

Among the many possible illustrations of this idea we can examine the entry for *ordre* (order) in the *Encyclopédie* by d'Alembert and Diderot. In it, a physiognomic expressiveness equal to that of the human face is attributed to the rigid stone facades of eighteenth-century *hôtels*.[22] According to the author of the entry, the Chevalier de Jaucourt, the order of society prompts us to seek in the order of architectural styles the medium that is most fitting to represent them, in the belief that there always exists a sensible form most in keeping with the individual social content. Military character is martial: therefore, among the formal repertoires available in the tradition one will look for the style—the Doric—that best expresses the idea of martiality, through its linear, symmetrical solid forms. To define the ecclesiastical style, instead, one will avoid ornaments and other signs of frivolity in favor of forms that express a composed dignity. And all this with due regard for the overall symbolic proportion, which grants the right to represent the highest standing in the hierarchical order, in both social and aesthetic terms, to the king alone.

Now, if the social order can be represented thanks to stylistic differentiation, why not also test out an argument that runs opposite and complementary to that of the encyclopedist? This reverse reasoning would consist in asking ourselves, on the basis of the theory of aesthetic mediation set out in the first part of this book, to what extent the *Stiltrennung* is not the factor that conditions social content. Might style be what creates distinction and classification—revealing itself to be the production site for classifications and symbolic hierarchies? Its status-creating function lies precisely in the ability to distinguish, distribute, and structure the material of the sensible world. Style separates, differentiates, and orders by virtue of form: it's the formal device of every hierarchy. For this reason, every division into classes corresponds naturally to a division in styles, and vice versa: the two concepts coincide. Concealed in this correspondence is what Adorno and Horkheimer called, in *Dialectic of Enlightenment*, the most guarded aspect of "style's secret: obedience to the social hierarchy."[23]

The difference between the two perspectives, between the *sociology and semiotics of style* and the *social aesthetics of style*, seems minimal. In reality, it is crucial. In the first case it is assumed that status exists prior to its representation, and that the sensible form is chosen more or less arbitrarily as a *sign* for expressing the social standing. The noble is noble, the bourgeois bourgeois (the definition of the "real" changes, then, depending on the interpretation: a Marxist will define it on the basis of economic position, a lawyer on the basis of titles, and so forth). These real categorizations look for the means to show themselves and be recognized in the realm of shared appearances, in the symbolic order, as well. From the sociological perspective, which converges with that of semiotics, the realm of appearances is only a language that society uses to express and communicate its content, but the contents are already constituted before the semiotic moment arrives. Conversely, from the social-aesthetic perspective, the moment when a social entity is formed coincides with its aesthetic representation. Society comes into existence, it is ordered, and this is when sensory material *takes form*, out of which the shared world is composed.[24]

Within the scope of social aesthetics, the "division of appearances" fulfills a function similar to that which the division of labor and the institution of private property fulfill in the sphere of political economy. (It must be remembered that I argue from a standpoint that *rejects any idea of a hierarchy between levels of reality, of which one is thought ultimately to determine the others*; rather, I think in terms of interaction between material and nonmaterial dimensions of life. The explanation provided in this book is no more idealistic than it is materialistic.) The importance of "the division of appearances" cannot and must not be underestimated, as the rulers of the Ancien Régime knew very well. They drafted their *sumptuary laws*—the political–aesthetic rules by which styles were defined to correspond to the various social categories and identities—with the greatest of care, and incongruous appearances were censured.[25] These rules did not simply regulate luxury for moral reasons or to oblige certain individuals or groups, such as prostitutes, Jews, and beggars, to wear distinguishing or stigmatizing signs: in reality, sumptuary laws *regulated the appearance of the social world as a structured whole*. Deciding on the legitimacy of public appearances—not only of clothes, shoes, and adornments but also of manners and styles of behavior, haircuts, the size and decorum of homes, the conspicuousness of consumption—made them genuine techniques of "social design": taxonomic aesthetic rules that determine the place of each individual and group in the system of common appearances, the reciprocal relations between their social images, and the criteria of exclusion and inclusion.

Modernity has not entirely abolished sumptuary laws, as one might first think; it has *reinterpreted* them and shifted them into a different domain. The normative restriction of social appearances has been largely removed from legal control and transferred to the social sphere, where only theoretically is it less repressive, and where the laws of the state do not apply but those of recognition and social differentiation do. Parallel to the crisis and ending of the Ancien Régime, along with the birth, or rather the promise of greater social mobility, the formal possibility of dressing more freely took hold, and therefore the possibility of formulating a style of one's own more in keeping with one's felt or desired identity. We no longer seek to appear in a way that conforms to our rank and social category; instead, we want to express our singularity and individual difference: this is the reigning sensation, legitimized and nurtured by individualistic ideology.[26] In reality, this greater freedom does not cancel out the normative pressure, which imposes itself on subjects no longer or not only in obedience to the codes imposed by rulers but in subjection to imitative–distinctive social dynamics.[27] According to Arjun Appadurai, modern consumers are victims of fashion as much as the consumers of primitive or traditional societies are victims of sumptuary laws. Moreover, even in modernized Western countries, laws pertaining to individual appearance persist and are designed to punish those who violate the style assigned to them (the French debate over the veil, for example, although the American Constitution is also full of normative references to clothing).[28] More often, though, the division of the sensible relies on morals and codes of propriety, educational precepts, or simple trends. It is, in any case, still a social-aesthetic censure, whose task is to mold and organize the *facies* of society: *deciding how human beings must appear to one another also means governing them.*

In short, style is the aesthetic device through which a set of appearances, which corresponds to a social identity and has acquired a determinate and particular formal configuration, is situated in a relationship of hierarchical interdependence with other forms within a system. As a world of internally structured appearances, every society always corresponds to a system of styles. This insight was familiar to the great sociologists, like Veblen, Elias, Simmel, and Bourdieu, who viewed the concept of "lifestyle" as a key to the study of social stratification and differentiation.[29] For social aesthetics, as a way of appearing perceived and recognized by others, *a lifestyle coincides with a way of being* and thus contributes to defining the ontology of the social. If it is true, then, as a great taxonomist once asserted, that the style is the person,[30] it is even more true that *the style is the society*.

15

PRESTIGE AND OTHER MAGIC SPELLS

Aesthetic Power

Appearances not only play a fundamental role in the creation of social value but also wield an illusionistic capacity, a force or power that acts on the psyche and the human body through the medium of sensibility. Perhaps nobody has formulated this truth more effectively than Pascal:

> Our judges have understood this mystery well. Their red gowns, the ermine skins which they wrap themselves in like stuffed cats, the courts where they pass judgment, their fleurs de lys, this whole impressive accoutrement was strictly necessary. And if doctors had no long robes or mules, if professors did not wear square caps and gowns four times too big, they would never have duped the world, which cannot resist such an authentic display.[1]

What in ordinary language we call social prestige is none other than this *display* (in French, *mise en scène*) of appearances, which strike the senses and the imagination—a faculty with such unique powers that it is defined by Pascal as *la reine du monde* (the queen of the world).[2] Pierre Bourdieu, whose later work developed specifically from these observations of

Pascal, has rightly described this ability to impress as a form of power that compels us and moves us even beyond our own intentions, leading to subjugation, acquiescence, and recognition, also against our interest: "the power, which certain people have, *to impose their own self-image as the objective and collective image of their body and being.*"[3] In this passage from *Distinction* Bourdieu continues by comparing this ability to impose one's image on others to charisma—which represents the subjective and active side of what, in the vocabulary of his theory, takes the name of symbolic power: "The charismatic leader ... 'makes' the opinion which makes him; he constitutes himself as an absolute by a manipulation of symbolic power which is constitutive of his power since it enables him to produce and impose his own objectification."[4] However, the innovative contribution of Bourdieu's sociology does not concern the study of the forms of extraordinary authority linked to specific personal qualities—charisma proper, as in Weber. The originality of his approach consists in showing how power also and especially acts in *impersonal, diffuse, invisible, and ordinary forms*. This is due to the hidden pressure that institutions and social stratification exert on the psyche and on the human body, through the symbolic order.[5] In Bourdieu's eyes, charisma actually exists in an objective form, as prestige freed from personal qualities: for power to exist there is no need for exceptional individuals blessed by grace. Thanks to the respect for social hierarchies and status, the ability to impose on others one's desired image need only be exerted in a diffused manner that goes largely unnoticed in games of recognition and systems of classification. Whatever packs respect and social consideration onto itself is prestigious, that is, symbolically powerful. Prestige is not an exceptional gift: it is *charisma without heroes*. Like the judge's gown and the doctor's white coat, it resembles a *garment*, a uniform that symbolizes a special status and whose action begins only when it is worn in the appropriate context: its power is a "status effect."

Unlike Bourdieu, however, I will not be talking about symbolic power but about *aesthetic power*, to underline the fact that this force acts on the basis of aesthetic, sensory, and sensible dynamics. These dynamics maintain an intimate relationship (suggested explicitly by the passage cited from *Distinction*) with the question of the "effectiveness" or "capacity to act" of images. This is a familiar question to scholars in visual theory and studies, but one that is rarely considered by philosophers and social theorists and scientists.[6] My social-aesthetic perspective aims to reconcile the two fields of knowledge through the intermediary of the sensible logic. The power that Pascal recognizes in the fleurs-de-lys, which Proust attaches to the princess's pearls and, more generally, to the fascinating lifestyle of the Guermantes "clan," or which van Dyck embodies in the extra finger bone added to his models' hands, is display. Since display acts in and on reality, causing particular effects that involve and stimulate human feelings and behavior, it is perhaps a type of "image act" (*Bildakt*), according to Horst Bredekamp's definition, which refers to a specific "power of images" and equally specific "visual agency."[7] Like the image act, prestigious representations or stagings do not act through mechanical contact and exert physical pressure on bodies but through *actio in distans* (action at a distance). This form of action, more similar to a seduction than a constraint, makes more fluid and ambiguous the one-directional and asymmetrical relationship between active and passive that is implicit in traditional concepts of power—or, even better, "in the notions of common sense," since *any* relationship of authority and subordination is based on reciprocity and therefore on an "active," spontaneous contribution on the part of the dominated.

This and other characteristics of the so-called *agency* of images have been focused on throughout a long tradition in the history of Western thought, with alternating success: Begun in antiquity and triumphing in the Renaissance through the strong influence of Neo-Platonic theurgy, during the Enlightenment interlude the idea underwent a hiatus when the problem of action at a distance (according to the version of scholars who are convinced that modernity cultivates an iconoclastic intent) was put aside in embarrassment,[8] because of its relationship with the irrational and its disturbing proximity with magic. Rising up again in the romantic period and reasserting itself in the early decades of the twentieth century, thanks to the foresight of pioneers of visual studies such as Warburg and Benjamin, the agency of images has come back powerfully into fashion in recent decades—a period known for its *iconic turn*: the effectiveness of images has become a crucial key to deciphering an ever more "spectacular" contemporary culture.[9] The reasons for this revival are certainly understandable, although its modes are often charged with hyperbole and some philosophical naivety.

The reflections on prestige that follow can be considered a partial contribution to this discussion from the point of view of social philosophy. They aim to clarify the social power of images, and more broadly that of sensible appearances, through the social-aesthetic chiasmus, by adopting a middle position between rationalist and materialist reductionism and "animism," in which a certain contemporary iconic theory indulges. (It behooves us to recall once again that from the social-aesthetic perspective the image is also a synecdoche of the entire realm of sensible appearances, and therefore what is true for images and for the sight can be rethought, while giving due respect, of course, to the specific modes of each sense and to the related forms of art.) The attention given to the aesthetic dimension aims to grasp the specific sensible logic with which appearances act—their sensory appeal, their specific aesthetic value—without flattening it into that of other motives such as utility, understood economically. The contribution of philosophical anthropology, psychology, and social philosophy, on the other hand, helps to clarify the terrain of human sensibility on which this appeal hinges: the search for sensory pleasure, taste, affects or passions, imagination, seduction, imitation, the desire for recognition and distinction, and so forth. As I recalled at the beginning of this book, behind a mesmerizing spectacle there always exists a human hand that has prepared the staging and that guides it—"showing is a practice"—even if the practice and the hand are not necessarily expressed in an intentional, personalized way. Once the old eighteenth-century metaphor of the invisible hand is brought back to earth, which is to say, deprived of its divine aspect and consequent teleological and providential purpose, it offers a good depiction of how social-aesthetic dynamics also act through impersonal and unconscious factors of stylization such as habits, the power of suggestion, fashions, and so on. Recognizing that images have their own powers should not make us forget that this power would make no sense and would be of no political interest without a constant mutual action from the side of the human beings who produce them and look at them. *The life of images is still a human life, and the power of images acts thanks to human practice and to the effect that the sensible qualities of things exert on human sensibility and sensoriality.* When one forgets this simple principle, one inevitably falls into the illusion of fetishism condemned by Marx: "It is nothing but the defined social relations between men themselves which assumes here, for them, the fantastic form of a relation between things. In order, therefore, to find an analogy we must take flight into the misty realm of religion. There the products of the human brain appear as autonomous figures endowed with a life of their own, which enter into relations both with each other and with the human race."[10]

The difference in the approach I take in this book is that Marx relates the fantastic forms to the economic domain, which he himself likened to "freezing" water, in that it excludes any qualitative connotations, while social aesthetics also seeks to relate the nature of fantastic forms to their sensible dimension—a realm that is always "colored," always qualified by sensible and emotional values, and always stylized in some form. To preserve this ambiguous perspective we will continue to use the term *prestige*, which Bourdieu, heir of Marxian and Enlightenment rationalism, considered to be too compromised by ordinary language and therefore lacking in rigor: "If we have to talk about 'symbolic capital,' it's not for the pleasure of forging a concept; 'symbolic capital' is better than 'prestige,' which destroys what it designates by making it banal."[11] The concept of symbolic capital, which is the objective counterpart of symbolic power as subjective power (prestige–charisma), carries with it the opposite disadvantages because it *banalizes* the aesthetic dimension. As we have seen in previous chapters, Bourdieu's approach to value, which is close to that of structuralism, tends to reduce the symbol to its function as a distinctive sign, without acknowledging any genuine aesthetic cachet or independent expressiveness.[12] Bourdieu's value is a *status symbol*, which proves in turn to be more properly a *status sign*—purely conventional, arbitrary, and positional. It has nothing of the substance, fascination, or evocativeness of the symbol in the strictest sense of the word. Gold is a sign of distinction because it is an economically exclusive good, not because it is a material endowed with certain sensory qualities. It is valuable because it is rare and because it is an elitist possession, not because its reflections and color recall the warm rays of the sun and how these rays enlighten the subject's field of perception. From Bourdieu's perspective, a work of art is always valuable because of the exclusivity involved in acquiring and appreciating it, not for its inner expressiveness and beauty. A form acquires worth only in relation to its position with respect to another form that is easier to interpret—not for its coherence or originality. Unlike Simmel, to explain how phenomena in the aesthetic sphere interact with those of power, Bourdieu does not examine the specific logic of the senses and the way it interacts with the economic sphere in determining value. Instead, he relates the sensible logic to the economic logic of the accumulation of utility (players compete to win advanced power positions within a field). In a nutshell: *appearances as such do not possess any specific aesthetic effectiveness*. Their power is quantitative (that of a "capital" of empty values, of "distinctions"), not qualitative. To explain why human beings allow themselves to be deceived by display requires that one resort to the logic of utilitarian interest, thereby denying the very issue of "enchantment": "If, as Mauss indicates, it is 'impossible to understand magic without the magic group,' it is because the power of the magician is a legitimate imposture, collectively misrecognized, and hence recognized."[13] *Magic* is a word that recurs almost obsessively Bourdieu's works on art. The illusion of art consists in magic; the task of the sociologist of art is to demystify it.

My point of departure will be different: I will not destroy magic a priori; rather, I will try to explain it as a social-aesthetic issue, which integrates the representational perspective with a perspective focused on techniques of artistic elaboration. These are what create the aesthetic illusion and lend aesthetic value to things and their representations. It makes sense, then, to retain the word from ordinary language because it preserves traces of a precious etymology and of an equally precious semantic history that is almost identical in all the main European languages.

Prestige

According to the most authoritative explanation,[14] *prestige* comes from the Latin *praestigium*, "trick," "illusion," "spell," which the Romans used mainly in the plural (*praestigia, -orum, praestigiae, -arum*) in a similar way to the Italian expression *giochi di prestigio*, and the French and English *prestidigitation*, the technical term used by illusionists to define sleights of hand. In this regard, popular culture evokes a second Latin derivation, *praesto* and *digitus*, which refers to the ability to move one's fingers very quickly. (One is immediately struck by the references to an "invisible hand" that creates a magic effect.) In games of prestige based on sleight of hand, such as the three-card trick, magicians used only their own manual skill, without any rigged props or equipment. Unlike jugglers, virtuosos whose goal is to impress the audience with genuine physical skills, prestidigitators attempt to deceive their spectators entirely with the illusion of their art.

Fundamentally connected with negative associations, then, prestige alludes to a trick designed to intentionally deceive a public of spectators. The origin of the word *praestigium* refers in turn to the verb *praestringere*, which means "to capture," "to bind tightly," as in the expression familiar to ancient Romans, *praestringere oculos*, "to dazzle the eyes or blindfold them." These etymologies, which relate prestige to illusionist techniques practiced for the purposes of seduction and manipulation, become even more interesting if we consider the semantic history of the word, which can be resumed in three phases.[15] In the first, the word *prestige* indicated illusions of supernatural origin, "prodigies" that violated the predictable order of nature and resisted any rational explanation. An intermediate phase gave rise to "seductive trickery," arts of human origin but with mysterious workings, which serve to produce captivating illusions: rhetoric, poetry, and the theatrical arts. Finally, in the sense that would become established in the eighteenth century, the word came to mean "the power to seduce and make an impression on the imagination of others with a remarkable act or a brilliant situation or one that is judged to be such": in other words, human attributes that arouse veneration and respect in public perception, such as social position, authority, and charisma.

To sum up, *prestige* is a word that passed from a metaphysical use to an anthropological and sociological one, to indicate human prodigies who, despite belonging to the ordinary experience of our world, seem to preserve something magical about them: the authority of a leader, the attraction of a movie star or celebrity, or even the simple fascination exerted by brilliant people or uniformed military personnel. The linguistic continuity appears to be justified by reference to the common phenomenological substrate preserved in the Latin etymology. This could be defined as the "phenomenon of *illusio*." The reference to this experience that is universally known and familiar but difficult to conceptualize is what has allowed the powers of a magician, the persuasive force of a rhetorician, the atmosphere of an exclusive milieu, and the charisma of a leader to be qualified in the same way in the evolution of language. It has also allowed the particular forms of human relationships that we call suggestion, seduction, influence to be grouped together in a single category despite their differences. An examination of the word *prestige* and its derivatives serves as an index for recognizing the phenomena that belong to this family of "everyday spells."

Several words akin to *prestige* in the main European languages have undergone the same semantic evolution: *charm, glamour, fashion* (English); *fascino, malia* (Italian); *charme, fascination* (French); *Zauber, Scharm* (German); *encanto, hechizo* (Spanish); *fascinação, encantamento* (Portuguese). All these words are used in reference to fashion (many have lent their names to popular magazines), the star system, advertising, fanaticism, high society, celebrities, and the communications and media side of politics: in a word, the social "spectacle" demonized by Debord, to which the conventional wisdom contained in ordinary language seems to have a paradoxical reaction. The fact that the lexicon of magic is used to denote this entire phenomenal realm is actually a symptom of our perplexity in the face of a swarm of appearances that are simultaneously attractive and threatening to us, which seem to enslave our psyches and seduce our imaginations: whatever manages to dominate us without the use of physical constraint appears to us as some sort of spell or sorcery. However, considered in a historical and social perspective, this linguistic usage proves to be paradoxical: the phenomena that we denote using the metaphor of magic illusion are precisely those that exponents of social critique consider responsible for contemporary forms of alienation and attribute to aesthetic capitalism's colonization of life. On the one hand, we can only lament the inability of the conventional wisdom demonstrated by language: by giving up on defining and hence on understanding more precisely that which exercises such a great power over us and affects us so intimately, it merely settles for evoking an ineffable *je-ne-sais-quoi* (but maybe this inability is in itself proof of the problem's importance: that which is more difficult to objectivize always touches us more deeply). On the other hand, we cannot fail to recognize the inconsistency of the collective self-representation: a society that tends to define itself as rationalized, scientific, and economic agrees to cohabit with an irreducible sphere of magical experience, blatantly putting the lie to Weber's thesis on the disenchantment of the world. What is at stake is not simply a hidden and repressed ground of irrationality that threatens to return when the dialectic of the Enlightenment reaches its last stage. Magic seems to have triumphed in all fields of social life in which appearances play a role: we are constantly immersed in its hypnotic spell.

Magnetism, Suggestion, and "Influencers": Ideas from the Belle Époque

In light of this linguistic and semantic history, I can now return to the question of prestige. Bourdieu's example is representative. Contemporary social theory has in fact abandoned or neutralized the concept in the name of a more "scientific" approach, which identifies prestige with status (considering it, therefore, as the positional value within the stratification hierarchy) and relates it to the logic of the economy (economy of prestige, symbolic capital, social capital, capital of *visibility*—the only term to preserve some reference to the field of *aisthesis*).[16] In reality, there was a period between the end of the nineteenth century and the early decades of the twentieth century when the concept was at the center of social and political discussion, from a much more original and philosophically more meaningful perspective. We find it in the lexicon of almost all the most important social thinkers of the time—Gabriel Tarde, Gustave Le Bon, Thorstein Veblen, Georg Simmel, Max Weber—who used it to tackle issues that seemed to be unrelated but were actually all linked in some way to the phenomenon of *illusio*: imitation and social distinction, charisma, suggestion and hypnosis, the particular behavior of crowds, and the psychology of groups. Another aspect common to these works is what we would today call their interdisciplinary approach: the problem of prestige is effectively addressed by fruitfully interlacing theoretical assumptions with studies of individual and social psychology, history and sociology of religions, political theory, and so forth.[17] In this method aesthetics does not appear officially as a discipline, but the references to the power of images and representations, examples taken from rhetoric, from the psychology of the passions and the imagination, from the history of arts and fashion, abound, so much so that it would not be far-fetched to hold these studies up as examples of social aesthetics *ante litteram*. Allow me therefore to retrace some crucial moments in this twentieth-century debate in pursuit of ideas to inspire this inquiry into the contemporary world.

We owe the first pioneering analysis to Gabriel Tarde, who has deservedly returned to the attention of current intellectual discussion.[18] In chapter 3 of his *Laws of Imitations* (1890), Tarde wonders about the way human relations, of an entirely imitative nature, take form on a microscopic level according to the laws of magnetism. The direction and intensity of the mimetic flows are always conditioned by the attraction of *prestige*, a force that acts as a social magnet, sparking the active forces of belief and desire in the magnetized subjects. Followers of prestige are not subjected to physical violence or even terror and deception; they turn spontaneously toward the model that appears superior to them in the desire to get closer to him and be more like him. This is why prestige has represented a formidable form of authority since ancient times: "in the beginning of every old society, there must have been, a fortiori, a great display of authority exercised by certain supremely imperious and positive individuals. Did they rule through terror and deception, as alleged? This explanation is obviously inadequate. They ruled through their *prestige*." And Tarde concludes: "The example of the magnetiser alone can make us realise the profound meaning of this word. The magnetiser does not need to lie or terrorise to secure the blind belief and the passive obedience of his magnetised subject. He has prestige that tells the story."[19]

Prestige is irrational and immaterial, a "nonlogical force" that, like all forces, shows itself and is knowable by virtue of its effects: its ability to attract by awakening and stirring up the latent forces in magnetized subjects. The status of these subjects is likened by Tarde to that of "sleepwalkers"; but this does not mean that the contribution of those who are affected by the force of prestige (all social actors, since imitation is a universal law) is only passive. Indeed, it could be said that the opposite movement also applies, so that the prestigious model, who seemingly triggers the magnetization process, is actually responding reactively to the stimulus of the person who is fascinated by him. Prestige, in other words, is not a univocal relationship between an active and a passive individual. It is an *interactive, one-to-one* relationship (a *Wechselwirkung*, in Simmel's terms):

> There is in the magnetised subject a certain potential force of belief and desire which is anchored in all kinds of sleeping but unforgotten

memories, and that this force seeks expression just as the water of a lake seeks an outlet. The magnetiser alone is able through a chain of singular circumstances to open the necessary outlet to this force. All forms of prestige are alike; they differ only in degree. We have prestige in the eyes of anyone in so far as we answer his need of affirming or of willing some given thing.[20]

These analyses are extraordinarily applicable to today's society, which pivots around the figure of the "influencer": the sociability of new media appears to paradigmatically embody Tarde's mimeticism. To grasp more closely how relevant his ideas are, two clarifications from the *Laws of Imitation* may be helpful. The first concerns the transindividual nature of the mimetic principle, which is not consciously acted on by individuals as if their subjectivity were an autonomous action center, but which passes through them, splitting and fragmenting them from inside.[21] The second uses the mimetic mechanism to explain the production of distinctive differences, not only of memes, which are positive imitative units. True imitation goes instantly in the direction of the most prestigious influence, while distinction is a counterimitation, which consists in doing the opposite or something different with respect to the prestigious model (for example, by adopting an anticonformist or rebellious behavior).[22] Prestige remains the magnet-model of the action but in a negative way. Tarde finally distinguishes between two sociohistorical forms of mimetism: custom-magnetization (*magnétisation-coutume*), or the vertical, unilateral, and hierarchical imitation typical of traditional societies. The latter is oriented toward the hierarchically highest model, the most ancient and venerable, who focuses all the force of suggestion on himself according to a pyramid or "waterfall" principle. In fashion-magnetization (*magnétisation-mode*), which prevails instead in the most egalitarian societies, the distribution of the magnets is instead multicentric, individual force fields are less intense, and imitation follows criteria that are more horizontal, disseminated, and reciprocal. Fathers, age-old traditions, teachers, priests, and aristocrats are no longer imitated but brothers and sisters, friends, minor trends, and models that resemble us and our peers are imitated. The imitated and the imitator can therefore continually exchange roles, which is impossible in hierarchical imitation (as in today's street style, which influences the creation of *haute couture*, or in the case of parents who dress like their teen-age children). In other words, while in traditional, vertical societies prestige remains an elitist concept ("paternal prestige, the source of custom"),[23] in modernity prestige is a democratic, mass concept. It still remains charged with the power of attraction but as it loses power and adapts to its new, multiple, horizontal status it takes other names. Tarde describes what we now call *trendy, glamour, cool*.[24]

In the chapter of his *Psychology of Crowds* (1895) on the means of persuasion employed by the *meneur*—the leader and enchanter of crowds—Gustave Le Bon certainly had Tarde's analysis in mind. He develops it by giving even more attention to the effects of passivity exercised by this form of power and especially to their explicitly *political* effects. The problem now is that of subordination, of forms of domination that exert themselves in particular on what Le Bon, in a negative sense, views as the psychology of "the masses." In this approach, prestige is the leadership that is exerted on the people, who are gathered together in a gregarious form. Its force is comparable to magnetism, exercised not only by individuals but also by ideas and things, which exerts a "fascination" (another term from the magical family) on the psyche, thereby paralyzing the critical faculties and arousing an admiration charged with respect:

> Prestige in reality is a sort of domination exercised on our mind by an individual, a work, or an idea. This domination entirely paralyses our critical faculty, and fills our soul with astonishment and respect. The sentiment provoked is inexplicable, like all sentiments, but it would appear to be of the same kind as the fascination to which a magnetised person is subjected. Prestige is the mainspring of all authority. Neither gods, kings, nor women have ever reigned without it.[25]

Simmel's reflection on authority as the fascination exerted by the leader will be found in the section of his *Sociology* (1908) on domination and subordination. The word *prestige* is used to discuss the form of subjective and personal authority associated with the individuality of the leader, which is contrary to the authority proper founded on the objectivity of norms: "prestige emanates just as much from the purely personal factors as does authority from the objectivity of norms and powers."[26] Simmel seems to faithfully restate the ideas of Tarde (whom he admired unconditionally) and probably also of Le Bon (whose elitist premises he does not seem to share, however). He explicitly mentions the principle underlying this form of power, which can "captivate others," whip up enthusiasm, and, above all, be combined with a feeling of spontaneity—a feeling that is perhaps illusory but sufficient to prove the existence of some form of collaboration between dominated and dominator. "We cannot often defend ourselves against authority; the élan, however, with which we follow the prestigious individual contains a persistent consciousness of spontaneity."[27] The qualification of prestige as a "warmer" bond than that based on objective norms, because it is more intimate and more charged with emotional implications, is a good example of the "coloring" and "temperature" that Simmel recognizes in all social relations. It makes every social form also an aesthetic entity—and an economic one, according to the affinity between the two sensible logics, a concept already mapped out in the previous chapters.

Prestige is characterized, then, as a form of power because of its *psychagogic* effectiveness; for its capacity, that is, to lead and captivate the psyche. This capacity is exercised through a form of "sweet" coercion. A contemporary best seller calls it *soft power*, a power that gently influences the preferences of others so that they want to do what we want them to do.[28] Ordinary language, in turn, speaks of *seduction*. Thanks to its force of attraction, prestige *se-duces*, irresistibly leads toward itself, by arousing desire, reverence, and imitation. Whoever experiences it turns toward leaders with docility and freely and willingly follows them. According to Le Bon, this is demonstrated by two typical examples of "voluntary servitude" to prestige. The first is imitation in painting: the painter copies the model who is considered the most prestigious and signals a superior aesthetic appeal. The second is snobbery, or the exaggerated respect that the British have for their aristocrats, based on their titles and manners. The obvious aesthetic component and complementarity between art proper and the unconscious dynamics of social life shown by these examples make them of great interest to my investigation: What do the snobs described by Thackeray do except imitate the lifestyle of the upper classes exactly the same way artists imitate the style of the masters?

According to Le Bon, a prodigy essentially consists in the ability to elicit effective illusions and to make oneself admired and desired. Indeed, prestige acts through images, which force the psyche to think and thus act through them: "Crowds being only capable of *thinking in images are only to be impressed by images. It is only images that terrify or attract them and become motives of action.*"²⁹ In this case, too, as in Tarde, this is a power that acts by means of irrational associations: "A crowd thinks in images, and the image itself immediately calls up a series of other images, having no logical connection with the first."³⁰ (It is worth nothing that Le Bon and Tarde share a definition of *logic* as a method associated exclusively with reason, a definition that social aesthetics rejects decisively, revealing the existence of a *sensible logic*.) As in Tarde again, the state of those who come under the influence of the power of prestige is compared to that of a sleepwalker or someone who has been hypnotized—with the difference that for Tarde this state is proper to all social actors, while Le Bon, in the most dated comments of his theory, restricts this analysis to the "barbaric" psychology of the masses and to the inferior psyche, which, in his opinion, characterizes them. The reason the leader acts is to prevent the irrational, infantile mob from getting the upper hand. To this end, all techniques that call up fascinating images in the senses and popular minds are indispensable weapons. "An orator in intimate communication with a crowd can evoke images by which it will be seduced. If he is successful his object has been attained, and twenty volumes of harangues—always the outcome of reflection—are not worth the few phrases which appealed to the brains it was required to convince."³¹

Le Bon recognizes the power of images and, more broadly, of appearances and he explicitly offers a theory of this aesthetic power: "*Appearances have always played a much more important part than reality in history, where the unreal is always of greater moment than the real.*"³² However, he views this power as a weapon for enticing inferior beings—"the masses." His social psychology thus suffers from a twofold prejudice: it disdains the image, placing it naively in competition and contradiction with rational thought and granting no other status to appearances than that of simple unrealities; and he limits his analysis of prestige to the "popular mind," which in his eyes would be more sensitive to irrational suggestion owing to the effects of amplification caused by contagion and by the psychophysical proximity between people in crowds. There is nothing to stop me, however, from interpreting his social-aesthetic insights as valid even more universally, without class distinctions; all the more so if contemporary "mass society" can be viewed as a democratic, media version of certain aspects of the proto-twentieth-century crowd.³³

Let us look more closely at the form of seduction exerted by prestige, by recalling that Le Bon's *Psychologie des foules* (*The Crowd: A Psychology of the Popular Mind*) was published the same year that movies were invented: the first projection of the Lumière Brothers took place on December 18, 1895. His theory of the power of appearances owes much to the model of the magic lantern: the fascination of prestige is based on the *projection of appearances* in a dark room, in a Platonic cave where the irrational nonlogic of *illusio* and of the unreal take over: "These image-like ideas are not connected by any logical bond of analogy or succession, and may take each other's place like the slides of the magic-lantern which the operator withdraws from the groove in which they were placed one above the other. This explains how it is that the most contradictory ideas may be seen to be simultaneously current in crowds."[34] A little later, in pages whose sociological relevance is rarely remembered, Proust would use the same metaphors. To illustrate what the magical prestige of the aristocratic family of the Guermantes was for his upper-middle-class imagination as a child, the narrator compares it to the projections of the magic lantern and to the reflections of the medieval stained-glass windows in the cathedral of Combray: "like the image of Geneviève de Brabant, ancestress of the Guermantes family, which the magic lantern sent wandering over the curtains of my room or flung aloft upon the ceiling—in short, invariably wrapped in the mystery of the Merovingian age and bathed, as in a sunset, in the amber light which glowed from the resounding syllable 'antes.'"[35] Proustian prestige is also a social-aesthetic projection. However, compared to Le Bon's version, Proust's has the advantage not only of no longer being dependent on the personal charisma of the leader but also of being adapted along lines that run closer to ordinary social psychology. Proust has a deeper grasp of the imaginative, spontaneous aspect of the phenomenon, seen from below. Throughout *In Search of Lost Time* the power of suggestion that prestige possesses is proportional to the young age of the narrator, to the power of his imagination. Prestige is the magic of what seems to be fantastic and superior, which fascinates the child inside us all.

To conclude this digression on twentieth-century theories of prestige, I would like to return to Le Bon and emphasize that the specific interest of his ideas partly consists in the particular attention he pays to *techniques* (arts) that have the capacity to arouse and manipulate seductive images and to construct a dramatic staging. The art of operating the magic lantern involves an obsessive repetition of the same formula, an affirmative method, a pathos, an ability to evoke images and emotions in the mind of the people and then have these images and emotions circulate, thanks to the force of contagion and irrational imitation. Le Bon himself notes how these techniques are shared by the languages of politics and advertising, a phenomenon that at that time was still in its infancy.[36] Starting in the 1950s and 1960s, his insights would make a comeback, now developed more systematically, often on sociological and psychoanalytic bases, in advertising and marketing theories and techniques as well as in works that seek to demystify and critique them.[37]

Social Arts

Further examination of the psychological foundations of prestige do not fall within the scope of this book, but it is helpful to recall that this direction was immediately suggested by Freud, whose criticism of Le Bon concerns precisely the need to integrate the question of *suggestion* with that of *libido*, that is, of eros as a desiring force, according to Plato's writings.[38] As shown in the previous chapter, a theory of a *social libido*, the will to please, lends itself even more effectively to this end, since it preserves the dynamics of pleasure while uniting them to the aesthetic ones of vanity. Intertwined with the libido line of development is another that follows the problem of *mimetic desire*, elaborating on Tarde's approach and putting it in dialog with that of René Girard, who provided stimulating studies on prestige:[39] the ontologically lacking *I* projects its inadequacy toward an ideal model, the other, who seems to be endowed with all perfections and thus becomes an object of comparison and envy. But this projection is totally illusory, because all human beings are the same and only God is their ontological superior. The value of prestige is ultimately revealed as an imaginary, empty, relative, and positional value: it is the sense of inferiority that we all project on others. This approach brings Girard's theory of mimetic desire close to that of Pierre Bourdieu.[40] The mimetic approach suggested by Tarde and Girard converges in another approach, already indicated by Pascal and perhaps the most indispensable, which deserves further examination: that of the *imagination*. The imagination should be investigated not only as a psychological faculty but also in its ontological dimension, using a contemporary viewpoint to reexamine the insights of Medieval and Renaissance philosophy, which granted imagination the active capacity to create reality.[41] At the same time, however, the Enlightenment objections must be taken into account (rather than simply bypassing and ignoring them, as does the neoanimistic current of thought). All three paths, whether leading toward the libido, mimesis, or the imagination, are open to the social-aesthetic approach, and they deserve to be pursued in individual studies. A full analysis of prestige should always be developed at three levels, because the phenomena of social enchantment form a triad: the level of power (exercised in a personal or impersonal manner), the level of those who experience it and are attracted by it, and the *medium* in which this power is exercised, takes shape, and becomes effective. It is especially in this third dimension, that of *aesthetic mediation*, that the original contribution of social aesthetics proves to be an original tool for analyzing sensible appearances and the arts required to "prestigidate" them.

I will now focus especially on this last aspect, in the conviction that there exists an aesthetic power that is particularly important today in our form of life, and whose specific principle of action lies in its sensory and sensible nature: only the imaginal dimension of power, only its relationship with forms and senses, only its perceptibility and its particular aesthetic seductiveness, explain the existence of a power capable of eliciting desire, recognition, and love in the subjects who experience it. Fundamentally, this was something well understood in ancient Greek culture, which viewed the *ars erotica* and rhetoric as complementary psychagogic arts, both founded on the power of attraction of "beautiful appearances." Proust, too, understood it, making Marcel "fall in love" with the duchess de Guermantes's social prestige. In short, *power also acts by means of aesthetics*: through the medium of appearances and the arts that are capable of transforming them. As the Louis XIV character in the film by Rossellini reminds us, echoing the wisdom of the baroque moralists, "one governs minds not with the profound nature of things but with appearances": with a new garment, with a grandiose, luxurious palace, or even with a small sound, such as the syllable "amber light," which glows from the resounding last syllable of de Guerm*antes*.[42] Those who have the ability to create these seductive sensations with their art hold in their hands the magic wand of prestige: writers, musicians, painters, the great aristocratic

Oriane, whose fascination is repeatedly compared to that of a fairy, or even Don Draper, the brilliant advertising protagonist of the television series *Mad Men*.

What I mean by *social arts* is all the techniques of social-aesthetic labor, without distinction and hierarchical value, and without attributing any romantic-religious aura to the word *art*. (I could define them simply as "techniques," but art maintains an allusion to the *capacity for stylization*, for bestowing form according to a specific *aesthetic logic*, which strikes me as indispensable.) Under this category, then, fall the "major" arts— the fine, noble arts consecrated by tradition, such as literature, painting, sculpture, and architecture—and the "middle" arts, as photography was called at one time. Even more important for grasping the micrological functioning of the social-aesthetic dynamics, though, are the "minor" arts, which are often not even recognized as such: rhetoric, the art of appearing in public, of presenting oneself and maintaining a fine posture, cosmetology, etiquette, fashion, advertising, design, stage design and interior decoration, the curatorship and installation of displays, exhibitions, and exhibition spaces, as well as dance, fencing, and the equestrian art (disciplines that have largely died out and are purely decorative today but that, in the modern age, contributed fundamentally to the physical and moral disciplining of the elite), as well as the *arte de prudencia* that Baltasar Gracián considered indispensable for surviving at court and that might have an equivalent today in the ability to regulate one's exposure in the new public space of social media. These various arts focus on the individual facets of appearances—language and demeanor, gestures, facial expressions, manners, makeup, clothes and adornments, reputation, posture, context, and habitat—by developing specific technical skills and specific codes of rules. Their system is the basis of what I define as *social design*—the art of producing socially relevant sensible appearances.

Like all arts, social-aesthetic techniques require experience, taste, and savoir faire. And, like all arts, they can be practiced both as an amateur and professionally. Artists are, in the first place, social actors themselves who work on their own appearance or that of others—which, because no social phenomenon escapes constant transformation and stylization of its appearance, happens every single moment of life in society. Amateurism is such only from the point of view of officialdom and not in terms of the results, since these can reach unparalleled levels of effectiveness, as shown in the case of the greatest seducers and arbiters of elegance. Still, there is also a professional social aesthetics, proper to specialists of public perception, who exercise their profession as a paid activity: tailors, jewelers, architects, and decorators; the ancient teachers of rhetoric, good manners, dance, and fencing; the artists of the Renaissance courts. Today this role is filled by photographers, stylists, cosmetic surgeons, marketing and image experts, retail clothing associates, influencers, lifestyle journalists and bloggers, advertising and communications consultants, exhibition installers and curators. The task of these professionals is vital for communications and creativity. On the one hand, experts mediate between different rungs on the social ladder. They make forms and stylistic motifs circulate throughout the social body by performing services for anyone who can afford to pay for their skills: by telling members of the middle class how prestigious people decorate their homes, by explaining to young women how to dress or style their hair to keep up with fashion trends, by revealing to the mass public the most exclusive mysteries of the lifestyles of the rich and famous. The aesthetic mediator, whose role is embodied today primarily in impersonal media such as blogs and gossip and lifestyle magazines, creates relations between social spaces that would otherwise be too distant to communicate directly and causes the flows of prestige to circulate between them.

This mercurial function has become essential in the modern world, because it administers the promise of mobility and, therefore, the intensity of mimesis between groups and classes. The power of these experts of appearances does not reside solely in this medial role, however: it lies above all in their artistic skill, in their mastery, which allows them to dominate the art of creating the illusion of the symbolic order. Andy Warhol will serve as an example to guide us through this final chapter on social aesthetics.

CONCLUSION

*Social Immaterialism or
the Philosophy of Andy Warhol*

Exposure, Worldliness, Publicity

Many critical studies share the opinion that the aesthetic form specific to our time is that of *total exposure*—a sort of overexposure or radicalization of the opening that characterizes the human relationship with the world. Interpretations diverge in what they see as its causes. For those who adopt a materialist viewpoint, as we have seen, the phenomenon has its origins in the capitalist economy and in the commodity-form: that is, in the extension of market mechanisms to intersubjective relations. For others, the origin lies in the growing power of the media, especially social media (which are becoming increasingly similar to Foucauldian surveillance devices).[1] These explanations capture one facet of the truth but they must presuppose a radicalization of the social-aesthetic chiasmus as their condition of possibility. Modern exposure, along with the amplification of the aesthetic domain that depends on it, goes hand in hand with the intensification of the dynamics of sociability, if not with the tendency to make *social existence* identical with *existence* tout court. It appears in the universalization of what I would define as the three "social forms" typical of late modernity—exposure, worldliness, publicity—which, throughout the twentieth century to the present day, have proven increasingly vital in determining the lifestyles of the Western urban world and in defining its peculiar forms of aestheticism.

If there exists a kind of transcendental mental perception of sociability—an awareness of our being together with others that accompanies us in every instant of shared life—it can be identified specifically with the feeling of being exposed to the perception of others: what in ordinary language is expressed as "feeling somebody's eyes on you." From an emotional standpoint, this feeling is not neutral. It is located in a polarized tension between positive and negative, as shown by the opposite examples of exhibitionists' pleasure in undressing in front of strangers to excite themselves and the recurring anxiety dream, shared by many, of being naked in public. Clothing is perhaps the most important of the medial surfaces: it is the perfect compromise between revealment and concealment, allowing us to show ourselves and satisfy the exhibitionist urge while at the same time limiting total exposure and keeping something secret. An absence of clothing leaves individuals in the grip of their representational nudity, stimulating the sensibility, as an aesthetic receptor, that lurks in the social experience and distinguishing *excitability* as one of its most characteristic possibilities.[2] Totally exposing oneself thus means not having any more masks to hide from the light of the public sphere, opening oneself up completely in the sensorium, and making oneself nothing but a percept in the senses of others. This practice of exposing oneself totally to the senses of others can be exciting in an ambivalent way.

One of the charms of *worldliness* (in the sense of the French *mondanité*) is rooted specifically in this exposure: it is the most aesthetic of the forms of sociability and the most modern (not surprisingly, it shares a common etymology with "fashion," la *mode*, and "modern," le *moderne*, not to mention its history, which began in the 1600s).[3] Subjects externalize themselves by opening up completely in the public space: they acquire an increasingly phenomenal being; they make themselves entirely into appearance, pure social image. This externalization of their nature also corresponds to the intensification of active sensoriality, the ability to perceive and feel pleasure, which is expressed so well by the famous verses of Voltaire's poem "Le Mondain" ("The Worldling" or "The Man of the World"): "I love luxury, and even laxness / All the pleasures, the Arts of all kinds, / Cleanliness, taste, adornments: / Every honest man has such feelings."[4] Luxury, sensuality, taste, pleasure for the arts, for the suitability of forms, and for decoration: the aesthetic sphere dominates worldliness, although in a sense that is never completely emancipated from the interests and ends of practical life. Indeed, contrary to what Simmel argues in his essay on *Geselligkeit*, in sociability aesthetics never become completely independent from the other dimensions of life (and much less so from the economy, whose kinship it always maintains) but it certainly leaves its imprint on them: it is their "dominant."[5]

Worldliness is therefore the quintessence of the aesthetic dimension of the social: the virtual space where one neither works nor produces but spends time with others, conversing, having fun, playing, dancing, flirting, and consuming. The state of sensory intensification that characterizes every worldly encounter is generated by a dialectical interplay—both active and passive—between the two aspects of perceiving and being-perceived. It is a dialectic of which a key moment is the *party* (not in the sense of a Rousseauian republican celebration or a Dionysian event, which are its specular opposites). During a party, worldly society gathers together in an occasion for intense self-perception. The entire social-aesthetic arsenal is mobilized: special outfits (we don evening gowns to go "into society," cocktail attire, theater clothing, and so on), showy makeup, stronger fragrances more freely diffused, flashy jewelry and adornments, reflected appearances (it's important to be accompanied by the right people), copious consumption (food, alcohol), shiny, reflective lights, and accessories (jewelry, sequins, the silver-lined Warholian Factory or the rotating mirror ball of discos and night clubs, a splendid symbol of worldliness in the 1970s and 1980s),[6] whose purpose is to attract attention and increase the intensity and range of the subjects' field of sensible irradiation. Virginia Woolf, who called herself ironically a *social festivity snob* and was enamored of brightly lit drawing rooms, spangles, and effervescent atmospheres, claimed that these were essential ingredients for a worldly gathering: "any group of people if they are well dressed, and socially sparkling and unfamiliar will do the trick; sends up that fountain of gold and diamond dust which I suppose obscures the solid truth."[7]

In worldly society, the *Lebenswelt* takes on an aestheticized aspect. Simmel's theory of *Geselligkeit* emphasizes the positivity of this peculiar experience, thus offering a useful counterweight to the moralistic criticism of "entertainment" and "disengagement." However, by falling victim to a still-Kantian notion of the autonomy of aesthetics, it conceives the triumph of the aesthetic dimension as a sphere of sublimation and liberation. Sociability seems to liberate human beings from their drives, thereby realizing Kant's ideal of the relationship between faculties: that of *free play*. As we have said, this stark antagonism between what is useful and what is an end in itself seems to reaffirm the opposition that we are attempting to make more fluid, by bringing aesthetics back into a realm that is immanent to society, where aesthetic forms and qualities are neither captive nor separated from it, but are part and parcel of society.[8]

A party is not only an experience of active perception, sensory pleasure enjoyed in the first person and shared engagingly with others, but also the moment of exposure to the perception of others. Many of the names given to worldly events today—shows, receptions, exhibitions, expositions, openings, open bars—or the expressions that refer to them emphasize the image of an "opening" and their "exhibitionist" and voyeuristic appeal. This confirms the insight of Saint-Preux, the protagonist of Rousseau's *Julie, or the New Heloise*, who, in the letters sent to Julie about Paris, remarked that nobody goes to a show for the pleasure of the show but rather to see the people gathered there and be seen by them. People dress more revealingly when they go to receptions and society events than they do in everyday life, as if the social overexposure into which one inevitably heads had an objective correlation in the quantity of bare skin that can legitimately be offered to view: low necklines, slits, and miniskirts rediscover their original purpose, their natural locus, in the worldly exteriority and opening of the public sphere. The sensible irradiation that derives from this collective being-on-show is intensified by the aesthetics of the surroundings (music, lights, and atmosphere) and by the food and intoxicants (smoke, drugs, alcohol), which are an essential ingredient of the social *aisthesis*. However, this exhilaration is not to be confused with Dionysian ecstasy.[9] In many ways, the worldliness of society life is the opposite of the barbaric: it is an experience not of depth, of descent into the unconscious and return to origins, but of superficiality and extreme phenomenalization. The social actors do not seek to lose their individuality, merge with the earth, and rediscover a common core; they simply want to stand out by flirting with the people around them. The elation does not come from the emotion of being swept through by a current of deep shared feelings and sensations so much as from the thrill of immaterialism and the will to please: the awareness of being seen and sensed by others, of owing the perception of one's own value (or even existence) to others. True, this pleasure, which arises from being dependent on others, innervates every experience of social recognition: it is an ingredient of love as well as the taste of glory. However, in worldliness it has an even more superficial and frivolous dimension and is sought as an end in itself. It is a *cupio percipi* (will to be perceived), which generates a syndrome of known, recognizable symptoms: the tendency to be present at every social event in order to get noticed; exhibitionism; snobbery; the pursuit of visibility and publicity at all costs; the desire to be included on every invitation list; the frenzy to appear in the news; depression from loneliness. Melancholy is a typical syndrome caused by publicity, and it is not surprising that historians have traced the origins of this romantic attitude to the courtly space, which is one of the original staging places of modern worldliness.[10]

Publicity—from now on intended in the active and performative sense, not as an opening to the world and presence in the *Öffentlichkeit* but as the capacity to attract public attention and interest to oneself and, consequently, also as advertising—reveals itself as the irrepressible reverse of worldly exposure in its passive aspect. To publicize themselves, individuals attempt to increase their perceptibility through appropriate means, which can only be aesthetic: the important thing is to be noticed, to attract attention, to stand out. The "shop-window quality of things" (*Schaufenster-Qualität*), in which, as we have seen, Simmel recognized the essential characteristic of commodities in the epoch of the great exhibitions, becomes the mode of being not only for things but also for human beings in modern advertising—it impels them to behave like display products and to emphasize their staging value. The force of attraction in publicizing oneself lies in the aesthetic potential, and the power of seduction is proportional to the ability to put oneself in the right light, to make oneself noticed with an attractive appearance, with an elegant or even vulgar flair, provided that it is provocative, that it attracts looks, and that it *makes a sensation*. *Self-display*: it brings to mind the art of courtesans, the demimondaines who are the experts at social seduction techniques, but also contemporary artists and art curators, who increasingly strive to win public attention through the spectacle of their art. Commercial advertising is therefore the performative side of publicity: there is no substantial difference between the shouts with which shopkeepers praise their goods and the clothes, attitudes, and poses with which worldly people seek to be socially seductive. All these are marketing and curtain-raiser techniques—which helps to explain the pertinence of the successful metaphor of the "Fair": the public sphere of vain appearances is not simply a show for its own sake but, more properly, an exhibition market.

It should be noted that in the modern world characterized by capitalist relations, for people as for commodities, exhibition conditions are necessarily linked to the rise of competition as well as to the phenomenon of the relativity and interdependence of positions and values (another proof of the deep affinity between aesthetics and economics). In an advertising regime, when an individual captures attention, the value of neighboring individuals is simultaneously depreciated in a single system of valuation, which allows values to be compared and respective positions to be placed in a hierarchy. Every system of social competition based on public appreciation is identical to the model of the stock exchange: the success of one inevitably coincides with the defeat of another. The scene of the rural festival in the *Discourse on Inequality* comes back to mind, in which Rousseau imagined an all-out war breaking out at the climax of the worldly entertainment, in order to please others and outshine rivals. The convergence between exposure, seduction, and open or covert agonism is the dark side of every experience of intense publicity.[11]

Social Disease

The most lucid understanding of the dynamics of worldly publicity inherent in the urban experience of late modernity belongs certainly to Andy Warhol. He was able to interpret these dynamics not only in their alienating effects—which, understood romantically as forms of loss of self, were widely denounced by critical philosophy of all backgrounds—but also in terms of their hedonistic, self-realizing, and even liberating aspects. This dialectical sensibility makes his work extremely pertinent to my inquiry. Although Warhol received no philosophical training, he had extraordinary theoretical insight: Arthur Danto, in a judgment that I share, considered him "the nearest to a philosophical genius that twentieth-century art had brought forth." Warhol's poetics, founded entirely on the social-aesthetic hendiadys, was entirely constructed on social appearances: on the centrality of images and sensible value in the construction of the real, on a vision of art as a professional and commercial practice of aesthetic labor that serves to transform them, and on the indissoluble intertwining between aesthetic and economic values. To conclude this survey on the forms of contemporary social aesthetics and take stock of its future development, I will therefore turn to the voice of the artist who, sixty years ago, was its most prophetic and unprejudiced interpreter, and whose vision of the relations between art and society can still today—indeed, more than ever today—be considered *paradigmatic*.[12]

The theme of *exposure* dominates Warhol's vision of the world: as he quipped, "I'll go to the opening of anything, including a toilet seat." Before being compelled to change his lifestyle, after Valerie Solanas's attempt on his life in 1968, he conceived his New York home as an *open house*—open to any passerby at any time of day or night. The most fascinating document of this worldly poetics, the photo album with which Warhol documented the life of partygoers in the early 1970s, makes the reference to opening and public exposure explicit, starting from the title, *Exposures*: the double meaning (photographic and social) seems to allude equally to the lifestyle shown in his images, in the complete sensible externalization of self, and to the essence of sensibility as an aesthetic receptor. Just as in photographic film, the self makes impressions by opening itself up and exposing itself to the power of sensible forms.

This *bal des têtes* of the pop celebrity—about whom the critic Robert Hughes wrote in the *New York Review of Books*, "Andy is climbing from face to face in a silent delirium of snobbery," which we now peruse with the same melancholy with which Proust recalled the lost splendors of faubourg Saint-Germain—begins with a provocative confession: "*I have Social Disease. I have to go out every night.*" Like a postmodern La Rochefoucauld or La Bruyère, Warhol illustrates his bleak worldly anthropology with a cynical and blatantly superficial tone:

> The symptoms of Social Disease: You want to go out every night because you're afraid if you stay home you might miss something. You choose your friends according to whether or not they have a limousine. You prefer exhilaration to conversation unless the subject is gossip. You judge a party by how many celebrities are there—if they serve caviar they don't have any celebrities. When you wake up in the morning, the first thing

you do is read the society columns. If your name is actually mentioned your day is made. Publicity is the ultimate symptom of Social Disease.[13]

To grasp how acutely the Factory's world predicted the form of social experience (a new "social media disease") that would prevail a few decades later, just think of Instagram or Facebook as the equivalent of "All Tomorrow's Parties."[14] But Warhol's foresight goes far beyond this. It does not escape him what the cure for the disease is—a cure that is nevertheless palliative, which only alleviates the symptoms without removing the cause and inevitably makes the patient increasingly obsessed with and addicted to his drug. The remedy for the desire for publicity lies in publicity itself, practiced on three complementary and convergent levels: as a professional activity, as an artistic form, and as an art of living.

Having landed in the empyrean of the art world through the job of adman and window dresser, Warhol *defends the absolute identity between art and advertising*, and his entire oeuvre could be interpreted in the light of the epoch-making assertion of Fortunato Depero in 1931: "The art of the future will be *powerfully advertising-like*." (In the first version of the manifesto in 1928, Depero had written "*fatally*," thus underlying the epochal aspect of the phenomenon.) But compared to the Futurist experimentations, Warhol's program takes on an aspect that is even more inseparable from everyday life, even more *powerfully social*. Depero had, in essence, nobilitated advertising by elevating it to the rank of avant-garde art, while Warhol completed the Futurist gesture through the opposite, double move: he not only lowers art to the level of advertising (and this cynical claim is what he is harshly berated for by his critics, who would never forgive him the profanation), but he also lowers publicity itself to the level of the most frivolous of social practices, worldly aestheticism. The socialite, the adman, and the artist are melded into a single persona. It is the most radical refutation of the sacred vision of art, epitomized by the poetics of the last and greatest romantic painting of the twentieth century, that of the abstract expressionists. The contrasting relationship with the school that is synonymous with metaphysical ambitions, authenticity, and the spirituality of art is a topos that Warhol mocked continuously. This refutation is also illustrated by comparing Warhol's poetics with the "moral of the story" of Proust's *In Search of Lost Time*. For Proust, the salvation of the individual lay in becoming a genuine artist and radically breaking all ties to snobs (those who systematically pursue social publicity) and aesthetes (those who do not create, like Swann, a man who remains *célibataire de l'art*). Warhol shamelessly asserts the indistinguishability between art, aestheticism, and universal snobbery. His concept of snobbery is to be understood in the sense René Girard gives it, as the universal mechanism of mimetic desire and quest for prestige. In no way relegated to the society of the Ancien Régime, snobbery is actually characteristic of modern democratic society and its intensity grows proportionally to the horizontal leveling of traditional hierarchies.[15]

"Esse est percipi aut percipere": The Social-Aesthetic Ontology

To fully understand the sense of this correspondence we must delve more deeply into Andy Warhol's "philosophy"—not to be confused with the ironic thought expressed in maxims, published in his book in 1975. *The Philosophy of Andy Warhol* was conceived as a work of collective authorship in collaboration with people connected to the Factory; it only represents one of the multiple expressions of Warholian philosophy, which is embodied, or better yet, *represented in sensible form*, throughout his entire artistic oeuvre. To show the ontological insight on which his philosophy is founded, and to explain the paradox of why his superficial obsession for celebrities is so philosophically acute and profound, Danto duly evoked the thought of Berkeley:

> Andy Warhol's career was a perpetual meditation on celebrity, money, nothingness, and art. It may be difficult to imagine that he had read the Bishop Berkeley, or even heard of him, but he had nevertheless intuitively and spontaneously understood that the fact of *not being perceived as an image by the collective consciousness is equivalent to being stripped of the only reality that matters*. This thought can help us to understand his tendency to reproduce indefinitely the same image of the same personality—Marilyn, Liz, Jackie, Elvis—as if only the reiterated repetition of their image could increase the substance of people who are in actuality no more than the brand image of themselves. To be is to be famous,

and to be famous means eliminating everything foreign to the familiar perception of one's image and that consequently does not reach popular awareness, because it is foreign to one's essence.[16]

It is worth pausing more carefully on the significance of this reference to Berkeley, which recurs frequently in contemporary theory and social criticism—mostly as a negative metaphor of an increasingly pervasive aestheticism and derealization; or, in Bourdieu, as an illustration of the petty-bourgeois vision of the world, to be criticized for its idealistic tendency, which denies the primacy of the economy.[17] Momentarily putting aside these uses, we will intend it in the strictly philosophical sense, as the concept I will define as *social immaterialism*. Paraphrasing the formula that is identified with the thought of Bishop Berkeley, I will adapt the Latin motto to the strictly social sphere: (*in societate*) *esse est percipi aut percipere*, in society, to exist is to be perceived and to perceive. An act of perception, active or passive, is equivalent to a change in the realm of being. The realm of being coincides with the realm of perception and hence with that of aesthetics, in the etymological sense of the word; aesthetics is shown in turn to have an immediate ontological correspondence. Social immaterialism is the social ontology that is founded on *aisthesis*, or, in other words, social-aesthetic ontology.

Andy Warhol's art is a perpetual meditation on this ontological equation. Its validity is revealed most purely in his multiples, perhaps the most typically Warholian invention: *more (social) images = more (social) perception = more (social) being*. Aesthetics merges with ontology because the social reality grows proportionally with the number of images that represent it and that circulate in the public space. The technique of silkscreen reproduction, which is serial, fast, and "light," is equivalent in mechanical terms to the principle that regulates the production of the social-aesthetic reality. Every new image (each of which presents small but significant variations) possesses an ontological effectiveness because, in the ethereal form of the impression left by silk, it adds a new layer of appearance to the world and brings with it an "increase in being."[18] Any artist who has the ability to produce and multiply these images and then disseminate them in the public space is therefore endowed with an almost divine faculty, the power to create social reality by transforming the shared perception of the world in which we live. Artists intervene *artificially* in the mechanism for producing social appearances—a mechanism already impregnated with artificiality—by manipulating them, using specific technical devices. It is the apotheosis of *aesthetic labor* and *social design*: art as the profession and technical ability of "prestidigitation" is interwoven with and superimposed on social art in producing and elaborating social appearances. Although his aesthetic labor focuses primarily on images, Warhol is aware of the synesthetic aspect of social perception and the fact that *esse est percipi aut percipere* unfolds ontologically when multiple senses are involved in the viewing. His interest in music and performances and his unstoppable experimentalism, aimed at broadening the scope of the aesthetic experience in every direction, can be explained as tension toward the "total work of art" (*Gesamtkunstwerk*). The famous series of multisensorial and multimedia events that he organized with the Velvet Underground & Nico between 1966 and 1967, with the title Exploding Plastic Inevitable, is a perfect example of this.

It should be noted that the image produced by Warhol always requires several levels of representation. His portraits are representations of the social reality already represented by appearances (for him, there is no such thing as a "natural" reality). Instead of representing the person who sat for it, the image represents the social figure that already exists and circulates in the public sphere. Warhol never portrays flesh-and-blood individuals; nor does he try to capture their soul, in which he has no interest whatsoever. Instead he lingers in an intentionally superficial fashion on the public image, the popular cliché that others see and recognize socially. This is why he always works from found images, such as photos taken with a Polaroid camera, illustrations cropped from magazines, film stills, ID photos, and especially the figurines that he collected as a child (which, in their seriality, mobility, and interchangeability, and thanks to their "minor" and highly stylized aspect, ascend to the rank of archetypes of social appearances: those Pirandellian images of ourselves that by definition represent us while alienating us from ourselves). This is what lies behind the proliferating mediations and the realization of that which, from the view of Platonic metaphysics, would be the nightmare of infinite production of copies of copies of copies, lacking any original model, in which any possibility of access to the "real" and to its authenticity would seem to be lost. The attempt to distinguish between original and copy is entirely insignificant in Warhol's work, because the model used to conceive the portrait is already an artificial product, a *representation*, the mask of a self. His work also signals the death of the aura, or at least of its romantic conception, given that, as we shall see, even in Warholian philosophy there is room for this concept.

Contrary to a still widely diffused interpretation that is split between contradictory views and that has inevitably run aground on the shoals of the "romantic" paradigm, Andy Warhol's philosophy forces us to overcome the stark opposition between illusion and reality. While critics were divided in their interpretation of Warhol's art, forcing his images to fit into the category of either simulacral or referential—an exaltation of postmodern derealization (the accusation made by Roland Barthes and Jean Baudrillard) or demystification in the name of authenticity and the referent (Thomas Crow)—the meaning of his theory of representation is that we must go beyond the metaphysics of the two worlds through a philosophy of aesthetic mediation. Because of this dialectical tension, perfectly described by Hal Forster, Warhol's art is just as much "referential" as it is "simulacral." And this ambivalence is what fuels the unending interest that his work holds for social aesthetics.[19]

Aesthetic Acts: *Ethel Scull Thirty-Six Times*

Through the multiple portrait, Warhol's art forcefully brings to light not only the production mechanisms of social ontology but also the fact that the aesthetic realm substantially interferes with the mechanisms of recognition, economics, and power by mediating them. First, the multiple portrait actively publicizes the model, making it more socially perceptible and increasing the exposure and extension of its social figure in proportion to the quantity and visibility of the circulating images. Each new aspect enriches the social figure, completing it almost to the point of suggesting its tridimensionality: not unlike the triple portraits of the seventeenth century (the one of Charles I painted by van Dyck or that of Richelieu created by Philippe de Champaigne), which were sent to Bernini so that the sculptor could create a marble bust from them.

Images can therefore propagate in the public space to the point of colonizing and saturating it. This is one of the most intuitive forms of propaganda exploited by power, from the time of Augustus's ancient Rome to the totalitarian regimes of the twentieth century, to which Debord followers allude when they interpret the "society of spectacle" and the "politics of glory" in a neototalitarian key.[20] In the world of Warhol, however, glorification through images is not a political prerogative of totalitarian "government," coordinated according to a univocal logic by the equivalent of a ministry for propaganda, so much as an anarchic social mechanism, working from above, but even more intensely from below, promoted and pursued by individuals, social classes, and minorities seeking visibility and prestige, with the complicity of experts in the social arts. From this point of view, the role of Warhol could be compared to that of the artists of early modern courts, such as van Dyck, who sold their aesthetic labor to sovereigns and princes or to status seekers wanting to nobilitate themselves and sublimate the material origins of their social success, such as rich Genoese bankers or the merchants of Flanders.[21] The analogy seems confirmed by the fact that the models of Warhol's portraits, like those of van Dyck, were already known celebrities or individuals on the rise who were seeking to increase their social worth. There is a significant difference between the two projects, though, represented by Warhol's identification with the common people, and by the greater social mobility promised by modernity and the myth of the "American dream." In actuality, the subjects ennobled by Warhol were not, as is often incorrectly remembered in a deploring tone, only the nouveaux riches who hoped to nobilitate themselves specifically thanks to the prestige promised by the artist and his aesthetic power. Warhol also portrayed marginalized individuals, transvestites and other "ignoble" subjects, who, through the artificial reinvention of their appearance, were granted the opportunity to re-create their social identity and aspire to a life that was more free and less subject to discrimination. This more democratic promise of ascent did not end with the experimental, more avant-garde phase of the 1960s; it persisted in the second and less radical phase of Warhol's work as well, exemplified by the exhibition *Ladies and Gentlemen*, held at the Palazzo dei Diamanti in Ferrara, Italy, in 1975.[22] Warhol portrayed unnamed black and Hispanic transvestites with the usual method of a free pose captured in a Polaroid, followed by a transfer of the image onto silk.

The show was reviewed by Pier Paolo Pasolini, who criticized the lack of psychology in Warhol's portraits and the stereotyping of their poses, which he saw as evidence of the standardization imposed by American ideology. In reality, stylization and typification are essential characteristics of the modern "status portrait" genre, which is meant to overshadow the individual psychology of the subjects in order to endow them with a recognizable and ennobling social *habitus*. Standardization is in reality a stylization intended to socially empower the portrait subjects. The obscure drag queens of the Gilded Grape club are intentionally represented in diva poses with the same style as the rich and famous because Warhol's principle is *what appears is real*. Pop art, whose archetype is plastic surgery, as in Warhol's first manifesto-work, offers anyone and anything (including a banal commodity from the supermarket) an opportunity to "be transfigured" and to create a better self-image, which, by dint of Berkeley's formula, once socially perceived becomes a shared social reality. And the "Factory" is the aesthetic industry that serves to make this dream come true.

It is important to remember this aspect of Warhol's poetics, which was defended and laid claim to by other radical artists associated with the Factory, such as Lou Reed.[23] It suggests a democratic and liberating potential for social immaterialism, which, when not accused of simply furthering capitalist interests, is most often dismissed as nonpolitical alongside the concept of "aestheticism." Aesthetic labor is a potentially dialectical concept; it may lend itself with the same suppleness to serving the interests of governments and the powerful as it does to improving the self-representation and quality of life of those who are low and distant from the centers of power, thanks to the force of imagination and fiction exerted from below. Of course, Marxist or moral arguments can be used to argue convincingly that this promise of democratic universal transfiguration is the usual ideological falsehood typical of the culture industry, or that it promises a narcissistic aesthetic enhancement of the self.[24] Still, we cannot deny that it has embodied something much more powerful, and thoughtful, than a simple practice of "commercial art" for wealthy business people.

The divine ontological power of the artist is not limited to the faculty of quantitatively producing a lot of images that contribute to fashioning reality; it also extends to the illusionistic capability, similar to the realm of magic, of "artificially" processing these images and transforming their surface to make them socially more impressive and attractive. A further comparison with the early modern portraitist famous for his ability to endow his subjects with social prestige may help to illuminate our understanding of Warhol. In addition to the treatment of hands, van Dyck's art included a choice of particular poses, such as that of the elbow resting on the hip, or the use of status symbols, such as columns, carpets, and fans. Warhol achieves a similar result through various "glamorization" techniques, which are his most characteristic invention and worth analyzing in detail.

Warhol's images undergo a sophisticated process of transfiguration and sublimation of their sensible appearance. The play of colors, the particular framing of the shots, the poses, and especially the *stylization*[25]—the secret of signage art, commercial advertising, and all *social arts* in general—give the model's appearance a quality that, in the language of pop art, defines *glamour*. The origins of the term—a magic spell or enchantment, cast over the eyes of the person perceiving it—refer to the family of prestige, a concept for which glamour is in a certain sense the modern, capitalistic, spectacular, hedonistic, and "sexy" embodiment: it is feminine and tinged with romantic–sexual connotations.[26] Compared to prestige, which operates through distinction and creating hierarchies, glamour is based on a less asymmetric relation between the dominating and the dominated. It plays on social envy and on the democratic promise of social ascent. In the prestigious representation, embodied ideally in the aristocratic portraits of the Ancien Régime, the subjects' seriousness and haughty, composed demeanor expressed their sovereignty, and a sense of coldness and distance predominates (*noli me tangere*). Conversely, the glamorous representation often displays an ecstatic and inviting smile: the subjects' happiness is a promise for viewers, who, while recognizing their own current inferiority, hope or delude themselves that they will be able to imitate and catch up with the models. John Berger writes in this regard: "Publicity persuades us of such a transformation by showing us people who have apparently been transformed and are, as a result, enviable. The state of being envied is what constitutes glamour. And *publicity is the process of manufacturing glamour.*"[27]

Like the various forms of prestige, glamour is a *sensational value* that further enhances the sensible substance of the image, boosts its irradiation, and renders it aesthetically and socially seductive. This is the "aura" Warhol gave to his objects, an aura that paradoxically represents the antithesis of authenticity and religious sacredness—which is individual and distant, and which Benjamin opposes to the technologically reproducible work of art: instead of killing off the aura, Warhol's mass-produced, mechanical technology creates a pop version of it with the capability of transfiguring the most banal object into something magical and seductive. The technological production of the aura is thus a form of aesthetic *super value*, which artists sell on the market, making themselves socially in demand: "Some company recently was interested in buying my 'aura.' They didn't want my product. They kept saying, 'We want your aura.' I never figured out what they wanted. But they were willing to pay a lot for it. So then I thought that if somebody was willing to pay that much for my it, I should try to figure out what it is."[28] Only if we conceive the aesthetic value as perfectly specular to the economic value—and therefore exchangeable with it—can we understand the meaning of Warhol's *commercial art*, its peculiar relationship to money (defined as desirable and representable as an artistic object), and the total identification of art with business. Two hundred years after their tragic, romantic divorce, Warhol celebrates the final reconciliation between aesthetics and economics. And it is a comedy of remarriage.[29]

Warhol's mastery of aesthetic power is represented in an exemplary way by one of his first and most successful multiples, perhaps the most famous American portrait of the 1960s: that of Ethel Scull, wife of the New York taxi magnate and art collector, through which Warhol—as it was said—transformed a random urban beauty into a superstar. The thirty-six glamorous images that compose it are so many socially ontological iconic acts, thirty-six magic tricks.[30]

Warhol not only understood that social reality—that is, the specific way of being that persons and things assume in society—is determined by public perception, he also sensed that the ontological question necessarily involves power. On the one hand, the power of the model: if we exist in society for others to the extent that we are perceived, those who manage to make themselves more perceived, more visible, more exposed, and more conspicuous on the social scene will necessarily exist more. And those who exist more are "empowered" to do more: they have more resources to influence the surrounding world, more "capital" of seduction and desirability.[31] Warhol thus *flips the Foucauldian principle*, now a commonplace in surveillance studies, which states that it is primarily the active position of the perceiving person who generates a position of power, especially when this position is not symmetric. According to Warhol's idea, it is being perceived and attracting attention that has more "power" to act, demonstrating a further analogy between the economic and spectacular aspects of value: the economy of attention and the financial practice of leverage obey the same logic of celebrity. On the other hand, there is the power of those who hold the aesthetic secret of aura creation: artists, advertisers, exhibitors, socialites. This is how Berkeley's formula acquires a political value, and how the theory of social immaterialism naturally converges with that of prestige.

Nevertheless, Warhol's gaze always remains ambivalent—here, too, is where his greatness lies—and a subtle dialectic crosses through every one of his representations. On further thought, Foucault's conception of power is not foreign to Warhol's vision, which emerges, for example, in the representation of suffering celebrity, such as Jackie or Marilyn, who confront death and mourning under the public gaze of the world. (I will come back to this point a little further on.) It is no coincidence that female figures are burdened with the sacrificial aspect of visibility and total exposure, given that in Western culture they embody primarily the passive and reifying side of *esse est percipi aut percipere*.

Unlike traditional prestige, therefore, the aura produced by Warhol is socially ambivalent and polarized: his ability to lift up is equal to his ability to pull down, and his auratic power always has a cynical and "vulgar" aspect to it (in the etymological sense of the word: "of the common people," and therefore easily and widely consumable). For this reason, another great philosophical insight of Pop Art is the indistinction that makes people and things equal in the world of publicity: in the popular imagination there is no difference between a can of soup and a famous actress. Social exposure makes them automatically a commodity and a slut, a "public woman" that everyone can look at and whose image they can even touch and perceive with their senses through the mediation of the represented figure. When seen from this angle, publicity is viewed as an aspect that corrupts, thereby implicitly confirming the theory of distinction: that which is open to everybody and can be looked at, touched, *perceived by everybody*, like a prostitute's body or a commercial product to which anyone can gain access for a small sum of money, automatically loses its social value. The aura no longer has a sacralizing effect, meant to mark the boundary with transcendence; instead it is irreverent or *profanatory*, erasing the "thin line between glamour and shit."[32]

Nevertheless, this indistinction not only offers a key for interpreting the processes of late-capitalist aestheticization and reification, as is normally thought, by judging reification as an exclusive outcome of publicity and the demands of economic production, it is actually a latent phenomenon of social experience in and of itself. The problem of publicity makes it possible to reinterpret the commodity issue from a philosophically and anthropologically wider perspective than that of a certain tradition of critical thought, which tends to relegate it exclusively to the historical dimension of aesthetic capitalism. The dynamics of economic production, capitalist competition, and the market should always be considered in relation to the social-aesthetic dynamics of appearing and seducing within a public sphere.

These latter considerations lead us to the figure of Marilyn Monroe, of which Warhol has left us a brilliant interpretation from the viewpoint of social immaterialism. We will bring this book to a close with her, by returning to that opposition between romanticism and social aesthetics from which this investigation into social appearances first began.

Marilyn Monroe: The Last Romantic Temptation

One of the reasons for the fascination that Marilyn Monroe still exerts is the way her public figure has successfully represented one of the most powerful tensions in modern culture. On the one hand, there is her disenchanted avowal of the correspondence between reality and appearance: in an interview from 1960 in *Marie-Claire* magazine, the actress who subjected herself to hours of makeup before every public appearance went on record as saying, "I am an artificial product." On the other hand, she represents one of the most powerful romantic rebellions against the alienating power of the social image (the loss of Rousseau's "natural self") in the name of authenticity and immediacy. Marilyn is the impossible synthesis between appearing and being, between art and nature, between identifying oneself consciously and entirely with one's sensible surface and suggestively claiming a hidden depth, a truth of the spirit or the soul that is inaccessible to public perception. One of the reasons for her myth lies hidden in this capacity to express two contradictory and incompatible messages, which correspond to a sort of double injunction of our culture—a culture still thoroughly seeped in romanticism. Although some figures of our contemporary star system and pop culture have ably managed to go beyond this ambivalence, to radically embody the *representative nature of social aesthetics* (David Bowie remains an unparalleled model of "eccentric" subjectivity and, in this respect, the perfect correlative of Warhol's artificialist poetics),[33] the yearning for authenticity and the theme of the tragic conflict between real life and its staging, between the real person and the mask, can still be perceived in the construction of even the most sophisticated performers, from Maria Callas to Madonna. To undo this double bind, then, we do well to return to the archetype that presents its purest embodiment.

Marilyn's figure lives in the same tension between natural self and social self that Rousseau made into a philosophical problem, and then later experienced in the first person with excruciating contradictions: it is the expression of two forces in conflict, the continuous oscillation between the lucid awareness of one's self-exhibition, accompanied by an intuitive use of seductive power, and the revolt against one's alienation, nurtured by nostalgia for an identity that is more innocent and closer to the origins. In an exemplary way, the figure of the actress also merges two different aspects of appearing that are complementary, perfectly superimposable masks: in addition to the mask generated by celebrity, there is another inherent in being a woman. Media popularity intensifies and seals the passivity implicit in the cultural relation between the female image and the male gaze. Marilyn's image is thus doubly public—doubly exposed and alienated—in other people's perception: her public figure is so "sensual" that, as Norman Mailer used to say, every American male had the impression of personally being able to feel her up.[34] The contrast between the diva sex symbol, celebrated and voyeuristically probed by the media, always ready to offer an even more provocative pose for the camera, and the childlike woman who wanted to be loved for what she was, touchingly revealing her suffering, is obvious to everyone. Yet nobody can say that they knew the "true" Marilyn or that they directly witnessed her presumed "nature," which seemed to glimmer behind the artificial social icon. Truman Capote suggested this impossibility in one of his most beautiful passages:

> **MARILYN:** Remember, I said if anybody ever asked you what I was like, what Marilyn Monroe was really like—well, how would you answer them? (Her tone was teaseful, mocking, yet earnest, too: she wanted an honest reply.) I bet you'd tell them I was a slob. A banana split.
> **TC:** Of course. But I'd also say . . .
> (The light was leaving. She seemed to fade with it, blend with the sky and clouds, recede beyond them. I wanted to lift my voice louder than the seagulls' cries and call her back: Marilyn! Marilyn, why did everything have to turn out the way it did? Why does life have to be so rotten?)
> **TC:** I'd say . . .
> **MARILYN:** I can't hear you.
> **TC:** I'd say you are a beautiful child.[35]

The romantic interpretation, which Capote plays with sophisticated grace (the real Marilyn remains an elusive yearning), was already established at the time of the actress's suicide. We find it sublimated by the tragic tone of the elegy that Pasolini inserted into his documentary *La Rabbia* (*Anger*) edited in 1962–63. Here, instead of being lost in the wind, the formula of the "beautiful child" is pronounced like a prayer by the strong, persuasive voice of Giorgio Bassani, which accompanies the images of the actress before and after her Hollywood triumph. Pasolini's Marilyn is the child of the people, whose genuine and true beauty, celebrated with Christian-Rousseauian rhetoric, was corrupted by the society that forced her to become conscious of her seduction and, consequently, inauthentic. In the moral of the story presented by *La Rabbia*, it is easy to recognize the umpteenth version of the *Vanity Fair* parable:

> You little younger sister,
> you wore that beauty humbly
> and your spirit of common people
> you never knew you had it,
> because otherwise it would not have been beauty.

It disappeared like a golden dust.
The world taught you it.
So your beauty became the world.³⁶

We are indebted to Elton John for his kitsch consecration of the romantic topos in the song "Candle in the Wind." Here, too, as the innocent victim of the perverse Hollywood machine, Marilyn is called significantly by her real name, Norma Jean, in tribute to the fragile, authentic woman and in protest against the deceitful image of the diva: "They set you on the treadmill / And they made you change your name . . . / Hollywood created a superstar / And pain was the price you paid / . . . Goodbye Norma Jean / From the young man in the twenty-second row / Who sees you as something more than sexual / More than just our Marilyn Monroe." The ease with which the singer recycled the same song for Lady Diana's funeral puts into question the sincerity of the tribute (which also raises suspicions of commercial exploitation) and even the coherence of the romantic maneuver itself. The authentic portrait of a unique human being should be as original and unrepeatable as the individual, as the incipit to Rousseau's *Confessions* reminds us: "I am not made like any of the ones I have seen; I dare to believe that I am not made like any that exist. If I am worth no more, at least *I am different*."³⁷ Claiming to honor a singular person and then borrowing the homage for multiple uses is equivalent to disavowing the value of the romantic gesture, to profaning individual sacrality.

In some works of Pop Art inspired by the death of Marilyn Monroe, the romantic topos of violated innocence remains in the background, but the artistic gaze begins to tip more toward social aesthetics, in a perspective that runs closer and closer to the Pirandellian theme of the alienated image: from the constructivist Marilyn by Allan D'Arcangelo (1962), a paper doll that the public is invited to put together with tabs and scissors, parroting the social construction of the public figure, to the fragmented Marilyn, upside down and reassembled with pieces of the Coca Cola logo by James Rosenquist (1962), and, finally, to *My Marilyn* by Richard Hamilton (the possessive adjective should be interpreted as a claim), which reproduces the photographic proofs that the actress discarded by marking them with a big cross (1965). However, Andy Warhol alone was able to represent the socially constructed artificiality of Marilyn Monroe without continuing to indulge in any romanticism. The silkscreen series dedicated to the diva during the 1960s is an extraordinary reflection on the status of the social image and its relationship with alienation. The more the actress is stereotyped in her public image, which everyone recognizes and expects from her, the more she seems to disappear into her "authentic" existential dimension. Warhol has accentuated this effect through the expert use of artistic techniques: by suggesting the sense of artificiality with the mechanical coldness of the screen-printing process; by always reproducing the same image of the actress, the promotional photo for the film *Niagara* (in which, contrary to her cinematic cliché of the sweet ingenue, Monroe plays an evil, conniving character); by focusing solely on the face, with the extreme stylization of its expression and features (reduced to identifying lines that make the face recognizable, such as the lascivious mouth, the half-opened eyelids, the hair style, the "seagull wing" eyebrows); and by using bright colors to trace out and spill over the made-up areas of the face, creating an alienating effect for the makeup, which would otherwise appear normalized. Warhol's Marilyn is thus a mask of a mask: an emphatic, caricature-like reproduction of the icon established in public media perception that has nothing to do with the real woman. This identification between social opinion and sacrality—which inverts the romantic triad of aura-sacrality-authenticity—becomes explicit in *Gold Marilyn Monroe* (1962), which evokes a Byzantine icon, a type of image that is to a great extent desubjectivized and stylized. The icon of Marilyn Monroe, which replaces the Madonna, serves as a counterpart to the Campbell soup can that embodies the sacred object, in an indistinguishability between social, aesthetic, and economic values.

Warhol has no interest in Marilyn's interiority, no piety toward the soul of Norma Jean, her troubled and painful life, her countless attempts to escape its canonical image by constructing another one—it, too, inevitably and equally affected. Artifice has by now definitively extinguished nature, even its memory or regret.

AFTERWORD

The story of Marilyn Monroe is a reminder that the relationship with the social image can spark fierce battles not only in conflict with others (envy, competition) but also within the individual conscience. The person who bore the cost of this inner war was actually Rousseau, the thinker who first wrote about social aesthetics and who proposed its moral critique on the basis of the opposition between *amour-propre* (the desire for recognition, love for one's image appreciated by others) and romantic authenticity ("I am me" and I don't care what others see and believe about me). Rousseau's ambivalent relationship with his social image curiously recalls that of Marilyn, starting from the identification with the familiarity and intimacy of his first name, which marks the birth of modern public figures and the beginning of the modern concept of celebrity.[1] With an inevitable but brazen paradox, for which his critics have never stopped berating him, after proclaiming to the entire world his rejection of the other's gaze and his disdain for appearances and the value of the social figure, Rousseau wrote a series of autobiographical works in order to leave the public with the authentic, true, and definitive public image of himself. In this pathology report, comprising the dialogs called *Rousseau, Judge of Jean-Jacques*, the proliferation of inner figures reaches a paroxysm: the character Rousseau has discussions with a generic

Frenchman to judge the defamed author Jean-Jacques. Contrary to what would happen to Norma Jean/Marilyn Monroe, here the birth name represents the stage name and thus becomes charged with the potential for alienation. The attempt to dissolve the opacities of the public mask with an act of radical authenticity not only proves to be impossible, it leads to absolute solitude, bordering on paranoia and madness. Madness and solitude represent recurring outcomes in the romantic tradition, which approached the problem of society primarily from the point of view of the subject—thus understanding alienation as a moral condition and not as a property of images and the sphere of reality, of the objective worlds that they contribute to creating. As we have seen, to reconceive the world of appearances, we need to liberate ourselves from this temptation. We must temporarily suspend the Platonic pursuit for the authentic reality that supposedly exists behind the phenomenological screen, starting from the myth of the natural self, in order to explore more carefully the realm of appearances in which the social aesthetic consists. However much critics attribute the iconoclastic tendency to the Enlightenment, the great battle against social image was in reality waged by romanticisms of all sorts.

This does not mean neutralizing or denying the existence of the moral question, or acritically accepting or celebrating the contemporary version of the social-aesthetic grammar—the social immaterialism so lucidly described by Warhol—as an inescapable destiny.[2] The lesson of Marilyn Monroe, who was unable to effectively preserve the "freedom of the mask," indirectly shows us how individuals who are (or feel) totally exposed and deprived of the capability to regulate their exposure experience the eccentric tendency of their own images as a loss of control over their lives. *But to learn how to dominate a phenomenon, we need to be familiar with its logic; otherwise the phenomenon will dominate us.* For this reason, before writing an ethics or politics of social appearances, we must first analyze the world of social appearances, without prejudices and according to its own principles. This book is intended as an introduction to social aesthetics and an initial exploration of the field.

APPENDIX

Illustrations Mentioned in the Text

Still frames from *Film*, script by Samuel Beckett, directed by Alan Schneider (1965). (Close-ups of Buster Keaton covering his face with his hands and revealing a blind eye.) Chapter 1, p. 15.

Ernst Ludwig Kirchner, *Five Women on the Street* (1913); Alex Katz, *Cocktail Party* (1965). (Artists often grasp and express the essence of a social phenomenon thanks to their sensitivity to the language of forms.) Chapter 3, p. 32.

Voltaire by Maurice Quentin de la Tour (1735); Allan Ramsay, *Jean-Jacques Rousseau in Armenian Costume* (1766). Michel Foucault; Jacques Lacan; Jacques Derrida in stylized poses. Chapter 4, p. 38.

Engraving showing Bunyan's "Vanity Fair," the cover of *Vanity Fair* by Thackeray, and the cover of the first issue and of a recent issue of *Vanity Fair*. Chapter 6, p. 64.

Guy Debord, still frame from *In girum imus nocte et consumimur igni* (1978). ("Ici les spectateurs, privés de tout, seront en outré privés d'images"). Chapter 8, p. 91.

Still frames from *The Leopard*, directed by Luchino Visconti (1963). (Angelica and Tancredi explore the abandoned rooms of the Donnafugata palace.) Chapter 10, p. 117.

van Dyck, *Portrait of George Gage with Two Attendants* (probably 1622–23). Chapter 14, p. 179.

Frans Hals, *The Officers of the St. Adrian Militia Company* (1633); August Sander, *Farming Generations* (1912). Chapter 14, p. 184.

Shepard Fairey, poster for Barack Obama's election campaign (2008). Chapter 14, p. 184.

Andy Warhol, cover of *Exposures* (1979). Chapter 15, p. 215.

van Dyck, *Charles I in Three Positions* (*The Triple Portrait of Charles I*) (1635 or 1636); Philippe de Champaigne, *Triple Portrait of Cardinal de Richelieu* (probably 1642). Chapter 15, p. 220.

Andy Warhol, *Ladies and Gentlemen* (1975). Chapter 15, p. 221.
Andy Warhol, *Before and After* (1961). Chapter 15, p. 222.
Andy Warhol, *Ethel Scull Thirty-Six Times* (1963). Chapter 15, p. 224.
Still from *La rabbia* (*Rage, the Anger*) by Pier Paolo Pasolini (1962). (The "natural" Marilyn.) Conclusion, p. 228.
Photo used by Andy Warhol as the foundation for his *Marilyn* series (1962). (The "artificial" Marilyn.) Conclusion, p. 230.

NOTES

PROLOGUE

Epigraph: "Sedulo curavi humanas actiones non ridere, non lugere, neque detestari, sed intelligere": "I have taken great care not to deride, bewail, or execrate human actions, but to understand them." Baruch Spinoza, *Political Treatise* (1677), in *Complete Works*, trans. Samuel Shirley, ed. and intro. Michael L. Morgan (Indianapolis: Hackett, 2002), 676–754, here chapter 1, §4, 681.

1. Peter Sloterdijk, *Spheres*, vol. 3, *Foams*, trans. Wieland Hoban (South Pasadena, CA: Semiotext[e], 2016), prologue.
2. See Martin Seel, *Aesthetics of Appearing*, trans. John Farrell (Stanford: Stanford University Press, 2005), who defines aesthetics as the domain of appearing, the reality that all aesthetic objects share, however different they may be.
3. Friedrich Nietzsche, *The Gay Science*, ed. Bernard Williams, trans. Josefine Nauckhoff (Cambridge: Cambridge University Press, 2001), 8–9, preface to the second edition.
4. See particularly Arnold Berleant, "Ideas for a Social Aesthetics," in *The Aesthetics of Everyday Life*, ed. Andrew Light and Jonathan M. Smith (New York: Columbia University Press, 2005), 23–38. In seeking the foundation of social harmony in the reconciliation enabled by the aesthetic form, and especially in the beautiful, Berleant takes his cue from *On the Aesthetic Education of Man* (1794) by Friedrich Schiller.
5. Georg Simmel, "Sociological Aesthetics," in *The Conflict in Modern Culture, and Other Essays*, ed. and trans. Peter Etzkorn (New York: Teachers College Press, 1968), 68–80. The reappraisal of this aspect of Simmel's work, embarked upon earlier by David Frisby and later developed in conversation with postmodern thought by Mike Featherstone, Scott Lash, and Michel Maffesoli, is being revived today by a new generation of sociologists. Compared to their orientation, my research asserts a more openly *philosophical*

aspiration. See Barbara Carnevali and Andrea Pinotti, "Social Aesthetics," in *Simmel Companion*, ed. Gregor Fitzi (London: Routledge, 2020).
6. Siegfried Kracauer, "The Mass Ornament," in *The Mass Ornament: Weimar Essays*, trans., ed., and intro. Thomas Y. Levin (Cambridge, MA: Harvard University Press, 1995), 75.
7. Georg Wilhelm Friedrich Hegel, *Aesthetics: Lectures on Fine Art*, trans. Thomas M. Knox (Oxford: Clarendon, 1988), 1:8 (my italics).

1. LIFE AS A SPECTACLE

1. These remarks take their inspiration from Georg Simmel, "Excursus on the Sociology of Sense Impression," in *Sociology: Inquiries Into the Construction of Social Forms*, 2 vols., trans. and ed. Anthony J. Blasi, Anton K. Jacobs, and Mathew Kanjirathinkal, intro Horst J. Helle (Leiden: Brill, 2009), 570–601; Helmuth Plessner, *Anthropologie der Sinne*, vol. 3, *Gesammelte Schriften*, ed. Günter Dux, Odo Marquard, and Elisabeth Ströker (Frankfurt: Suhrkamp, 1980–85); Maurice Merleau-Ponty, *Phenomenology of Perception*, trans. Donald A. Landes (New York: Routledge, 2012); Michel Serres, *The Five Senses: A Philosophy of Mingled Bodies*, trans. Margaret Sankey and Peter Cowley (London: Bloomsbury Academic, 2016). See also chapter 12.
2. For more on the media as "extensions of the senses," see, of course, Marshall McLuhan, *Understanding Media: The Extensions of Man* (Cambridge, MA: MIT Press, 1994). But on the necessary precautions to avoid an inflationary use of the word *medium*, see also Lambert Wiesing, "What Are Media?," in *Artificial Presence: Philosophical Studies in Image Theory*, trans. Nils F. Schott (Stanford: Stanford University Press, 2010), 122–33.
3. As in Carnevali, *Romantisme et reconnaissance: Figures de la conscience chez Rousseau*, trans. Philippe Audegean (Geneva: Droz, 2012), original Italian edition 2004.
4. Hannah Arendt, *The Life of the Mind*, vol. 1, *Thinking* (London: Secker and Warburg, 1978), 21. See also Hannah Arendt, *The Human Condition*, 2nd ed. (Chicago: University of Chicago Press, 1998), part 5: in this book, twenty years before developing a new political anthropology, Arendt discovered the aesthetic-political chiasmus through an idealized reinterpretation of the model of the Greek polis.
5. See Arjun Appadurai, ed., *The Social Life of Things: Commodities in Cultural Perspective* (Cambridge: Cambridge University Press, 1986).
6. See Lambert Wiesing, *Sehen lassen: Die Praxis des Zeigens* (Berlin: Suhrkamp, 2013), 105.
7. See Erving Goffman, *The Presentation of Self in Everyday Life* (London: Penguin Books, 1990). In rhetoric, the notion of *self-presentation* is central to the work of Ruth Amossy, who applies Goffman's theories to verbal discourse in *La Présentation de soi* (Paris: Presses Universitaires de France, 2015).
8. Adolf Portmann, *Animals as Social Beings*, trans. Oliver Coburn (New York: Viking, 1961).
9. Adolf Portmann, *Animal Forms and Patterns: A Study of the Appearance of Animals*, trans. Hella Czech, illustrated by Sabine Baur (New York: Schocken, 1967). See also Maurice Merleau-Ponty, *The Visible and the Invisible*, ed. Claude Lefort, trans. Alphonso

1. Life as a Spectacle 237

Lingis (Evanston, IL: Northwestern University Press, 1968); Jacques Dewitte, *La Manifestation de soi* (Paris: La Découverte, 2010).
10. As the representative of M.A.U.S.S. the antiutilitarian movement in social sciences, suggests. See www.revuedumauss.com.
11. The concept of reflexivity as I use it shares some similarities with that of "narcissism." As an essential element inherent in human subjectivity, narcissism is a key notion in psychoanalysis, and, from Freud on, psychoanalytical studies on narcissism have probed the ways it can evolve into both healthy and pathological forms. I have intentionally chosen not to use the term, however, so as to avoid the moralistic and negative connotations that the word has acquired in common use. In ordinary language, a "narcissist" is someone with egocentric attitudes who has little empathy and is largely indifferent to other people: an egotist.
12. Thomas Fuchs, "The Psychopathology of Hyperreflexivity," *Journal of Speculative Philosophy*, new series, 24, no. 3 (2010): 239–55.
13. See Philippe Rochat, *Others in Mind: Social Origins of Self-Consciousness* (Cambridge: Cambridge University Press, 2009).
14. Heinrich von Kleist, "On the Marionette Theater," trans. Christian-Albrecht Gollub, in *German Romantic Criticism*, ed. Amos Leslie Willson (New York: Continuum, 1982), 238–44. On "artificial naturalness," see Paolo D'Angelo, *Sprezzatura: Concealing the Effort of Art from Aristotle to Duchamp*, trans. Sarin Marchetti (New York: Columbia University Press, 2018). On reflection and its aporias, see Charles Larmore, *The Practices of the Self* (Chicago: University of Chicago Press, 2010).
15. See, for example, the studies by Gordon G. Gallup, starting with "Chimpanzees: Self-Recognition," *Science* 167 (1970): 86–87.
16. My use of philosophical anthropology is intended to be compatible with a naturalist perspective. See Jean-Marie Schaeffer, *La Fin de l'exception humaine* (Paris: Gallimard, 2007).
17. Arendt, *The Life of the Mind*, 1:19–20.
18. Helmuth Plessner, *Levels of Organic Life and the Human: An Introduction to Philosophical Anthropology*, trans. Millay Hyatt, intro. Jay M. Bernstein (New York: Fordham University Press, 2019). Other works by Plessner that have been translated into English include *The Limits of Community* (1924), *Political Anthropology* (1931), and *Laughing and Crying* (1941), which I will come back to later on in this book. Generally, Plessner's thought remains still fairly unknown in the English-speaking world. For a critical presentation of Plessnerian anthropology in dialogue with contemporary philosophy, in addition to the excellent introduction by Jay Bernstein to *Levels*, see Jos de Mul, ed., *Plessner's Philosophical Anthropology: Perspectives and Prospects* (Amsterdam: Amsterdam University Press, 2014); and the articles by Joachim Fischer, Hans-Peter Krüger in the special issue of *Iris* 1, no. 1 (2009), edited by Andrea Borsari, dedicated to philosophical anthropology; the articles by Richard Shusterman and Hans-Peter Krüger in *Journal of Speculative Philosophy*, new series, 24, no. 3 (2010). Shusterman situates Plessner's theory in relation to Husserl, Merleau-Ponty, and pragmatism.
19. Helmuth Plessner, *Laughing and Crying: A Study of the Limits of Human Behavior*, trans. James Spencer Churchill and Marjorie Grene (Evanston, IL: Northwestern University Press, 1970).

20. See Joachim Fischer, *Exzentrische Positionalität: Studien zu Helmuth Plessner* (Weilerswist: Velbrück Wissenschaft, 2016), especially 343ff., on the question of the boundaries between animal, human, and android beings, and 115ff., on the relationship between the concept of eccentric positionality and other theories of negativity and reflexivity.
21. Fischer, 287ff. Maurice Merleau-Ponty, whose theories were indirectly influenced by Plessner, arrives at similar conclusions. See, for instance, Merleau-Ponty, "The Child's Relations with Others," trans. William Cobb, in *The Primacy of Perception, and Other Essays on Phenomenological Psychology, the Philosophy of Art, History, and Politics*, ed. James M. Edie (Evanston, IL: Northwestern University Press, 1964), 96–155.
22. John Berger, *Ways of Seeing* (New York: Viking, 1973), 66. See Simone de Beauvoir, *The Second Sex*, trans. Constance Borde and Sheila Malovany-Chevallier (London: Jonathan Cape, 2009).
23. The film was interpreted in different terms by Gilles Deleuze in "The Greatest Irish Film (Beckett's Film)," in *Essays Critical and Clinical*, trans. Daniel W. Smith and Michael A. Greco (London: Verso, 1998), 23–26, and by Simon Critchley, "To Be or Not to Be Is Not the Question: On Beckett's Film," *Film-Philosophy* 11, no. 2 (2007): 108–21.
24. This hypothesis is suggested in Beckett's preparatory notes, which, while taking the form of a denial, allude to the protagonist's relationship with his mother.
25. Sensorial reflexivity is not exclusive to sight; it can be expressed through all the senses. We perceive ourselves through touch, the sound of our own voice, our body odors, and the taste of our bodily fluids, such as blood. This topic, which deserves a study all on its own, also rekindles the question of human-animal comparison, shifting the threshold of reflexivity on the basis of the senses that are more or less vital to each species: a dog that can't recognize itself in the mirror recognizes instantly the smell of its own urine.
26. Plessner, *Levels of Organic Life and the Human*.
27. See especially Plessner, "Zur Anthropologie des Schauspielers" (On the anthropology of the actor, 1948), and his other essays on mimesis and expression included in volume 7, *Ausdruck und Menschliche Natur*, in *Gesammelte Schriften*, ed. Günter Dux, Odo Marquard, and Elisabeth Ströker (Frankfurt: Suhrkamp, 1980–85). See also *Die Frage nach der Conditio Humana* (The question of human condition, 1961), in volume 8.
28. Some similarities with Sartre's philosophy of the self are analyzed in Marco Stahlhut, *Schauspieler ihrer selbst: Das Performative, Sartre, Plessner* (Vienna: Passagen, 2005).
29. Plessner, "Zur Anthropologie des Schauspielers," 418.
30. Regarding gender theory perspectives on appearances, theatricality, and the performative, see Judith Butler's work, especially *Gender Trouble: Feminism and the Subversion of Identity* (1990; New York: Routledge, 2006).
31. Friedrich Nietzsche, *Human, All Too Human: A Book for Free Spirits*, trans. R. J. Hollingdale, intro. Erich Heller (Cambridge: Cambridge University Press, 1996), 39–40.
32. This example is aptly commented on, although only in relation to external, and not internal, spectators, in Gloria Origgi, *Reputation: What It Is and Why It Matters*, trans. Stephen Holmes and Noga Arikha (Princeton: Princeton University Press, 2018).
33. See, for example, Helmuth Plessner, *The Limits of Community: A Critique of Social Radicalism*, trans. Andrew Wallace (Amherst, NY: Humanity, 1999).

34. According to Mauss, the notion of person derives from the Latin *persona*, which means "mask." See Marcel Mauss, "A Category of the Human Mind: The Notion of Person; the Notion of Self," in *The Category of the Person: Anthropology, Philosophy, History*, ed. Michael Carrithers, Steven Collins, and Steven Lukes (Cambridge: Cambridge University Press, 1985), 1–25.

2. MASKS AND CLOTHES

1. See George Santayana, "The World's a Stage" and "Masks," in *Soliloquies in England and Later Soliloquies* (New York: Scribner's, 1922), 126–32; Alessandro Pizzorno, "The Mask: An Essay" (1960), trans. Monica Greco, *International Political Anthropology* 3, no. 1 (2010): 5–28; Richard Weihe, *Die Paradoxie der Maske: Geschichte einer Form* (Munich: Wilhelm Fink, 2004); Hans Belting, *Face and Mask: A Double History*, trans. Thomas S. Hansen and Abby J. Hansen (Princeton: Princeton University Press, 2017).
2. This theoretical perspective opens up an original path in contemporary debate, in which authors tend either to substantialize authenticity, by treating representations as hypocritical masks and falsehoods, or to dissolve authenticity into the plurality of its representations. In what I propose, on the contrary, the self is an open concept whose creation obeys aesthetic dynamics, but whose foundation remains an entirely negative gesture that is unrepresentable par excellence.
3. This evocative image comes from Byung-Chul Han, *The Transparency Society*, trans. Erik Butler (Stanford: Stanford Briefs, 2015), chapter 1. Unfortunately, the book's thesis never breaks past the limits of the anticapitalist paradigm, which I will analyze in the second part of this book.
4. See Erving Goffman, *Asylums: Essays on the Social Situation of Mental Patients and Other Inmates* (Garden City, NY: Anchor, 1961); and Niklas Luhmann, *Grundrechte als Institution* (Berlin: Duncker und Humblot, 1965), for this notion of dignity as self-presentation.
5. Hans Blumenberg, *Beschreibung des Menschen* (Frankfurt: Suhrkamp, 2006), 860 and 865.
6. Georg Simmel, "The Secret and the Secret Society," in *Sociology* (Leiden: Brill, 2009), 307–21. On the moral landscape of modernity as it relates to the values of authenticity and sincerity, see Lionel Trilling, *Sincerity and Authenticity* (New York: Harcourt Brace Jovanovich, 1972); Charles Taylor, *Sources of the Self: The Making of Modern Identity* (Cambridge, MA: Harvard University Press, 1989); Charles Larmore, *The Practices of the Self* (Chicago: University of Chicago Press, 2010).
7. Erving Goffman, "The Nature of Deference and Demeanor," in *Interaction Ritual: Essays on Face-to-Face Behaviour* (1967; New York: Pantheon, 1982), 47–95.
8. See Thomas Nagel, "Public and Private," in *Concealment and Exposure, and Other Essays* (Oxford: Oxford University Press, 2002), 3–26. On tact, see Wolfram Hogrebe, *Riskante Lebensnähe: Die szenische Existenz des Menschen* (Berlin: Akademie, 2009); Ossi Naukkarinen, "Everyday Aesthetic Practices, Ethics and Tact," *Aisthesis* 7, no. 1 (2014): 23–44.

9. John C. Flügel, *The Psychology of Clothes* (London: Hogarth, 1930), 21.
10. Georg Wilhelm Friedrich Hegel, *Aesthetics: Lectures on Fine Art*, trans. Thomas M. Knox (Oxford: Clarendon, 1988), 1:31.
11. Elena Esposito, "The Fascination of Contingency: Fashion and Modern Society," in *Philosophical Perspectives on Fashion*, ed. Giovanni Matteucci and Stefano Marino (London: Bloomsbury Academic, 2017), 175–90. On fashion as the expression of two basic, oppositional tendencies that move toward either homologation or difference, see Georg Simmel, "The Philosophy of Fashion," in *Simmel on Culture*, ed. David Frisby and Mike Featherstone (London: SAGE, 1997), 187–206. Although the literature on clothing and fashion is practically limitless at this point, there is still a lack of a serious *philosophy of clothing*.
12. In the case of subcultures, such as punks or skaters, the expressive need is based on the need for recognition or categorization, but without the categories being imposed by tradition: this is the essential difference from premodern societies.
13. See Goffman, *Interaction Ritual*; Pierre Bourdieu, *Distinction: A Social Critique of the Judgement of Taste*, trans. Richard Nice (Cambridge, MA: Harvard University Press, 1984).
14. James Laver, *A Concise History of Costume* (London: Thames and Hudson, 1969), 241. See also Georg Simmel, "The Picture Frame: An Aesthetic Study," trans. M. Ritter, *Theory, Culture and Society* 11, no. 1 (1994): 121–33.
15. Hannah Arendt's political anthropology, which offers such a wealth of insights for my social aesthetics, is limited, in my opinion, by its tendency to emphasize the "disinterest" of aesthetic expression.
16. Helmuth Plessner, *The Limits of Community: A Critique of Social Radicalism*, trans. Andrew Wallace (Amherst, NY: Humanity, 1999), 133; and Plessner, *Political Anthropology*, trans. Nils F. Schott (Evanston, IL: Northwestern University Press, 2018), chapter 9, "The Exposure of the Human," 53–60. See Joachim Fischer, *Panzer oder Maske: "Verhaltenslehre der Kälte" oder Sozialtheorie der "Grenze,"* in *Plessners "Grenzen der Gemeinschaft": Eine Debatte*, ed. Wolfgang Essbach, Joachim Fischer, and Helmut Lethen (Frankfurt: Suhrkamp, 2002), 80–102.

3. AESTHETIC MEDIATION

1. On expression as a constitutively mediated phenomenon and as a typical manifestation of the anthropological law of "mediated immediacy," see especially Helmuth Plessner, *Laughing and Crying: A Study of the Limits of Human Behavior*, trans. James Spencer Churchill and Marjorie Grene (Evanston, IL: Northwestern University Press, 1970).
2. Jacques Derrida, *Voice and Phenomenon: Introduction to the Problem of the Sign in Husserl's Phenomenology*, trans. Leonard Lawlor (Evanston, IL: Northwestern University Press, 2011); Derrida, *Of Grammatology*, trans. Gayatri Chakravorty Spivak (Baltimore: Johns Hopkins University Press, 2016). See also the development toward semiology offered in Louis Marin, *On Representation*, trans. Catherine Porter (Stanford: Stanford University Press, 2001).

3. This is how one of the most powerful and shareable insights of Jacques Derrida could be summed up. See Derrida, *Dissemination*, trans. and intro. Barbara Johnson (Chicago: University of Chicago Press, 2017).
4. The idea that society is like a work of art encapsulates the teachings of Georg Simmel, as his students have pointed out. See M. S. Davis, "Georg Simmel and the Aesthetics of Social Reality," *Social Forces* 51 (1973): 320–29, which is where the sentence from Georg Simmel quoted in the epigraph of this book is taken from.

4. FIGURES

1. See Emanuele Coccia, *Sensible Life: A Micro-Ontology of the Image*, trans. Scott Alan Stuart (New York: Fordham University Press, 2016).
2. For more on the ideas that follow, in addition to the previously cited studies by Blumenberg and Belting, see Georg Simmel, "The Aesthetic Significance of the Face" (1901), trans. Lore Ferguson, in *Essays on Sociology, Philosophy and Aesthetics*, by Georg Simmel et al., ed. Kurt H. Wolff (New York: Harper Torchbooks, 1965), 276–81; Emmanuel Levinas, *Alterity and Transcendence*, trans. Michael B. Smith (New York: Columbia University Press, 1999); Jean-Jacques Courtine and Claudine Haroche, *Histoire du visage: Exprimer et taire ses émotions, XVIe–début XIXe siècle* (Paris: Rivages, 1988).
3. Thomas Macho, *Vorbilder* (Munich: Wilhelm Fink, 2011), 263ff. See also Gerburg Treusch-Dieter and Thomas Macho, eds., *Medium Gesicht: Die faciale Gesellschaft* (Berlin: Elefanten, 1996).
4. See Peter Brown, *The Cult of the Saints: Its Rise and Function in Latin Christianity*, 2nd ed. (Chicago: University of Chicago Press, 2015); Edgar Morin, *The Stars*, trans. Richard Howard (New York: Grove, 1960); Daniel Herwitz, *The Star as Icon: Celebrity in the Age of Mass Consumption* (New York: Columbia University Press, 2008).
5. See Antoine Lilti, *The Invention of Celebrity, 1750–1850*, trans. Lynn Jeffress (Malden, MA: Polity, 2017); and Jean-Louis Fabiani, *Qu'est-ce qu'un philosophe français?: La vie sociale des concepts, 1880–1980* (Paris: Editions de l'EHESS, 2010).

5. OUT OF CONTROL

1. On the concept of alienation and its revival in contemporary social philosophy, see Stéphane Haber, *L'Aliénation: Vie sociale et expérience de la dépossession* (Paris: Presses Universitaires de France, 2007); and Rahel Jaeggi, *Alienation*, trans. Frederick Neuhouser and Alan E. Smith (New York: Columbia University Press, 2014). For a criticism of the concept of alienation, a criticism that inspires my analysis of social romanticism, see the previously mentioned work by Helmuth Plessner, *The Limits of Community: A Critique of Social Radicalism*, trans. Andrew Wallace (Amherst, NY: Humanity, 1999). See also the article by Arnold Gehlen, "Über die Geburt der Freiheit aus der Entfremdung," *Archiv für Rechts- und Sozialphilosophie* 40, no. 3 (1952): 338–53; and Peter

Sloterdijk, "Luhmann, Devil's Advocate," in *Not Saved: Essay After Heidegger*, trans. Ian Alexander Moore and Christopher Turner (Cambridge: Polity, 2016), 155–263.
2. Guido Kreis, "Für eine Philosophie des objektiven Geistes," in *Lebenswelt und Wissenschaft*, Deutsches Jahrbuch Philosophie 2 (Hamburg: Meiner, 2011), 120–36.
3. Hannah Arendt, *The Human Condition*, 2nd ed. (Chicago: University of Chicago Press, 1998), 204.
4. See Hans Belting, *An Anthropology of Images: Picture, Medium, Body*, trans. Thomas Dunlap (Princeton: Princeton University Press, 2011).
5. See Georges Didi-Huberman, *The Surviving Image: Phantoms of Time and Time of Phantoms: Aby Warburg's History of Art*, trans. H. L. Mendelsohn (University Park: Pennsylvania State University Press, 2017).
6. See chapter 1.
7. See Axel Honneth, *The Struggle for Recognition: The Moral Grammar of Social Conflicts*, trans. Joel Anderson (Cambridge, MA: Polity, 1995). On the reputational goods and other issues raised in this chapter, see Gloria Origgi, *Reputation: What It Is and Why It Matters*, trans. Stephen Holmes and Noga Arikha (Princeton: Princeton University Press, 2018).
8. On Rousseau's ideal of authenticity, see chapter 7.
9. Jean-Paul Sartre, *Being and Nothingness: An Essay on Phenomenological Ontology*, trans. and intro. Hazel E. Barnes (New York: Philosophical Library, 1956), part 3, chapter 4, "The Look." See also Simone de Beauvoir, *The Second Sex*, trans. Constance Borde and Sheila Malovany-Chevallier (London: Jonathan Cape, 2009), passim.
10. Luigi Pirandello, *One, No One, and One Hundred Thousand*, trans. William Weaver (Boston: Eridanos, 1990), 3.
11. Pirandello, 5 and 7 (my italics).
12. Plessner became aware of Pirandello's work through the book by Löwith, which Plessner cites in the first note to his essay on the anthropology of the actor.
13. Pirandello, *One, No One, and One Hundred Thousand*, 15.
14. Pirandello, 15.
15. Pirandello, 17. Philippe Rochat and Dan Zahavi explore the issue using an approach similar to Pirandello's and examine the results of cognitive sciences in the light of Merleau-Ponty's suggestions. See Rochat and Zahavi, "The Uncanny Mirror: A Re-Framing of Mirror Self-Experience," *Consciousness and Cognition* 20 (2011): 204–13.
16. Jacques Lacan, "The Mirror Stage as Formative of the Function of the *I* as Revealed in the Psychoanalytic Experience" (1949), in *Ecrits: A Selection*, trans. Alan Sheridan (London: Tavistock, 1977), 1–8, here 2.
17. Lacan, 2. See also chapter 4.
18. Pirandello, *One, No One, and One Hundred Thousand*, 19–20.
19. Karl Löwith, *Das Individuum in der Rolle des Mitmenschen* (Munich: Drei Masken, 1928), §23, 175 [Translator's note: The quoted passage is translated from the Italian edition: *L'individuo nel ruolo del co-uomo* (Naples: Guida, 2009), 159–60].
20. Luigi Pirandello, *Shoot!: The Notebooks of Serafino Gubbio, Cinematograph Operator*, trans. C. K. Scott Moncrieff (Chicago: University of Chicago Press, 2005), 68.

21. Walter Benjamin, "The Work of Art in the Age of Its Technological Reproducibility," 2nd version, in *Selected Writings*, vol. 3, *1935–1938*, ed. Howard Eiland and Michael Jennings, trans. Edmund Jephcott et al. (Cambridge, MA: Harvard University Press, 2002), 112. For more on these issues, Francesco Casetti, *Eye of the Century: Film, Experience, Modernity*, trans. Erin Larkin and Jennifer Pranolo (New York: Columbia University Press, 2008).

6. "VANITY FAIR"

1. Jacques Derrida, *Of Grammatology*, trans. Gayatri Chakravorty Spivak (Baltimore: Johns Hopkins University Press, 2016), 35.
2. On these issues in ancient culture, see the classic work by Martha C. Nussbaum, *The Fragility of Goodness: Luck and Ethics in Greek Tragedy and Philosophy* (Cambridge: Cambridge University Press, 1986), especially the chapter on Aristotle, which, significantly, is called "Saving Aristotle's Appearances," 240ff.
3. Hannah Arendt, *The Human Condition* (Chicago: University of Chicago Press, 1998), 176 (my italics).
4. Georg Simmel, *Sociology* (Leiden: Brill, 2009), 335. On the will to please, see also chapter 13.
5. Thomas Hobbes, *Leviathan*, vol. 2, ed. Noel Malcolm (Oxford: Clarendon, 2012), chapter 13, 62. For more on this topic, see the classic work by Leo Strauss, *The Political Philosophy of Hobbes: Its Basis and Its Genesis*, trans. Elsa M. Sinclair (1936; Chicago: University of Chicago Press, 1996); and Barbara Carnevali, "Triumphs of the Mind: Hobbes and the Ambivalences of Glory," in *The Dark Side: Philosophical Reflections on the "Negative Emotions,"* ed. Paola Giacomoni, Sara Dellantonio, and Nicolò Valentini (Springer: New York, 2020).
6. Blaise Pascal, *A Letter to Further the Search of God*, in *Pensées, and Other Writings*, trans. Honor Levi, ed. Anthony Levi (Oxford: Oxford University Press, 1995), 160.
7. John Bunyan, *The Pilgrim's Progress*, ed. Roger Sharrock (London: Penguin, 1987), 136. On the history of this "runaway metaphor," which developed from an emblem of sin and persecution into a motif of urban experience and consumerism, see Kirsty Milne, *At Vanity Fair: From Bunyan to Thackeray* (Cambridge: Cambridge University Press, 2015).
8. Bunyan, *The Pilgrim's Progress*, 137.
9. William Makepeace Thackeray, *Vanity Fair: A Novel Without a Hero*, ed. John Carey (London: Penguin, 2006), 5.
10. Thackeray, 809.
11. See *La notion de "monde" au XVIIe siècle*, ed. Bernard Beugnot, special issue of *Littérature classique* 22 (1994). On worldliness as a typical modern and late-modern social form, see the conclusion.
12. See Roberto Simanowski, *Facebook Society: Losing Ourselves in Sharing Ourselves*, trans. Susan H. Gillespie (New York: Columbia University Press, 2018), which refers explicitly

to Proust; and Simanowski, *Waste: A New Media Primer*, trans. Amanda DeMarco and Susan H. Gillespie (Cambridge, MA: MIT Press, 2018).

13. Although Hobbes is not mentioned directly by Kojève, Leo Strauss reveals their deep connection in a footnote to his book on Hobbes: "M. Alexandre Kojevnikoff and the writer intend to undertake a detailed investigation of the connexion between Hegel and Hobbes." Strauss, *The Political Philosophy of Hobbes*, 58.
14. See also Axel Honneth, *Anerkennung: Eine europäische Ideengeschichte* (Berlin: Suhrkamp, 2018), chapter 2 (on vanity and *amour-propre* in the French moralists).
15. On "prestige," see also chapters 14 and 15.
16. Alexandre Kojève, *Introduction to the Reading of Hegel*, assembled by Raymond Queneau, ed. Allan Bloom, trans. James H. Nichols, Jr. (Ithaca: Cornell University Press, 1969), 226–27, and, on snobbery, see pp. 161–62.
17. For a reappraisal of the connection between appearances, play, and aesthetics, understood as a source of culture, see Johan Huizinga, *Homo Ludens: A Study of the Play-Element in Culture*, trans. R. F. C. Hull (London: Routledge and K. Paul, 1949).
18. Ernst Gombrich, *The Logic of Vanity Fair: Alternative to Historicism in the Study of Fashion, Styles and Taste* (La Salle, IL: Open Court, 1974).

7. AGAINST THE MASK

1. See Guillaume Navaud, *Persona: Le Théâtre comme métaphore théorique de Socrate à Shakespeare* (Genève: Droz, 2011).
2. See Louis Van Delft, *Les Spectateurs de la vie: Généalogie du regard moraliste* (Paris: Hermann, 2012); Barbara Carnevali, "L'Observatoire des mœurs: Les coutumes et les caractères entre littérature et morale," in *Pensée morale et genres littéraires: De Montaigne à Genet*, ed. Jean-Charles Darmon and Philippe Desan (Paris: Presses Universitaires de France, 2009), 159–78.
3. Baltasar Gracián y Morales, *The Art of Worldly Wisdom: A Pocket Oracle*, trans. Christopher Maurer (New York: Doubleday, 1992), 220, 282.
4. See John William Smeed, *The Theophrastan "Character": The History of a Literary Genre* (Oxford: Clarendon, 1985); Marc Escola, *La Bruyère I: Brèves questions d'herméneutique* (Paris: H. Champion, 2001); Vincent Descombes, *Proust: Philosophy of the Novel*, trans. Catherine Chance Macksey (Stanford: Stanford University Press, 1992).
5. My remarks in this chapter draw precious inspiration from the work of Jean Starobinski. In addition to his book on Rousseau, which I will draw from later on, see especially Starobinski, *Montaigne in Motion*, trans. Arthur Goldhammer (Chicago: University of Chicago Press, 1985); Starobinski, *Interrogatoire du masque* (Paris: Éditions Galilée, 2015); and Starobinski, "La Rochefoucauld et les morales substitutives," *Nouvelle Revue Française* 14 (1966): 16–34 and 211–29. See also Richard Weihe, *Die Paradoxie der Maske: Geschichte einer Form* (Munich: Wilhelm Fink, 2004), 333–35; Louis Van Delft, *Littérature et anthropologie: Nature humaine et caractère à l'âge classique* (Paris: Presses Universitaires de France, 1993).

6. See Brendan Donnellan, *Nietzsche and the French Moralists* (Bonn: Bouvier, 1982); and especially Robert B. Pippin, *Nietzsche, Psychology, and First Philosophy* (Chicago: University of Chicago Press, 2010).
7. For a long-duration reconstruction of the Aristotelian genealogy, see Barbara Carnevali, "Literary Mimesis and Moral Knowledge: The Tradition of *Ethopoeia*," *Annales: Histoire, Sciences Sociales* 2 (2010): 291–322, www.cairn-int.info/article-E_ANNA_652_0291 —literary-mimesis-and-moral-knowledge.htm.
8. For this interpretation of Rousseau, see Carnevali, *Romantisme et reconnaissance: Figures de la conscience chez Rousseau*, trans. Philippe Audegean (Geneva: Droz, 2012), original Italian edition 2004. On the question of recognition in Rousseau (an interpretation that picks up on the positive aspects of *amour-propre*, interpreting them from the perspective of German idealism), see also Frederick Neuhouser, *Rousseau's Theodicy of Self-Love: Evil, Rationality, and the Drive for Recognition* (Oxford: Oxford University Press, 2008).
9. Jean-Jacques Rousseau, *Discourse on the Origin and the Foundations of Inequality Among Men*, in *The Discourses, and Other Early Political Writings*, ed. and trans. Victor Gourevitch (Cambridge: Cambridge University Press, 1997), 218, note 15.
10. Rousseau, 187 (my italics).
11. Rousseau, 166 (my italics).
12. Faithful to the cultural stereotype of gender, Rousseau's condemnation makes vanity coincide with a reprimand against the effeminacy of modern customs.
13. Rousseau's insight, explained here in my own terms, can be compared with Rancière's concept of the "partage du sensible" (distribution of the sensible). See Jacques Rancière, *The Politics of Aesthetics: The Distribution of the Sensible*, trans. Gabriel Rockhill (London: Continuum, 2004).
14. For more on how symbolic inequality turns into material and economic inequality, and for a more detailed analysis of this long degenerative process, see Carnevali, *Romantisme et reconnaissance*, 128–35.
15. Jean-Jacques Rousseau, *Letter to M. d'Alembert on the Theater*, in *Politics and the Arts*, ed. Allan Bloom (Ithaca, NY: Cornell University Press, 1960), 81 (my italics). For a reading of Rousseau's treatment of the actor that intersects at several points with the thesis of this book, starting with its engagement with Plessner's work, see Juliane Rebentisch, *The Art of Freedom: On the Dialectics of Democratic Existence*, trans. Joseph Ganahl (Cambridge, MA: Polity, 2016), part 3.
16. The thesis that Leo Strauss developed about Hobbes—the naturalism of Hobbesian anthropology is belied by its Christian "moral basis," which is evidenced precisely by the prominence it gives to the problem of vanity—applies, therefore, all the more to the moralist Rousseau. See Leo Strauss, *The Political Philosophy of Hobbes: Its Basis and Its Genesis*, trans. Elsa M. Sinclair (1936; Chicago: University of Chicago Press, 1996). Rousseau's proximity with the Christian paradigm is also betrayed by how closely his moral arguments against theater mirror those of Tertullian in his *De spectaculis* (*The Shows*), written in the late second century. Tertullian's treatise, which had an inestimable influence on the "anti-theater" culture of the West, can also be read as a compendium of moral

prejudices that have impeded proper understanding of social appearances and of the spectacular dynamics underlying social life.

17. See Charles Larmore, *The Romantic Legacy* (New York: Columbia University Press, 1996). On Rousseau's ideal of authenticity, in addition to my *Romantisme et reconnaissance*, see Alessandro Ferrara, *Modernity and Authenticity: A Study in the Social and Ethical Thought of Jean-Jacques Rousseau* (Albany: State University of New York Press, 1993); Claude Romano, *Être soi-même* (Paris: Gallimard, 2019), chapter 14.

18. Pascal, *Pensées*, 147, 181.

19. Starobinski, "La Rochefoucauld et les morales substitutives."

20. Jean-Jacques Rousseau, *Discourse on the Sciences and Arts*, in *The Discourses, and Other Early Political Writings*, 7–8 (my italics).

21. Rousseau, 8. In reality, many philosophical and sociological explanations of trust, such as Simmel's, are actually based on the contrary assumption, by positing a constitutive dimension of opacity that makes transparent social relations impossible (and unsuitable).

22. The question of artifice in the thought of Rousseau presents intermediate tensions and solutions that are not wholly reducible to the romantic paradigm—a paradigm that I have adopted here in an ideal-type version in order to reconstruct and deconstruct the thought tradition of social romanticism. For an interpretation of Rousseau that is focused on the same issues but more attentive to internal waverings and nuances, see the classical studies by Jean Starobinski, in particular *Jean-Jacques Rousseau, Transparency and Obstruction*, trans. Arthur Goldhammer (Chicago: University of Chicago Press, 1988); and *Blessings in Disguise: or, The Morality of Evil*, trans. Arthur Goldhammer (Cambridge, MA: Harvard University Press, 1993).

23. Norbert Elias, *The Court Society*, trans. Edmund Jephcott (Dublin: University College Dublin Press, 2006), chapter 6.

24. Helmuth Plessner, *The Limits of Community: A Critique of Social Radicalism*, trans. Andrew Wallace (Amherst, NY: Humanity, 1999), 80. At the dawn of Nazism (the book was published in 1924), but also in polemic with communism, Plessner complained about the risks of the appeal to community and to an immediate bond. He also defended the representative-aesthetic culture of the mask and prestige typical of the Ancien Régime as the only culture able to preserve the vital space of the human in the properly social sphere. See chapter 12.

8. AGAINST THE SPECTACLE

1. Guy Debord, *The Society of the Spectacle*, trans. Donald Nicholson-Smith (New York: Zone, 1994). All citations from *The Society of the Spectacle* are indicated by their paragraph mark and are taken from this edition.

2. On the Lukácsian and Marxian roots of Debord's thought, see Anselm Jappe, *Guy Debord*, trans. Donald Nicholson-Smith (Berkeley: University of California Press, 1999).

3. Paul Ricœur, "Aliénation," in *Dictionnaire de la Philosophie* (Paris: Albin Michel, 2000), 47.
4. Guy Debord, *In girum imus nocte et consumimur igni*, in *Complete Cinematic Works*, ed. Ken Knabb (Oakland: AK, 2003), 154.
5. In Blake's preface to his edition of Milton, the artist asks himself in similar tones whether the divine presence showed itself in England in ancient times, before its hills were covered by "these dark, Satanic mills." Against the devastation, Blake engages in an eschatological fight for the construction of the new Jerusalem: "I will not cease from mental Fight / Nor shall my sword sleep in my hand / Till we have built Jerusalem / In England's green and pleasant land." For more on the current of romantic anticapitalism, see the overview by Michael Löwy and Robert Sayre, *Romanticism Against the Tide of Modernity* (Durham, NC: Duke University Press, 2001).
6. Debord, *In girum imus nocte et consumimur igni*, 164. See also Michael Löwy, "Consumé par le feu de la nuit (Le romantisme noir de Guy Debord)," *Lignes* 31 (1997): 161–69.
7. Giorgio Agamben, "Marginal Notes on *Commentaries on the Society of the Spectacle*," in *Means Without End: Notes on Politics*, trans. Vincenzo Binetti and Cesare Casarino (Minneapolis: University of Minnesota Press, 2000), 75.
8. Agamben reads Debord through the lens of Benjamin's work on the Parisian *passages* and display of merchandise, particularly through the notion of "phantasmagoria." The romantic origin of his anticapitalism, which in the critique of spectacle unites the French and German critiques of modernity, comes through in *Stanzas: Word and Phantasm in Western Culture*, trans. Ronald L. Martinez (Minneapolis: University of Minnesota Press, 1993).
9. Guy Debord, *Comments on the Society of the Spectacle*, trans. Malcolm Imrie (London: Verso, 1990), 9.
10. Agamben, *Means Without End*, 94.
11. See Barbara Carnevali, "*Gloria*: Sauver les apparences," in *Politique de l'exil: Giorgio Agamben et l'usage de la métaphysique*, ed. Anoush Ganjipour (Paris: Lignes, 2018), 69–98.
12. So much so that for over a century now it has defined itself as a "visual culture." The film theorist Béla Balázs (who spoke of *visuelle Kultur* in 1924) and the artist László Moholy-Nagy (1925, *optische Kultur*) celebrated the dawning of visual culture as early as the 1920s. See Andrea Pinotti and Antonio Somaini, *Cultura visuale: Immagini, sguardi, media, dispositivi* (Turin: Einaudi, 2016).
13. Jacques Rancière, *The Emancipated Spectator*, trans. Gregory Elliott (London: Verso, 2009), 44.
14. See also Daniel J. Boorstin, *The Image: A Guide to Pseudo-Events in America* (1961; New York: Vintage, 1992), whose complaints, although philosophically weaker and more moralistic than Debord's, historically precede his.
15. Debord, *In girum imus nocte et consumimur igni*, 144.
16. Siegfried Kracauer, *The Salaried Masses: Duty and Distraction in Weimar Germany*, trans. Quintin Hoare (London: Verso, 1998).

17. As suggested by Remo Bodei in his Italian presentation of Siegfried Kracauer, *La massa come ornamento* (Napoli: Prismi, 1982), 11.
18. Debord, *In girum imus nocte et consumimur igni*, 153–54.

9. AGAINST AESTHETIC VALUES

1. Jacques Rancière, *The Politics of Aesthetics: The Distribution of the Sensible*, trans. Gabriel Rockhill (London: Continuum, 2004), 12.
2. Slavoj Žižek, afterword to Rancière, *The Politics of Aesthetics*, 76.
3. Emile Durkheim, *The Division of Labour in Society*, 2nd ed., ed. Steven Lukes, trans. W. D. Halls (Basingstoke: Palgrave Macmillan, 2013), 43 (my italics).
4. Durkheim, "Teaching Aesthetics and History," in *Moral Education: A Study in the Theory and Application of the Sociology of Education*, trans. Everett K. Wilson and Herman Schnurer (New York: Free Press, 1973), 267–82, this quote 271.
5. For a more exhaustive analysis, see my contributions "Gloria: sauver les apparences," in *Politique de l'exil: Giorgio Agamben et l'usage de la métaphysique*, ed. Anoush Ganjipour (Paris: Lignes, 2018), 69–98 and "Bourdieu et l'esthétique" in *Bourdieu et les disciplines*, ed. Stéphane Dufoix and Christian Laval (Paris: Presses Universitaires de Paris Nanterre, 2018), 117–32.
6. Bourdieu, *Distinction: A Social Critique of the Judgment of Taste*, trans. Richard Nice (Cambridge, MA: Harvard University Press, 1984), 483 (my italics).
7. Pierre Bourdieu, *Pascalian Meditations*, trans. Richard Nice (Stanford: Stanford University Press, 2000), 166 (my italics). The quotation is Pascal, *Pensée* 404.
8. Bourdieu, *Distinction*, 11 (my italics).
9. Bourdieu, 44.
10. Bourdieu, 47.
11. See Mike Featherstone, *Consumer Culture and Postmodernism*, 2nd ed. (Los Angeles: SAGE, 2007); and Wolfgang Fritz Haug, *Critique of Commodity Aesthetics: Appearance, Sexuality and Advertising in Capitalist Society*, trans. Robert Bock (Cambridge: Polity, 1986). The original book, written in the 1960s, has been updated in a new edition: *Kritik der Warenästhetik: Gefolgt von Warenästhetik im High-Tech-Kapitalismus* (Frankfurt: Suhrkamp, 2009). See also Gernot Böhme, *Critique of Aesthetic Capitalism*, trans. Edmund Jephcott (Milan: Mimesis International, 2017); Gilles Lipovetsky and Jean Serroy, *L'Esthétisation du monde: Vivre à l'âge du capitalisme artiste* (Paris: Gallimard, 2013); and Peter Murphy and Eduardo de la Fuente, eds., *Aesthetic Capitalism* (Leiden: Brill, 2014).
12. Juliane Rebentisch stands out for her lack of prejudices. In a book that stays close to the Frankfurt School of critical theory, she has titled her introduction "Aesthetization: An Apologia": Rebentisch, *The Art of Freedom: On the Dialectics of Democratic Existence*, trans. Joseph Ganahl (Cambridge, MA: Polity, 2016).
13. Walter Benjamin, "The Work of Art in the Age of Its Technological Reproducibility," 2nd version, in *Selected Writings*, vol. 3, *1935–1938*, ed. Howard Eiland and Michael

Jennings, trans. Edmund Jephcott et al. (Cambridge, MA: Harvard University Press, 2002), 120–21 (my italics). The notion of the aestheticization of politics is central to several important historical interpretations of Nazism and Fascism. See Peter Reichel, *Der schöne Schein des Dritten Reiches: Faszination und Gewalt des Faschismus* (Munich: Hanser, 1991); Simonetta Falasca-Zamponi, *Fascist Spectacle: The Aesthetics of Power in Mussolini's Italy* (Berkeley: University of California Press, 1997); Jeffrey T. Schnapp, *Staging Fascism: 18BL and the Theater of Masses for Masses* (Stanford: Stanford University Press, 1996); Eric Michaud, *The Cult of Art in Nazi Germany*, trans. Janet Lloyd (Stanford: Stanford University Press, 2004). This approach was then extended to other totalitarian states: Boris Groys, *The Total Art of Stalinism: Avant-Garde, Aesthetic Dictatorship, and Beyond*, trans. Charles Rougle (Princeton: Princeton University Press, 1992).

14. Agamben's idea of the contemporary "civil war over face," commented on in the previous chapter, represents another attempt to reapply and extend Benjamin's analysis of fascist aestheticizing, through Carl Schmitt.
15. Böhme, *Critique of Aesthetic Capitalism*, 21.
16. See Martijn Konings, *Capital and Time: For a New Critique of Neoliberal Reason* (Stanford: Stanford University Press, 2018); and, on the "speculative" function of money and the relationship between aesthetic and economic values in modernity, Georg Simmel, *The Philosophy of Money*, trans. Tom Bottomore and David Frisby (1900; London: Routledge, 2004). Simmel shows exemplarily that, contrary to common thought, the process of derealization is characteristic of modernity and not postmodernity.
17. See Roland Barthes, *Writing Degree Zero*, trans. Annette Lavers and Colin Smith (New York: Hill and Wang, 2012).
18. See Gernot Böhme, *The Aesthetics of Atmospheres*, ed. Jean-Paul Thibaud (London: Routledge, 2017). In the third part of this book, these concepts will be developed from the novel perspective of social aesthetics.

10. TWO BAPTISMS AND A DIVORCE

1. For a systematic presentation of this renewal of aesthetics, see Wolfgang Welsch, "Aesthetics Beyond Aesthetics," *Proceedings of the XIIIth International Congress of Aesthetics* (1995), www2.uni-jena.de/welsch/papers/W_Welsch_Aesthetics_beyond_Asthetics.html; Jean-Marie Schaeffer, *Art of the Modern Age: Philosophy of Art from Kant to Heidegger*, trans. Steven Rendall (Princeton: Princeton University Press, 2000); and Schaeffer, *Beyond Speculation: Art and Aesthetics Without Myths*, trans. Daffyd Roberts (London: Seagull, 2015).
2. Benedetto Croce, "Le due scienze mondane: L'estetica e l'economica (1931)," was translated as "The Two Profane Sciences: Aesthetics and Economics," in *My Philosophy, and Other Essays on the Moral and Political Problems of Our Time*, trans. E. F. Carritt (London: Allen and Unwin, 1949), 140–52, this quote 144. The translations of the title and the quotation have been modified to more accurately reflect the Italian original.
3. Croce, 144.

4. This idea, which appears in Croce's first formulation of his aesthetics (the *Theses of Aesthetics* from 1900 and then the lengthy *Aesthetics* of 1902), was gradually toned down in the later, markedly more idealistic developments of his philosophy. See Paolo D'Angelo, "Estetica ed economia in Croce," in *Il problema Croce* (Macerata: Quodlibet, 2015), 35–44.
5. The picture provided here is not solely intended to shed light on a disciplinary taxonomy: it makes no claim to reducing all modern aesthetic theories within the same schemas or to rooting the origins of aestheticism in Kant's *Critique of Judgment*, as a commonplace introduced by Bourdieu would have it. Paolo D'Angelo makes some welcome cautionary comments on this topic in *Estetica* (Rome: Laterza, 2011), 66–67.
6. Giorgio Agamben, *Taste*, trans. Cooper Francis (New York: Seagull, 2017), 67–68.
7. Arno J. Mayer, *The Persistence of the Old Regime: Europe to the Great War* (New York: Pantheon, 1981), 105–6 (my italics).
8. Theodor W. Adorno, "Short Commentaries on Proust," in *Notes to Literature*, ed. Rolf Tiedemann, trans. Shierry Weber Nicholson (New York: Columbia University Press, 1992), 2:174–84, this quote 179.
9. Hippolyte A. Taine, *History of English Literature*, vol. 2, trans. H. Van Laun (New York: Henry Holt, 1874), 383. See Carnevali, "Snobbery: A Passion for Nobility," in *Navigatio vitae: Saggi per i settant'anni di Remo Bodei*, ed. Luigi Ballerini, Andrea Borsari, and Massimo Ciavolella (New York: Agincourt, 2010), 112–37.
10. Luc Boltanski and Eve Chiapello, *The New Spirit of Capitalism*, trans. Gregory Elliott (London: Verso, 2005), esp. "The Test of the Artistic Critique," 419–82. See also Andreas Reckwitz, *The Invention of Creativity: Modern Society and the Culture of the New*, trans. Steven Black (Cambridge: Polity, 2017).
11. Goethe, *Wilhelm Meister's Theatrical Calling*, trans. and intro. John R. Russell (Columbia, SC: Camden House, 1995), 56–57.
12. Goethe, 80.
13. See in particular the excursus "The Demise of the Representative Publicness Illustrated by the Case of Wilhelm Meister," in Jürgen Habermas, *The Structural Transformation of the Public Sphere: An Inquiry Into a Category of Bourgeois Society*, trans. Thomas Burger (Cambridge: Polity, 1992), 12–14.
14. Johann Wolfgang Goethe, *Wilhelm Meister's Apprenticeship*, ed. and trans. Eric A. Blackall in cooperation with Victor Lange (Princeton: Princeton University Press, 1995), 175, book 5, chapter 3.
15. Goethe, 174.
16. Franco Moretti, *The Bourgeois: Between History and Literature* (London: Verso, 2013), 39. A number of important Marxist critics have focused on these literary themes. See also György Lukács, *Goethe and His Age*, trans. Robert Anchor (London: Merlin P., 1968); and Herbert Marcuse's doctoral dissertation *Der deutsche Künstlerroman* (1922), of which the introduction is translated as "The German Artist Novel: Introduction," in *Art and Liberation: Collected Papers of Herbert Marcuse*, ed. Douglas Kellner, vol. 4 (London: Routledge, 2007), 71–81.
17. Norbert Elias, *The Court Society*, trans. Edmund Jephcott (Dublin: University College Dublin Press, 2006), 124–25.

18. Hippolyte A. Taine, *The Ancient Régime*, trans. John Durand (1876; New York: Holt, 1896), 131. Taine had made the "theater" the emblem of the nostalgic spirit of Ancien Régime.
19. Goethe, *Wilhelm Meister's Apprenticeship*, 88–89, book 3, chapter 2.
20. Pierre Bourdieu, *Distinction: A Social Critique of the Judgement of Taste*, trans. Richard Nice (Cambridge, MA: Harvard University Press, 1984), 483.
21. Siegfried Kracauer, *The Salaried Masses: Duty and Distraction in Weimar Germany*, trans. Quintin Hoare (London: Verso, 1998). Bourdieu himself ultimately acknowledges that the obsession for one's image is the most characteristic complex of the lower-middle class: "the petit bourgeois is haunted by the appearance he offers to others and the judgment they make of it." Bourdieu, *Distinction*, 253.

11. THE OPENING

1. See Gregory Nagy, *The Best of the Achaeans: Concepts of the Hero in Archaic Greek Poetry* (Baltimore: Johns Hopkins University Press, 1979); Christian Meier, *Politik und Anmut: Eine wenig zeitgemässe Betrachtung* (Stuttgart: Hohenheim, 2000); Louis Gernet, *The Anthropology of Ancient Greece*, trans. John Hamilton and Blaise Nagy (Baltimore: Johns Hopkins University Press, 1981).
2. See, in addition to Norbert Elias's *Court Society*, Jean-Marie Apostolidès, *Le Roi-Machine: Spectacle et politique au temps de Louis XIV* (Paris: Minuit, 1981).
3. Eiko Ikegami, *Bonds of Civility: Aesthetic Networks and the Political Origins of Japanese Culture* (Cambridge: Cambridge University Press, 2005).
4. Alexandre Kojève, *Introduction to the Reading of Hegel*, assembled by Raymond Queneau, trans. James H. Nichols, Jr. (Ithaca: Cornell University Press, 1969), 161–62; Roland Barthes, *Empire of Signs*, trans. Richard Howard (New York: Hill and Wang, 1982).
5. Jun'ichirō Tanizaki, *In Praise of Shadows*, trans. Thomas J. Harper and Edward G. Seidensticker (London: Cape, 1991); Kuki Shūzō, *Reflections on Japanese Taste: The Structure of Iki*, trans. John Clark (Sydney: Power, 1997).
6. See, among her many works, Yuriko Saito, "Everyday Aesthetics in the Japanese Tradition," in *Aesthetics of Everyday Life: East and West*, ed. Liu Yuedi and Curtis L. Carter (Cambridge: Cambridge Scholars, 2014), 145–64.
7. The differences between the two phenomena are in any case greater and, most importantly, more significant than the similarities.
8. On the importance of visibility and the social-aesthetic dimension in Melanesian anthropology, see, for example, Marilyn Strathern, *The Gender of the Gift* (Berkeley: University of California Press, 1988); or Simon Harrison, *The Mask of War* (Manchester: Manchester University Press, 2003). On the Amazonian area, Eduardo Viveiros de Castro, *From the Enemy's Point of View: Humanity and Divinity in an Amazonian Society* (Chicago: University of Chicago Press, 1992). My thanks to Stéphane Breton for these suggestions.
9. See Remo Bodei, *The Logics of Delusion*, trans. Giacomo Donis (Aurora, CO: Davies Group, 2006), ix.

10. Georg Simmel, *The Philosophy of Money*, trans. Tom Bottomore and David Frisby (London: Routledge, 2004), 54.
11. Georg Simmel, *Sociology* (Leiden: Brill, 2009), 570–601. See chapter 1.
12. See Barbara Carnevali and Andrea Pinotti, "Social Aesthetics," in *International Handbook of Simmel Studies*, ed. Gregor Fitzi (London, Routledge, 2020).
13. Plessner arrived at this point by way of an original anti-Cartesian route and an interpretation of Kantian transcendental philosophy that he proposed to complete through a "critique of the senses." On the relationship between Simmel's and Plessner's aesthesiologies, see Joachim Fischer, "Simmels Sinn der Sinne: Zum vital turn der Soziologie," in *Die Sinnlichkeit des Sozialen: Wahrnehmung und materielle Kultur*, ed. Hanna Katharina Göbel and Sophia Prinz (Bielefeld: Transcript, 2015), 423–40.
14. See chapter 9.
15. See Gunter Gebauer and Christoph Wulf, *Mimesis: Culture, Art, Society*, trans. Don Reneau (Berkeley: University of California Press, 1995); and Gebauer and Wulf, *Spiel—Ritual—Geste: Mimetisches Handeln in der sozialen Welt* (Reinbek bei Hamburg: Rowohlt, 1998).
16. Georg Simmel, "The Metropolis and Mental Life," in *Simmel on Culture*, ed. David Frisby and Mike Featherstone (London: SAGE, 1997), 174–85. See Vincenzo Mele, ed., *Sociology, Aesthetics & the City* (Pisa: Pisa University Press, 2012).
17. See Gregor Fitzi, *The Challenge of Modernity: Georg Simmel's Sociological Theory* (New York: Routledge, 2018).
18. See Werner Sombart, *Luxury and Capitalism*, trans. W. R. Dittmar (Ann Arbor: University of Michigan Press, 1967). Sombart's insights have been picked up on by Grant McCracken, *Culture and Consumption* (Bloomington: Indiana University Press, 1988).
19. Erich Auerbach, "La Court et la Ville," trans. Ralph Manheim, in *Scenes from the Drama of European Literature* (Minneapolis: University of Minnesota Press, 1984), 133–82.
20. Reinhart Koselleck, *Critique and Crisis: Enlightenment and the Pathogenesis of Modern Society* (Cambridge, MA: MIT Press, 1988). See also Antoine Lilti, *The World of the Salons: Sociability and Worldliness in Eighteenth-Century Paris*, trans. Lydia G. Cochrane (Oxford: Oxford University Press, 2015).
21. Even these historical contextualizations have a limit. As recalled at the end of chapter 8, Erving Goffman demonstrated that the model of spectacular interaction possesses a general, transcontextual dimension, since it also works in the nonurban and antimodern social context of a small island.
22. The field of sensory studies now has a wealth of specialized journals and monographs. See especially Constance Classen, *Worlds of Sense: Exploring the Senses in History and Across Cultures* (London: Routledge, 1993); Anthony Synnott, *The Body Social: Symbolism, Self and Society* (London: Routledge 1993); David Howes, *Sensual Relations: Engaging the Senses in Culture and Social Theory* (Ann Arbor: University of Michigan Press, 2003); Phillip Vannini, Dennis Waskul, and Simon Gottschalk, *The Senses in Self, Society, and Culture: A Sociology of the Senses* (New York: Routledge, 2012).
23. See Andreas Reckwitz, *The Invention of Creativity: Modern Society and the Culture of the New*, trans. Steven Black (Cambridge: Polity, 2017); and Reckwitz, *The Society of*

11. The Opening 253

Singularities: On the Structural Transformation of Modernity (Cambridge: Polity, 2020). See also Lucien Karpik, *L'Economie des singularités* (Paris: Gallimard, 2007); Nathalie Heinich, *L'Elite artiste: Excellence et singularité en régime démocratique* (Paris: Gallimard, 2005); Nathalie Heinich, *De la visibilité: Excellence et singularité en régime médiatique* (Paris: Gallimard, 2012); *De l'artification: Enquêtes sur le passage à l'art*, ed. Nathalie Heinich and Roberta Shapiro (Paris: Editions de l'EHESS, 2012).

24. Hans Blumenberg, *Höhlenausgänge* (Frankfurt: Suhrkamp, 1989), 76–81.
25. See Ernst Bloch, *The Principle of Hope*, trans. Neville Plaice, Stephen Plaice, and Paul Knight (Cambridge, MA: MIT Press, 1986).
26. See the chapter on Andy Warhol and the exemplary case of the Factory's transsexual regulars who are immortalized in Lou Reed's song "Walk on the Wild Side." The film *Midnight Cowboy* (1969) by John Schlesinger shows how this version of the American dream can flip into its opposite.
27. Hannah Arendt, however, would not subscribe to the *social-aesthetics* formula, because her political anthropology excludes the modern and economic realm of the "social," which is instead central to my approach. For Arendt, the opening in which human beings live does not give rise to a mediated exchange, to the conflictual interaction of particular interests. The same caveat applies to Giorgio Agamben's concept of "the open," which takes its inspiration from Heidegger and Arendt, identifying aesthetics with politics and radically excluding the economic realm. Agamben's theory lacks a social sphere, and it is expressed in idealistic and romantic terms: the open is realized in poetry. This and its messianic and eschatological bent make it inapplicable to my perspective. See Giorgio Agamben, *The Open: Man and Animal*, trans. Kevin Attell (Stanford: Stanford University Press, 2004).
28. See Jean-Marie Guyau, *L'Art au point de vue sociologique* (Paris: Fayard, 2001), 24–25.
29. The invention of the two ideal types is notoriously owed to Gustav Tönnies, but the way I intend the opposition from the viewpoint of social aesthetics is inspired once again by the reflection of Helmuth Plessner in *The Limits of Community*.
30. The writings of Jacques Rancière, for example, are marbled with a romantic view of popular art: see Rancière, *Aisthesis: Scenes from the Aesthetic Regime of Art*, trans. Zakir Paul (London: Verso, 2013). See also two writers who are very different from each other in terms of their orientation but who share a similar Dionysian romanticism: Manfred Frank, *Der kommende Gott* (Frankfurt: Suhrkamp, 1982); and Michel Maffesoli, *The Time of the Tribes: The Decline of Individualism in Mass Society*, trans. Don Smith (London: Sage, 1996).
31. On art as a medium of communication, from a rigorously nonromantic perspective, see Niklas Luhmann, *Art as a Social System*, trans. Eva M. Knodt (Stanford: Stanford University Press, 2000), chapter 1.
32. See the already cited works by Jacques Derrida, and chapter 3.
33. The English text of *Quaestio* 28 of Newton's *Optics* (in Latin text 20) reads: "there is a Being incorporeal, living, intelligent, omnipresent, who in infinite Space, as it were in his Sensory, sees the things themselves intimately, and thoroughly perceives them, and

comprehends *them wholly by their immediate presence to himself*: Of which things the Images only carried through the Organs of Sense into our little Sensoriums are there seen and beheld by that which in us perceives and thinks" (my italics).

34. See especially the historic chapter "Sensus Communis, Taste, Judgment," in Hans Gadamer, *Truth and Method*, trans. Joel Weinsheimer and Donald G. Marshall (London: Bloomsbury, 2013), 17–36; and Hannah Arendt, *Lectures on Kant's Political Philosophy*, ed. Ronald Beiner (Chicago: University of Chicago Press, 1992). On the aesthetic nature of the public sphere, from a perspective that is critical of Habermas's normative viewpoint and that highlights of publicity the asymmetries and nonidealistic aspects of publicity that are tied to power, see also Ari Adut, *Reign of Appearances: The Misery and Splendor of the Public Sphere* (Cambridge: Cambridge University Press, 2018).
35. Arendt, *Lectures on Kant's Political Philosophy*, 222.
36. Jacques Rancière, *The Politics of Aesthetics: The Distribution of the Sensible*, trans. Gabriel Rockhill (London: Continuum, 2004), 12.

12. AISTHESIS

1. In *Discourse on Inequality* Rousseau identifies the first exchange of glances as the historical event that founds human sociability and initiates the struggle for recognition. In *Emile*, the metaphor returns to describe the dawning of social sentiments in the adolescent, the delicate moment of transition during which the young man leaves the "age of things" to enter into the "age of men": "The eye becomes animated and looks over other beings. One begins to take an interest in those surrounding us; one begins to feel that one is not made to live alone. It is thus that the heart is opened to the human affections and becomes capable of attachment." Jean-Jacques Rousseau, *Emile: or, On Education*, trans. Allan Bloom (New York: Basic, 1979), 218.
2. Jean-Paul Sartre, *Being and Nothingness: An Essay on Phenomenological Ontology*, trans. Hazel E. Barnes (New York: Philosophical Library, 1956), 916–17.
3. Georg Simmel, *Sociology* (Leiden and Boston: Brill 2009), 571.
4. *The Play of the Eyes* is the title of the third volume in *The Memoirs of Elias Canetti* (New York: Farrar, Straus and Giroux, 1999), which recounts his love affair with Anna, the daughter of Gustav and Alma Mahler.
5. Another etymology points to *invitare* (invite) and calls up the result of this tension: throw out a challenge, invite to battle. See Helmuth Schoeck, *Envy: A Theory of Social Behaviour*, trans. Michael Glenny and Betty Ross (New York: Harcourt, Brace and World, 1969); George. M. Foster, "The Anatomy of Envy: A Study in Symbolic Behavior," *Current Anthropology* 13 (1972): 165–202; Richard H. Smith, ed., *Envy: Theory and Research* (Oxford: Oxford University Press, 2008).
6. Marcel Proust, *Swann's Way*, in *In Search of Lost Time*, vol. 1, trans. C. K. Scott Moncrieff and Terence Kilmartin, rev. D. J. Enright (New York: Modern Library, 1992), 166ff.;

and Ralph Ellison, *Invisible Man*, ed. Harold Bloom (New York: Bloom's Literary Criticism, 2010). Ellison's novel is commented on in this key by Axel Honneth, "Invisibility: On the Epistemology of 'Recognition,'" *Aristotelian Society Supplementary Volume 75*, no. 1 (2001): 111–26.

7. Erving Goffman, *Relations in Public: Microstudies of the Public Order* (New York: Basic, 1971).
8. *Le parfum*, vv. 7–14, in Charles Baudelaire, *Œuvres complètes*, vol. 1 (Paris: Gallimard, 1975), 39; English translation: "The Perfume," in *Les Fleurs du Mal*, trans. Richard Howard (Boston: Godine, 1982), 43. See also "The Cat": "And from head to heels / A subtle scent, a dangerous perfume, / rises from her brown flesh" (40). On the olfactive relationship between mother and child, see, for example, Florence Lafine, *Du Sensoriel au sens social: Naissance de la pertinence et de la normativité sociale chez le bébé* (Paris: L'Harmattan, 2015).
9. See Simmel, *Sociology*, 570, which picks up from Kant's *Anthropology from a Pragmatic Point of View*, bk. 1, §16, trans. and ed. R. B. Louden (Cambridge: Cambridge University Press, 2006), 46.
10. Simmel, *Sociology*, 571.
11. Just think about the role that sight and hearing play in Hannah Arendt's political philosophy, by making gestures and speech publicly perceptible, or the role that the sight of the other's face has in the ethics of Levinas.
12. See the classic book by Axel Honneth, *The Struggle for Recognition: The Moral Grammar of Social Conflicts*, trans. Joel Anderson (Cambridge, MA: MIT Press, 1996); and Paul Ricoeur, *The Course of Recognition*, trans. David Pellauer (Cambridge, MA: Harvard University Press, 2005).
13. See, for instance, the previously cited book by Nathalie Heinich, *De la visibilité: Excellence et singularité en régime médiatique* (Paris: Gallimard, 2012), and, for the normative approach, Honneth, "Invisibility."
14. Taste and smell are chemical senses because they involve contact between chemical stimuli and chemosensory receptors in the nose and mouth. See Barry C. Smith, "The Chemical Senses," in *The Oxford Handbook of Philosophy of Perception*, ed. Mohan Matthen (Oxford: Oxford University Press, 2015), www.oxfordhandbooks.com/view/10.1093/oxfordhb/9780199600472.001.0001/oxfordhb-9780199600472-e-045. Smith explains that the traditional distinction between higher and lower senses was based on whether the associated stimuli were proximal or distal. Aquinas and Kant both thought that the lower senses (touch, taste, and smell) could only provide us with information about ourselves—they produce mere bodily sensations, rather than enabling us to perceive the world around us. By contrast, vision and audition connect us with distal objects, revealing their perceiver-independent properties and so offering objective knowledge of our environment. In reality, Smith argues that our chemosensory perception informs us and connects us with objective features just as much as the other senses do, but for this social inquiry of ours the Kantian concept proves to be more fruitful, specifically because of its slant toward the subjective side.

15. On the philosophical history of smell and on the prejudices and epistemological obstacles that have prevented it from being properly appreciated, see especially Chantal Jaquet, *Philosophie de l'odorat* (Paris: Presses Universitaires de France, 2010).
16. See Smith, "The Chemical Senses."
17. Kant, *Anthropology from a Pragmatic Point of View*, 50 (my italics).
18. Simmel, *Sociology*, 578. Italics added and translation slightly modified to better reflect the original.
19. This idea of sight has dominated the Western philosophical tradition, from Plato to Husserl. There does exist a secondary tradition, beginning with Democritus, which conceives of the gaze as a passive, introverted sense.
20. Kant, *Anthropology from a Pragmatic Point of View*, 50.
21. As Proust teaches, a privileged connection with the memory is shared with the other chemical sense: taste.
22. Simmel, *Sociology*, 577. In this context where he talks about Jews, Simmel is probably playing on the double meaning of "Nasenfrage" as nasal question and question of the nose. See also Simmel, "Sociological Aesthetics," in *The Conflict in Modern Culture, and Other Essays*, ed. and trans. Peter Etzkorn (New York: Teachers College Press, 1968), 68–80.
23. On the sociology, anthropology, and social and cultural history of smell, see Gale Peter Largey and David Rodney Watson, "The Sociology of Odors," *American Journal of Sociology* 77, no. 6 (1972): 1021–34; Alain Corbin, *The Foul and the Fragrant: Odor and the French Social Imagination*, trans. M. Kochan, R. Porter, and C. Prendergast (Cambridge, MA: Harvard University Press 1986); Constance Classen, David Howes, and Anthony Synnott, *Aroma: The Cultural History of Smell* (London: Routledge, 1994); Kelvin Low, *Scents and Scent-Sibilities: Smell and Everyday Life Experiences* (Newcastle: Cambridge Scholars, 2009).
24. George Orwell, *The Road to Wigan Pier* (1937; London: Penguin, 2001), 197–98.
25. See especially Nussbaum, *Hiding from Humanity: Disgust, Shame, and the Law* (Princeton: Princeton University Press, 2006). On disgust see also Aurel Kolnai, *On Disgust*, ed. Barry Smith and Carolyn Korsmeyer (Chicago: Open Court, 2004).
26. Friedrich Nietzsche, *Ecce Homo: How One Becomes What One Is*, trans. Walter Kaufmann (New York: Vintage, 1967), "Wise," §8.
27. Simmel, *Sociology*, 578. On the concepts of air and atmosphere, see also Peter Sloterdijk, *Spheres*, vol. 3, *Foams*, trans. Wieland Hoban (South Pasadena, CA: Semiotext[e], 2016), chapter 1.
28. On the history of the word *atmosphere* and on the family of "atmospheric" terms, I refer to Carnevali, "Aura e Ambiance: Léon Daudet tra Proust e Benjamin," *Rivista di estetica* 33, no. 3 (2006): 117–41. The semantic history of this conceptual family has been traced in Leo Spitzer, *Classical and Christian Ideas of World Harmony: Prolegomena to an Interpretation of the Word "Stimmung,"* ed. Anna Granville Hatcher (Baltimore: Johns Hopkins University Press, 1963).
29. As I have already recalled in the previous chapters, the theory of atmospheres serves to support Gernot Böhme's critique of aesthetic capitalism. For the phenomenological approach, see also Böhme, *The Aesthetics of Atmospheres*, ed. Jean-Paul Thibaud

(London: Routledge, 2017); Tonino Griffero, *Atmospheres: Aesthetics of Emotional Spaces*, trans. Sarah de Sanctis (Farnham: Ashgate, 2014); and Griffero, *Quasi-Things: The Paradigm of Atmospheres*, trans. Sarah de Sanctis (Albany: State University of New York Press, 2017); a metaphysical and artificialist use of the concept is central to Sloterdijk. On the necessary precautions to be taken before using the concept of atmospheres, see Martin Seel, *Aesthetics of Appearing*, trans. John Farrell (Stanford: Stanford University Press, 2005), 92–94.

30. Sloterdijk, *Foams*, x. Sloterdijk replaces the concept of aura with others that are more compatible with the artificialism of his anthropotechnics: "air conditioning" and "latency."
31. Simmel, *Sociology*, 332–42. This is a cardinal principle of Simmel's sociological aesthetics, a principle we will return to when talking about the issue of value.
32. Simmel, 579.
33. See Carnevali, "Aura e Ambiance." On people's air, see also chapters 1 and 4.
34. Eugène Minkowski, *Vers une cosmologie: Fragments philosophiques* (Paris: Payot et Rivages, 1999), 115. The concept of atmosphere, which has a kinship with the phenomenological notion of *Umwelt*, would play a key role in the great compendium of the *Traité de psychopathologie* (1966; Paris: Institut Synthélabo, 1999).
35. Hubertus Tellenbach, *Geschmack und Atmosphäre: Medien menschlichen Elementarkontaktes* (Salzburg: O. Müller, 1968).
36. Some of Tellenbach's analysis has been supported by empirical results in neuroscience and psychology. See Smith, "The Chemical Senses."
37. Léon Daudet, *Mélancholia* (Paris: Grasset, 1928), 63.
38. See John Dewey, "Qualitative Thought," in *The Later Works*, vol. 5 (Carbondale: Southern Illinois University Press, 1984), 243–52.
39. On *Stimmung* in Heidegger, see *Being and Time*, trans. Joan Stambaugh, rev. Dennis J. Schmidt (Albany: State University of New York Press, 2010), part 1, chapter 5, §29.
40. See Axel Honneth, *Reification: A New Look at an Old Idea*, with commentaries by Judith Butler, Raymond Geuss, and Jonathan Lear, ed. and intro. Martin Jay (Oxford: Oxford University Press, 2008). On the relationship between *Stimmung* and empathy, Andrea Pinotti, *Empatia* (Rome-Bari: Laterza, 2013).
41. Axel Honneth and Stéphane Haber, "Réification, connaissance, reconnaissance: Quelques malentendus," *Esprit* 7 (2008): 96–107, quote at 103.
42. Nonetheless, as Simmel notes repeatedly in *Sociology*, this does not stop our affective knowledge of individual people from being mediated through "types."
43. Joseph Brodsky, *Nobel Lecture*, 1987, in *Brodsky's Poetics and Aesthetics*, ed. Lev Loseff and Valentina Polukhina (New York: Palgrave Macmillan, 1990), 4–5.

13. SOCIAL TASTE AND THE WILL TO PLEASE

1. The affinities between the works of Simmel and Bourdieu are striking, starting with their shared interest in studying group lifestyles. Although German and Anglo-American readers often point out the closeness of the two authors, rarely, if ever, is their proximity

mentioned in France, probably because of how poorly Simmel's work was received in that country. In fact, Bourdieu only explicitly mentioned his debt to Simmel in an interview on *Distinction* that he gave on German television. Answering a question about his relation to Simmel and Elias, he says he "read Simmel a lot," and "particularly liked his analyses in the sociology of culture," but he also expresses reservations about Simmel's method, which he judges to be "too confident in its subtle insights but a little superficial." He concludes that he feels closer to Elias, notably to his *Court Society*. See Pierre Bourdieu, "Die feinen Unterschiede, oder: Die Abhängigkeit aller Lebensäußerungen vom sozialen Status," *L'80* (28 November 1983): 131–43. An affinity of method "from a phenomenological angle" was also noted by Axel Honneth in his obituary for Bourdieu published in *Le Monde* (5 February 2002), titled "Une synthèse de Georg Simmel et de Max Weber."

2. The idea that fashion is a strategy internal to the struggle of the elite against the petty bourgeoisie is, significantly, the most dated aspect of his analysis and has attracted the criticism of fashion studies. See Georg Simmel, "The Philosophy of Fashion," in *Simmel on Culture*, ed. David Frisby and Mike Featherstone (London: SAGE, 1997), 187–206.

3. Pierre Bourdieu, *The Logic of Practice*, trans. Richard Nice (Stanford: Stanford University Press, 1992).

4. For this reason, too, Simmel's legacy should always be rethought in dialogue with that of Plessner or Merleau-Ponty, and using the interpretive model of visibility that was introduced by Blumenberg. See also chapters 1, 2, and 12 of this book.

5. The word *Stimmung* derives from *Stimme*, "voice," while the verb *stimmen*, in German, designates a plurality of forms of agreement: the correct way of being, relevance to the facts, and also agreement and harmony between musical instruments, opinions, and tastes, between two or more people, between the elements of a style and an atmosphere (for example, the assortment of colors or accessories in a setting or interior decoration).

6. I do not mean a "judgment of taste" in the Kantian sense, because this refers to a transcendental and more universal dimension. At question here is rather a completely individual and idiosyncratic experience that is both immediate and empirical. For a different approach to the social role of taste, which owes a great deal to Simmel and the Kantian legacy, see Jukka Gronow, *The Sociology of Taste* (London: Routledge, 1998).

7. Simmel's comments are dispersed across various essays, but the social anthropology they sketch out is consistent and clear. To flesh it out more fully, it can be read in dialog with the modern moralistic tradition of vanity and *amour-propre*, which developed in the courts and salons of the Ancien Régime and of which Simmel represents the most worldly, most metropolitan, most humanistic, and least "dark" version.

8. See chapter 6 and the conclusion.

9. Georg Simmel, "The Sociology of Sociability," in Frisby and Featherston, *Simmel on Culture*, 120–29, quote at 125.

10. See Georg Simmel, "Flirtation," in *On Women, Sexuality, and Love*, trans. and intro. Guy Oakes (New Haven: Yale University Press, 1984), 133–52; and the essays collected in Daniel Hoffman-Schwartz, Barbara Natalie Nagel, and Lauren Shizuko Stone, eds.,

Flirtations: Rhetoric and Aesthetic This Side of Seduction (New York: Fordham University Press, 2015).

11. And which, according to Simmel, tends toward progressive sublimation, so that the pure form of sociability, like pure aesthetics for Kant, is "liberated" of its material, economic, and other motives, attaining the form of "free play." This aspect is ultimately what makes Simmel's definition of sociability subject to criticism and unsatisfactory for the purposes of a new social aesthetics. It bears noting that Ernst Bloch's criticisms of his teacher were focused precisely on this essay by Simmel, which Bloch sees as demonstrating a broader philosophical disengagement: Ernst Bloch, "Weisen des 'Vielleicht' bei Simmel" (1958), in *Philosophische Aufsätze zur objektiven Phantasie* (Frankfurt: Suhrkamp, 1969), 57–60.
12. See chapter 7.
13. Jean-Jacques Rousseau, *Emile: or, On Education*, ed. Allan Bloom (New York: Basic, 1979), 214.
14. Georg Simmel, *Sociology* (Leiden: Brill 2009), 332. The essay on adornment was written and published as an independent essay in 1908, hence at the same time as the one on the sociology of the senses, and later included in *Sociology*.
15. See Barbara Carnevali, "Social Sensibility: Simmel, the Senses, and the Aesthetics of Recognition," *Simmel Studies* 21, no. 2 (2017): 9–39.
16. Simmel, *Sociology*, 332. On the conceptual model of strategic recognition, from Hobbes to Bourdieu, passing through Rousseau and Veblen, see Barbara Carnevali, "Glory: La lutte pour la réputation dans le modèle hobbesien," *Communications* 93 (2013): 49–67.

14. AESTHETIC LABOR AND SOCIAL DESIGN

1. Richard A. Lanham, *The Economics of Attention: Style and Substance in the Age of Information* (Chicago: University of Chicago Press, 2006); Yves Citton, *The Ecology of Attention*, trans. Barnaby Norman (Cambridge: Polity, 2017).
2. Georg Simmel, *Sociology* (Leiden: Brill 2009), 333.
3. See chapter 12, which explains that sensible irradiation was attributed to perfume, the olfactory adornment.
4. Marcel Proust, *The Guermantes Way*, in *In Search of Lost Time*, vol. 3, trans. C. K. Scott Moncrieff and Terence Kilmartin, rev. D. J. Enright (New York: Modern Library, 1992), 35–36.
5. "Size, color and perfection of form help to influence the value attached to pearls, but it was their 'orient' which made them outstandingly attractive to men of many civilisations." Grahame Clark, "Pearls," in *Symbols of Excellence: Precious Materials as Expressions of Status* (Cambridge: Cambridge University Press, 1986), 78. Pearls have always been the focus of sumptuary laws, the target of complaints, and subject to severe norms that restricted their use to sovereigns and princes. Some interesting observations on the concept of prestige value as a specific form of utility, distinct from that of use value and exchange value, are to found in Lindley M. Keasbey, "Prestige Value," *Quarterly Journal*

of Economics 17, no. 3 (1903): 456–75. The author interprets prestige value in relation to shared social properties and values, but independently from an aesthetic and representational perspective.
6. Clark, *Symbols of Excellence*.
7. See also Eric Michaud, "Capitalisation du temps et réalité du charisme," in *Travailler avec Bourdieu*, ed. Pierre Encrevé and Rose-Marie Lagrave (Paris: Flammarion, 2003), 281–88, which rightly notes that Bourdieu's sociology of art is founded on a big absence: that of the person who produced the material object and gave it a value.
8. See chapter 9. See also Alexis Merle du Bourg, *Antoon van Dyck: Portraits* (Paris: Musée Jacquemart-André/Fonds Mercator, 2008), 37.
9. Georg Simmel, "The Berlin Trade Exhibition," in *Simmel on Culture*, ed. David Frisby and Mike Featherstone (London: SAGE, 1997), 255–58. In this essay Simmel comments on the industrial exhibition of Treptow, which was held in May 1896. The article must be read together with a complementary one on art exhibitions, "Über Kunstausstellungen" (1890), a report of the artistic scene in Berlin around 1890.
10. Simmel, "The Berlin Trade Exhibition," 257.
11. See chapter 9.
12. See chapter 10.
13. Fernand Léger, "L'esthétique de la machine, l'objet fabriqué, l'artisan et l'artiste" (1924), in *Fonctions de la peinture* (Paris: Gonthiers, 1965), 56.
14. Michaud, "Capitalisation du temps et réalité du charisme," 286 (from which I took the preceding quotation). For an analysis of the growing trend in self-exhibition on the part of contemporary artists, see Boris Groys, *Going Public* (Berlin: Sternberg, 2010), 21–37.
15. According to the idea of George Dickie, who reinterprets Arthur Danto's concept of *The Artworld* by recasting it in sociological terms. On curating, see Paul O'Neill, *The Culture of Curating and the Curating of Culture(s)* (Cambridge, MA: MIT Press, 2012).
16. "character, n." OED Online, Oxford University Press, June 2019, www.oed.com/view/Entry/30639.
17. On the relationship between style, type, and character, see Andrea Pinotti, *Il corpo dello stile: Storia dell'arte come storia dell'estetica a partire da Semper, Riegl, Wölfflin* (Milan: Mimesis, 2011). On the possibility of extending the notion of style to the social sciences, see also Marielle Macé, *Styles: A critique de nos formes de vie* (Paris: Gallimard, 2016), who reinterprets, and reromanticizes, some of the ideas on social aesthetics I developed in the Italian edition of this book (published in 2012).
18. See the classics by Dick Hebdige, *Subculture: The Meaning of Style* (1979; London: Routledge, 2003); and Hebdige, *Resistance Through Rituals: Youth Subcultures in Post-War Britain*, ed. Stuart Hall and Tony Jefferson (1975; London: Routledge, 2006). On the importance of style in religious orders, see Vincenzo Lavenia, "Signs and Religious Distinction in Early Modern Europe: A Sketch," *storicamente.org* 16 (2020); Louis Trichet, *Le Costume du clergé: Ses origines et son évolution en France, d'après les règlements de l'Eglise* (Paris: Editions du Cerf, 1986); Giancarlo Rocca, *La sostanza dell'effimero: Gli abiti degli ordini religiosi in Occidente* (Rome: Edizioni Paoline, 2000).

19. Georg Simmel, "Germanic and Classical Romanic Style," *Theory, Culture and Society* 24, nos. 7–8 (2007): 47–52, quote at 47. See also by Simmel, "The Problem of Style," in Frisby and Featherstone, *Simmel on Culture*, 211–18; and Barbara Carnevali and Andrea Pinotti, "Social Aesthetics," in *Simmel Companion*, ed. Gregor Fitzi (London: Routledge, 2020).
20. Jacques Séguéla, who created the Mitterrand campaign and the famous slogan "la force tranquille" (the quiet force), lists three fundamental traits that advertising needs to give a product: the physical (*appearance*), *character*, and *style*. See also Virginia Postrel, *The Substance of Style: How the Rise of Aesthetic Value Is Remaking Commerce, Culture, and Consciousness* (New York: HarperCollins, 2003).
21. It is sometimes forgotten that one of the first cases of corporate identity was that of a public body, the London Underground. See Robert Jones, *Branding: A Very Short Introduction* (Oxford: Oxford University Press, 2017); Mark Ovenden, *London Underground by Design* (London: Penguin, 2013).
22. See "Ordre," in *Encyclopédie, ou dictionnaire raisonné des sciences, des arts et des métiers*, ed. Denis Diderot and Jean Le Rond d'Alembert (Stuttgart: Frommann, 1988), 11:609–12.
23. Max Horkheimer and Theodor W. Adorno, *Dialectic of Enlightenment: Philosophical Fragments*, trans. Edmund Jephcott (Stanford: Stanford University Press, 2002), 103–4.
24. See chapter 3.
25. See Alan Hunt, *Governance of the Consuming Passions: A History of Sumptuary Law* (New York: St. Martin's, 1996). On stigmatizing clothing, see, for example, Michel Pastoureau, *The Devil's Cloth: A History of Stripes and Striped Fabric*, trans. Jody Gladding (New York: Columbia University Press, 2001).
26. See the classic work by Elizabeth Wilson, *Adorned in Dreams: Fashion and Modernity* (1985; New Brunswick, NJ: Rutgers University Press, 2003). See also Gilles Lipovetsky, *The Empire of Fashion: Dressing Modern Democracy*, trans. Catherine Porter (Princeton: Princeton University Press, 1994).
27. See Arjun Appadurai, ed., *The Social Life of Things: Commodities in Cultural Perspective* (Cambridge: Cambridge University Press, 1986), 32.
28. Regarding the American constitution, see Ruthann Robson, *Dressing Constitutionally: Hierarchy, Sexuality, and Democracy from Our Hairstyles to Our Shoes* (New York: Cambridge University Press, 2013). On the use of the veil in Turkey and France, see Nilüfer Göle, *The Daily Lives of Muslims: Islam and Public Confrontation in Contemporary Europe*, trans. Jacqueline Lerescu (London: Zed, 2017).
29. See also Ernst H. Gombrich, "Style," in *International Encyclopedia of the Social Sciences* (New York: Macmillan, 1968), 15:352–61.
30. The original wording is "le style est l'homme même": Georges-Louis Leclerc Buffon, *Discours sur le style* (Castelnau-le-Lez: Éditions Climats, 1992), 30.

15. PRESTIGE AND OTHER MAGIC SPELLS

1. Blaise Pascal, *Pensées, and Other Writings*, trans. Honor Levi, ed. Anthony Levi (Oxford: Oxford University Press, 1995), 18.

2. On the relevance of Pascal's approach to the question of power and on his fragments on the imagination, in addition to the writings of Bourdieu (*Pascalian Meditations*, trans. Richard Nice [Stanford: Stanford University Press, 2000]), see the studies by Louis Marin—especially *La Critique du discours* (Paris: Minuit, 1975); *Le Portrait du roi* (Paris: Minuit, 1981); and *Pascal et Port-Royal* (Paris: Presses Universitaires de France, 1997). See also Gérard Ferreyrolles, *Les Reines du monde: L'imagination et la coutume chez Pascal* (Paris: Champion, 1995).
3. Pierre Bourdieu, *Distinction: A Social Critique of the Judgement of Taste*, trans. Richard Nice (Cambridge, MA: Harvard University Press, 1984), 208. See also Bourdieu, *Pascalian Meditations*, 164ff.
4. Bourdieu, *Distinction*, 208.
5. The distinction between personal prestige and the prestige of status was developed earlier by Le Bon, while Weber distinguishes between two forms of charisma. See Jean-Claude Monod, *Qu'est-ce qu'un chef en démocratie?: Politiques du charisme* (Paris: Seuil, 2016), 35–37.
6. With some exceptions, like the studies mentioned earlier by Andreas Reckwitz, which attribute aesthetic power to the performance of singularities (including aesthetic entities such as brand and styles). See also Jeffrey C. Alexander, *Performance and Power* (Cambridge: Polity, 2011); and Jeffrey C. Alexander, Dominik Bartamański, and Bernhard Giesen, eds., *Iconic Power: Materiality and Meaning in Social Life* (New York: Palgrave, 2012).
7. See Horst Bredekamp, *Image Acts: A Systematic Approach to Visual Agency*, trans. Elizabeth Clegg (Berlin: de Gruyter, 2018), especially for the definition, 29ff. The concept of iconic act is inspired by Searle's, and even earlier Austin's, linguistic acts—although with a necessary word of caution: in the iconic act, the image does not occupy the place of the language utterance but that of the actor who pronounces it.
8. W. J. T. Mitchell, *What Do Pictures Want?: The Lives and Loves of Images* (Chicago: University of Chicago Press, 2005).
9. On the current debate that has accompanied the Warburg renaissance, in addition to the work of Mitchell, see David Freedberg, *The Power of Images: Studies in the History and Theory of Response* (Chicago: University of Chicago Press, 1989); and Gottfried Boehm, "Representation, Presentation, Presence: Tracing the Homo Pictor," in Alexander, Bartamański, and Giesen, *Iconic Power*, 15–23. While Boehm adopts a philosophical perspective influenced by phenomenology and hermeneutics, Freedberg takes an anthropological direction, which in his latest works leads into the cognitive sciences. On the iconic turn and the term visual culture, see note 12 in chapter 8 of this book.
10. Karl Marx, *Capital: A Critique of Political Economy*, trans. Ben Fawkes (London: Penguin, 1990), 165. The image of the "hand" that produces and moves the images (= the commodities) also derives from this.
11. Pierre Bourdieu, "La Noblesse: Capital social et capital symbolique," afterword to *Anciennes et nouvelles aristocraties de 1880 à nos jours*, ed. Didier Lancien and Monique de Saint Martin (Paris: Maison des Sciences de l'Homme, 2007), 385–97, quote at 389.

12. See chapters 9 and 14. To understand Bourdieu's reductive move against the symbolic, it helps to study his interpretation of Cassirer, whose three-volume work *Philosophy of Symbolic Forms* he had translated into French for the Seuil collection "Le sens commun." As I have already pointed out, however, Bourdieu's later anthropology, particularly his *Pascalian Meditations*, incorporated the question of recognition by giving greater weight to the importance of being perceived, to the need for approval, and consideration, and to the dynamics of the affective life.
13. Pierre Bourdieu, *The Rules of Art*, trans. Susan Emanuel (Stanford: Stanford University Press, 1995), 169.
14. Alfred Ernout and Alfred Meillet, *Dictionnaire étymologique de la langue latine* (Paris: Klincksieck, 1939); *Oxford English Dictionary Online*, Oxford University Press, December 2018, www.oed.com/view/Entry/150864.
15. The remarks that follow are based on the entry *prestigio* in the *Grande Dizionario Utet della Lingua Italiana* (Torino: Utet, 1961–2002); *prestige* in the *Grand Robert de la langue française*, 2nd ed. (Paris: Le Robert, 1985); and *prestige* in the *Oxford English Dictionary Online*.
16. See, for example, Heinz Kluth, *Sozialprestige und sozialer Status* (Stuttgart: F. Enke, 1957); Bernd Wegener, *Kritik des Prestiges* (Opladen: Westdeutscher, 1988); Henryk Domański, *Prestige*, trans. Patrycja Poniatowska (Frankfurt: Peter Lang, 2015). For the economic vocabulary of "capital," in addition to the classic by Bourdieu and Coleman, see the book cited earlier on visibility by Nathalie Heinich. See also the article by Lindley M. Keasbey, "Prestige Value," *Quarterly Journal of Economics* 17, no. 3 (1903): 456–75, which explains prestige value as an intermediate value between use value and exchange value, tied to possession and its social significance, and characterized by a form of utility. The use of the term in the human and social sciences corresponds mostly to these two reductions with a few happy exceptions, such as the studies of Gregory Nagy, which focus on the relationship between prestige and poetry as a sensible medium. See, in particular, Nagy, "The 'Professional Muse' and Models of Prestige in Ancient Greece," *Cultural Critique* 12 (1989): 133–43.
17. See also a monograph that is somewhat methodologically vague but significant for its intention to provide an exhaustive explanation of the phenomenon from a social-psychological point of view: Lewis Leopold, *Prestige: A Psychological Study of Social Estimates* (London: T. F. Unwin, 1913).
18. In an ideal line that interprets it as a forerunner of a post-Durkheimian age, and that runs from Gilles Deleuze to Bruno Latour and Actor-Network Theory. See, for example, the contribution in Matei Candea, ed., *The Social After Gabriel Tarde: Debates and Assessments* (Abingdon: Routledge, 2016); David Toews, "The New Tarde: Sociology After the End of the Social," *Theory, Culture and Society* 20, no. 5 (2003): 81–98. Peter Sloterdijk also refers to Tarde in his work.
19. Gabriel Tarde, *The Laws of Imitations*, trans. Elsie Clews Parsons (New York: Henry Holt, 1903), 78.
20. Tarde, 78.

21. See Bruno Karsenti's introductory essay to Gabriel Tarde, *Les Lois de l'imitation* (Paris: Kiné, 1993).
22. This principle would be revived, with appropriate differences due to different theoretical premises, by René Girard with his criticism of the "romantic lie" of individual originality and by Pierre Bourdieu, in the very definition of distinction as a social principle. But it had already been noted by Simmel, in his writings on fashion, in which he spoke about the distinctive counterimitation of those who exhibit indifference to fashion.
23. Tarde, *The Laws of Imitation*, 276.
24. On imitation, see also the synthesis by Gunter Gebauer and Christoph Wulf, *Mimesis: Culture, Art, Society*, trans. Don Reneau (Berkeley: University of California Press, 1995).
25. Gustave Le Bon, *The Crowd: A Study of the Popular Mind* (Mineola, NY: Dover, 2002), 81.
26. Georg Simmel, *Sociology* (Leiden: Brill, 2009), 131–32.
27. Simmel, 132.
28. Joseph S. Nye, *Soft Power: The Means to Success in World Politics* (New York: Public Affairs, 2004). This political science book is not entirely without interest for our perspective, given that the core issue for the definition of soft power—the export of the American way of life in a nonviolent form, that is, not imposed by wars and economic sanctions but through consumption and the media, especially movies—is also a matter of social appearances: this is the power, says the author, that comes through the *image of America*, and that must use its force of attraction to prevail.
29. Le Bon, *The Crowd*, 35 (my italics).
30. Le Bon, 15.
31. Le Bon, 52.
32. Le Bon, 35.
33. See Remo Bodei, *Destini personali: L'età della colonizzazione delle coscienze* (Milano: Feltrinelli, 2002); and Christian Borch: *The Politics of Crowds: An Alternative History of Sociology* (Cambridge: Cambridge University Press, 2013). It is significant that Borch forged these ideas in the direction that is attentive to the political use of aesthetics and atmospheres. See Christian Borch, ed., *Architectural Atmospheres: On the Experience and Politics of Architecture* (Basel: Birkhäuser, 2014).
34. Le Bon, *The Crowd*, 30–31.
35. Marcel Proust, *Swann's Way*, in *In Search of Lost Time*, vol. 1, trans. C. K. Scott Moncrieff (New York: Modern Library, 1992), 241–42. For more on these topics, please see my works on Proust, including Carnevali, "Sur Proust et la philosophie du prestige," *Fabula LHT* (Littérature, histoire, théorie) 1 (February 2006): www.fabula.org/lht/1/Carnevali.html.
36. Le Bon, *The Crowd*, 74–75.
37. As in the classic by Vance Packard, *The Hidden Persuaders* (1957; Brooklyn, NY: Ig, 2007).
38. See Sigmund Freud, *Group Psychology and the Analysis of the Ego*, trans. James Strachey (New York: W. W. Norton, 1975), 21–22, 33–40.

39. This is the case despite Girard's close ties with existentialism and the twentieth-century philosophy of the subject, whereas, as we have noted, part of the interest contemporary social theory has in Tarde consists in the transindividual potential of his theory.
40. See René Girard, *Deceit, Desire, and the Novel: Self and Other in Literary Structure*, trans. Yvonne Freccero (1961; Baltimore: Johns Hopkins University Press, 1965); and Girard, *Things Hidden Since the Foundation of the World*, research undertaken in collaboration with Jean-Michel Oughourlian and Guy Lefort, trans. Stephen Bann and Michael Metteer (Stanford: Stanford University Press, 1987).
41. See, for example, Henry Corbin, *Alone with the Alone: Creative Imagination in the Ṣūfism of Ibn 'Arabī*, trans. Ralph Manheim (Princeton: Princeton University Press, 1998); Giorgio Agamben, *Stanzas: Word and Phantasm in Western Culture*, trans. Ronald L. Martinez (Minneapolis: University of Minnesota Press, 1993).
42. *La Prise de pouvoir par Louis XIV* (*The Taking of Power of Louis XIV*), directed by Roberto Rossellini (1966).

CONCLUSION

1. See the chapters on Debord and Co. in part 2 of this book. See, for example, Bernard E. Harcourt, *Exposed: Desire and Disobedience in the Digital Age* (Cambridge, MA: Harvard University Press, 2015). The two discourses (anticapitalist and antimedia) easily converge, as in Byung-Chul Han, *The Transparency Society*, trans. Erik Butler (Stanford: Stanford Briefs, 2015).
2. Excitation is latent, therefore, in every society, not just the society of spectacle and consumption. The thesis by Christoph Türke, *Erregte Gesellschaft: Philosophie der Sensation* (Munich: C. H. Beck, 2012), which offers a synthesis of the Frankfurt critique of capitalism along with that of Debord, in the umpteenth example of the pathological approach to social aesthetics, must therefore be integrated with this anthropological observation.
3. Marc Fumaroli, "Premiers témoins du parisianisme: Le 'monde' et la 'mode' chez les moralistes du XVIIe siècle," in *La notion de "monde" au XVIIe siècle*, ed. Bernard Beugnot, special issue of *Littérature classique* 22 (1994): 165–90. See also André Morize, *L'Apologie du Luxe au XVIIIe siècle et "Le Mondain" de Voltaire* (Geneva: Slatkine, 2014); Eugenia Paulicelli, *Writing Fashion in Early Modern Italy: From Sprezzatura to Satire* (Farnham: Ashgate, 2014). On the secularization of the theological notion of *mundanitas* see the remarks in chapter 6. There is no satisfying theoretical bibliography on worldliness. In addition to Hannah Arendt's youthful pages on Rahel Varnhagen's salon and the works of Goffman (in particular *Behavior in Public Places*), Simmel's essay on *Geselligkeit* remains the essential reference. Roland Barthes's essay "La Bruyère" (in *Critical Essays*, trans. Richard Howard [Evanston, IL: Northwestern University Press, 1972]), which explains the particular relationship that seems to exist between worldliness and semiology, must also be mentioned. See also Patrick Mauriès, *Le Mondain* (Paris: Seuil, 1984).

4. Voltaire, "Le Mondain," vv. 9–12, in Morize, *L'Apologie du Luxe au XVIIIe siècle et "Le Mondain" de Voltaire*, 133. Original text: "J'aime le luxe, et même la mollesse / Tous les plaisirs, les Arts de toute espèce / La propreté, le goût, les ornements / Tout honnête homme a de tels sentiments."
5. See Georg Simmel, "The Sociology of Sociability," in *Simmel on Culture*, ed. David Frisby and Mike Featherstone (London: SAGE, 1997), 120–29.
6. See the catalog *Night Fever: Designing Club Culture 1960–Today*, ed. Mateo Kries, Jochen Eisenbrand, Catharine Rossi, and Kirsten Thietz (Weil am Rhein: Vitra Design Museum, 2018).
7. Virginia Woolf, *"Am I a Snob?,"* in *Moments of Being* (London: Hogarth, 1985), 210.
8. In "The Sociology of Sociability" Simmel still reasons within the eighteenth-century episteme, which conceives art as an activity and a "free" condition in relation to the necessities of life, and which opposes the autonomy of the aesthetic form to the determinacy of material content. In his theory of sociability, social interaction is motivated by content: drives, needs that serve the purpose of life (erotic instincts, material interests, religious beliefs, and so forth). By acting with a view to given objectives, these contents bring people closer together and create relationships of dependency and mutual trade between them. When the gathering together of human beings is made autonomous from this content and becomes an end in itself, sociability is born—which is the pleasure of being together without a specific purpose, in the pure social form of passing time together.
9. In the manner of Michel Maffesoli, an exponent of the neo-Dionysian view of the sensorium. See chapter 11.
10. Wolf Lepenies, *Melancholy and Society*, trans. Jeremy Gaines and Doris Jones (Cambridge, MA: Harvard University Press, 1992). Elias had earlier explained the origin of romantic attitudes at the end of the eighteenth century as a reaction to the superfetation of worldly sociality: see the penultimate chapter of *The Court Society*, trans. Edmund Jephcott (Dublin: University College Dublin Press, 2006), 214–67, "On the Sociogenesis of Aristocratic Romanticism in the Process of Courtisation."
11. On seduction as the key to the consumer society and spectacle, see Jean Baudrillard, *Seduction*, trans. Brian Singer (New York: St. Martin's, 1990). Gilles Lipovetsky, *Plaire et toucher: Essai sur la société de séduction* (Paris: Gallimard, 2017), views seduction as the typical aestheticized social form of liberal hypermodernity.
12. This was superbly demonstrated in the recent retrospective at the Whitney Museum. See the catalog Donna De Salvo, ed., *Andy Warhol: From A to B and Back Again* (New York: Whitney Museum of American Art, 2018), which includes contributions by Jessica Beck, Okwui Enwezor, Trevor Fairbrother, Hendrik Folkerts, Bill Horrigan, Bruce Jenkins, Branden Joseph, Barbara Kruger, Glenn Ligon, Michael Sanchez, and Lynne Tillman.
13. *Andy Warhol's Exposures* (New York: Grosset and Dunlap, 1979), introduction. See Victor Bockris, *Andy Warhol: The Biography*, 75th anniversary ed. (New York: Da Capo, 2003).
14. See Roberto Simanowski, *Facebook Society: Losing Ourselves in Sharing Ourselves*, trans. Susan H. Gillespie (New York: Columbia University Press, 2018). I refer of course to the song from 1967 by the Velvet Underground & Nico, written by Lou Reed, who took inspiration from the Warhol clique.

15. Proust intended snobbery in the same way, as Nathalie Sarraute grasped in her book *L'Ere du soupçon* (Paris: Les Essais, 1956). Proustian redemption through art is effectively a redemption from this universal social disease in the name of a romantic recapturing of authenticity.
16. Arthur C. Danto, "Qui était Andy Warhol?," in *Les Cahiers du Musée National d'Art Moderne* 34 (1990): 5–9, quote at 5 (my italics); and Danto, *Andy Warhol* (New Haven: Yale University Press, 2009). There are some convergent observations in Jean Baudrillard, "Le snobisme machinal," in *Les Cahiers du Musée National d'Art Moderne*, 35–43.
17. "*The Berkeleian—i.e., petit-bourgeois-vision which reduces social being to perceived being, to seeming.*" Bourdieu, *Distinction: A Social Critique of the Judgment of Taste*, trans. Richard Nice (Cambridge, MA: Harvard University Press, 1984), 483 (my italics). Bourdieu suggests the social-aesthetic chiasmus, but then breaks the symmetry between the two orders by reasserting the ultimate primacy of the materialist dimension. As regards his aside on the class origin of social immaterialism, his explanation appears to be biased because it is devoid of any historical dimension. If it is true that the obsession for decorum, which conceals or denies the reality of material factors, can be defined as petit-bourgeois (or, even better, as bovarism), the vision that tends to identify being with perceiving and to give the utmost importance to aesthetic representations seems, in a much broader and more general way, to be a typically late-modernist tendency that lacks any specific class connotation. It suffices to think of the way social media has universalized practices of presentation and self-promotion, transforming aesthetic labor on one's own image into a daily practice.
18. One might compare Warhol's process with that of Cézanne, whose technique for variations was interpreted by Gottfried Boehm as an "increase in being" (*Zuwachs an Sein*) in Boehm, *Paul Cézanne, Montagne Sainte-Victoire* (Frankfurt: Insel, 1988). From Boehm's hermeneutic and phenomenological perspective, he would likely reject the comparison and accuse Warhol's images of being pure simulacra devoid of the "embodied" substrate that allows the painter's eye to reveal the sensible profundity of the world; or, perhaps, although acknowledging their ability to create meaning without being pure reproductions, he would not consider them to be "strong images." However that may be, from the perspective of social immaterialism, the romantic claim to authenticity no longer makes sense, and every single Warholian image-variation actually increases the social reality (and the perspectivism that passes through it).
19. See Hal Forster, *The Return of The Real* (Cambridge, MA: MIT Press, 1996), 127–70. Unlike what I have argued in these pages, Forster believes that the ambivalence of Warhol's images can be reconciled using the theory of Jacques Lacan's "traumatic device." My thanks to Angela Mengoni for suggesting that I bring up this issue.
20. See Paul Zanker, *The Power of Images in the Age of Augustus*, trans. Alan Shapiro (Ann Arbor: University of Michigan Press, 1988). See chapters 9 and 10.
21. See Alexis Merle du Bourg, *Antoon van Dyck: Portraits* (Paris: Musée Jacquemart-André/Fonds Mercator, 2008). On Warhol as a postmodern equivalent of the court artist, see the essays collected in the exhibition catalog *Le Grand Monde d'Andy Warhol* (Paris: RMN, 2009).

22. See *Andy Warhol: Ladies and Gentlemen* (New York: Skarstedt Gallery, 2009).
23. In addition to the song "Walk on the Wild Side," already mentioned in chapter 11, see the tribute album *Songs for Drella* with John Cale, which offers one of the most acute interpretations of Warhol's poetics and comes from a perspective similar to my own.
24. On the ambivalences of Warhol's attitude in *Ladies and Gentlemen*, see the essay by Glenn Ligon in De Salvo, *Andy Warhol*, 78–81.
25. "I have the style it takes": Andy's motto in the song by the same name by Reed and Cale.
26. See John Berger, *Ways of Seeing* (New York: Viking, 1973). See also Stephen Gundle, *Glamour: A History* (New York: Oxford University Press, 2009); Virginia Postrel, *The Power of Glamour: Longing and the Art of Visual Persuasion* (New York: Simon and Schuster, 2013).
27. Berger, *Ways of Seeing*, 204–5.
28. Andy Warhol, *The Philosophy of Andy Warhol (From A to B and Back Again)* (Orlando: Harcourt, 1975).
29. See chapter 10.
30. Bockris, *Warhol*, 167.
31. The metaphor-concept of "capital of visibility" returns not only in sociology studies on celebrity and sexuality but also in the language of advertising and mass culture, which talks about the capital of beauty and erotic capital. See the work of Eva Illouz, including *Why Love Hurts: A Sociological Explanation* (Cambridge: Polity, 2012). The notion of trick is a technical term from the advertising lexicon.
32. Barbara Kruger, "Contempt and Adoration," in De Salvo, *Andy Warhol*, 83. For this use of the concept of profanation, see the article by Wolfgang Ullrich, "Transzendenzskepsis: Andy Warhol und der Calvinismus," in *An die Kunst glauben* (Berlin: Klaus Wagenbach, 2011), 66–89.
33. See Simon Critchley, *On Bowie* (London: Serpent's Tail, 2016); and Carnevali, "Loving the Alien: La grâce de Bowie," *Vacarmes* 83, no. 2 (2018): 76–81. Among contemporary artists, Lady Gaga has been most consistently inspired by the poetics of the Factory, in what she herself defines as a "reverse Warholian" phenomenon in pop culture. However, in her performances there are moments of romantic revolt against the world of spectacle—and it is no coincidence that these are the same times when the name of Marilyn is evoked.
34. Norman Mailer, *Marilyn: A Biography* (New York: Grosset and Dunlap, 1973).
35. Truman Capote, "A Beautiful Child," in *Music for Chameleons* (New York: New American Library, 1981), 244–45.
36. Original text: "Tu sorellina più piccola, / quella bellezza l'avevi addosso, umilmente, / e la tua anima di figlia di piccola gente, / non hai mai saputo di averla, / perché altrimenti non sarebbe stata bellezza. / Sparì, come un pulviscolo d'oro. / Il mondo te l'ha insegnata e così la tua bellezza divenne sua." The English translation is from Colleen Ryan-Scheutz, *Sex, the Self, and the Sacred: Women in the Cinema of Pier Paolo Pasolini* (Toronto: University of Toronto Press, 2007), 36ff. For a reading sympathetic to Pasolini's, see Georges Didi-Huberman, "*Rabbia poetica*: Note sur Pier Paolo Pasolini," *Poe&sie*

143, no. 1 (2013): 114–24. The author, who compares Pasolini's poetics with Warhol's film *Sleep*, does not note the chronological and thematic connection between Pasolini's homage to Marilyn Monroe and the Warhol series.
37. Translation by Christopher Kelly, italics added.

AFTERWORD

1. Rousseau was known by his public as "ami [friend] Jean-Jacques," and Rousseau interpreters still refer to him charmingly by this name to underline the strong autobiographical element of his work but also a sort of intimacy and complicity that the reader enters into with the author. On Rousseau as one of the first public figures to experience the ambivalence of recognition and celebrity, in addition to my *Romantisme et reconnaissance*, see Antoine Lilti, *The Invention of Celebrity, 1750–1850*, trans. Lynn Jeffress (Malden, MA: Polity, 2017).
2. See, for instance, the fine criticism of the injunctions of *esse est percipi* by Pierre Zaoui, *La Discrétion ou L'art de disparaître* (Paris: Autrement, 2013).

INDEX

adornment, 160, 175, 180–88
Adorno, Theodor W., 88, 97, 117–18, 148–49, 187, 250n8, 261n23
Adut, Ari, 254n34
advertising, 181–85, 197, 205, 207, 208, 213, 214, 216, 223
aesthesiology. *See* social sensibility
aesthetic capitalism, 104–10
aestheticism, 96–104
aestheticization, 96–105, 131–36
aesthetic labor, 106, 109, 137, 175–89
aesthetic mediation, 29–33, 134, 144, 146, 147, 158–59, 186, 220
aesthetic power, 190–208
aesthetic public sphere, 146–49
aesthetics and economics, 111–16
aesthetics of recognition, 154–58, 161–65, 173–74
aesthetic values, 96–110, 175
Agamben, Giorgio, 87–91, 100–1, 103, 115–16, 119, 247nn7, 8, 247nn10, 11, 248n5, 249n14, 250n6, 253n27, 265n41
d'Alembert, Jean Le Rond, 75, 145, 186, 245n15
Alexander, Jeffrey C., 262n6
alienation, 14–18, 41–53, 75–83–88, 232

Althusser, Louis Pierre, 83
Amossy, Ruth, 236n7
D'Angelo, Paolo, 237n14, 250nn4, 5
D'Annunzio, Gabriele, 105
Apostolidès, Jean-Marie, 251n2
Appadurai, Arjun, 188, 236n5, 261n27
D'Arcangelo, Allan, 229
Arendt, Hannah, xiii, 6, 8, 10, 43, 59–60, 66–67, 71, 89, 121, 132, 142, 146–48, 236n4, 237n17, 240n15, 242n3, 243n3, 253n27, 254nn34, 35, 255n11, 265n3
Aristotle, 59, 237n14, 243n2
atmospheres, 5, 109, 112, 143, 153, 157, 159–61
Auerbach, Eric, 139, 252n19
Augustine of Hippo, 71, 76
Augustinian, 61, 71, 76, 77, 171
Augustus, 220, 267n19
Austin, John Langshaw, 262n7
authenticity, 21–23, 30, 31, 45, 75–91, 219–20, 226–32

Balázs, Béla, 247n12
Barthes, Roland, 132, 220, 249n17, 251n4, 265n3
Bataille, Georges, 106, 177

Baudelaire, Charles Pierre, 108, 152, 157, 255n8
Baudrillard, Jean, 107–8, 220, 266n11, 267n16
Baumgarten, Alexander Gottlieb, xiv, 111
De Beauvoir, Simone, 13, 238n22, 242n9
Beck, Jessica, 266n12
Beckett, Samuel, 14–15, 238nn23, 24
Belting, Hans, 239n1, 241n2, 242n4
Benjamin, Walter, xv, 46, 53, 88, 97, 105, 138, 140–41, 157, 192, 224, 243n21, 247n8, 248n13, 249n14, 256n28
Berger, John, 13, 223, 238n22, 268nn26, 27
Berkeley, George (Bishop), 217–18, 222, 225, 267n17
Berleant, Arnold, 235n4
Bernstein, Jay, 237n18
Blake, William, 86, 247n5
Bloch, Ernst, xv, 97, 141, 253n25, 259n11
Blumenberg, Hans, 22–23, 46, 71, 138, 140–41, 239n5, 241n2, 253n24, 258n4
Bockris, Victor, 266n13, 268n30
Bodei, Remo, 134–35, 248n17, 250n9, 251n9, 264n33
Boehm, Gottfried, 262n9, 267n18
Böhme, Gernot, 106–7, 108, 109–10, 137, 181, 248n11, 249n15, 249n18, 256n29
Boltanski, Luc, 119, 250n10
Le Bon, Gustave, 198, 201–5, 262n5, 264n25, 264nn29, 30, 264n31, 264n32, 264n34, 264n36
Boorstin, Daniel J., 247n14
Borch, Christian, 264n33
Borsari, Andrea, 237n18, 250n9
Bourdieu, Pierre, xiii, 100–4, 108, 118, 125–27, 158–59, 166–68, 169, 170–71, 172, 173, 178, 179, 189, 190–91, 194–95, 198, 205, 218, 240n13, 248nn5–10, 250n5, 251n20, 251n21, 257n1, 258n3, 259n16, 260n7, 262nn2–4, 262n11, 263nn12, 13, 263n16, 264n22, 267n17
Du Bourg, Alexis Merle, 260n8, 267n21
Bowie, David, 227, 268n33

Bredekamp, Horst, 109, 192, 262n7
Breton, Stéphane, 251n8
Brodsky, Joseph, 164, 168, 257n43
Brown, Peter, 241n4
La Bruyère, Jean de, 70, 71, 215, 244n4, 265n3
Bunyan, John, 62–63, 243n7, 243n8
Butler, Judith, 238n30, 257n40

Cale, John, 268n23, 268n25
Callas, Maria, 227
Canetti, Elias, 151, 254n4
Capote, Truman, 64, 228, 268n35
Carnevali, Barbara, 235n5, 236n3, 243n5, 244n2, 245n7, 245n8, 245n14, 247n11, 248n5, 250n9, 252n12, 256n28, 257n33, 259nn15, 16, 261n19, 264n35, 268n33, 269n1
Della Casa, Giovanni, 125
Casetti, Francesco, 243n21
Cassirer, Ernst, 263n12
Castiglione, Baldassare, 125
Cézanne, Paul, 267n18
Von Chamisso, Adelbert, 14
Chiapello, Eve, 119, 250n10
Christian, xi, xvi, 14–15, 37, 57, 60, 62, 64, 76, 77, 90, 91, 94, 107, 245n16, 256n28
Christianity, 30, 58, 85, 241n4
Christian-romantic, xii
Christian-Rousseauian, 83, 228
Citton, Yves, 259n1
Clark, Grahame, 178, 259n5, 260n6
Classen, Constance, 252n22, 256n23
clothing, 24–27, 39, 58, 160, 188, 210 and passim
Coccia, Emanuele, 241n1
Coleman, James, 263n16
commodity, 83, 84, 87–90, 104–9, 116, 139, 209, 222, 225, 226 and passim
Condillac, Etienne Bonnot de, 115
Corbin, Alain, 256n23,
Corbin, Henry, 265n41
Courtine, Jean-Jacques, 241n4

court sociability and aesthetics, 69, 79, 95, 121, 122, 124–27, 132, 137, 139, 140, 208, 213, 221
Critchley, Simon, 238n23, 268n33
Croce, Benedetto, 112–13, 115, 249nn2, 3, 250n4
Crow, Thomas, 220
culture of appearances, 124–27, 132

Danto, Arthur, 214, 217, 260n15, 267n16
Daudet, Léon, 161–62, 256n28, 257n37
Debord, Guy, xvii, 71, 81–95, 97, 100–1, 105–6, 107, 109, 119, 134, 141–42, 148, 197, 221, 246nn1, 2, 247n4, 247n6, 247nn8, 9, 247nn14, 15, 248n18, 265nn1, 2
Deleuze, Gilles, 115, 238n23, 263n18
Van Delft, Louis, 244n2, 244n5
Depero, Fortunato, 216
Derrida, Jacques, 29, 58, 79, 115, 240n2, 241n3, 243n1, 253n32
Descombes, Vincent, 244n4
Des Esseintes, 99
Dewey, John, 162, 257n38
Dewitte, Jacques, 236n9
Diana, Princess, 229
Dickie, George, 260n15
Diderot, Denis, 186
Didi-Huberman, Georges, 242n5, 268n36
distinction, 100, 101, 104, 108, 118, 125, 127, 137, 157, 158, 166, 169, 171, 173, 179, 181, 186, 193, 194, 195, 200, 225
Domański, Henryk, 263n16
Donnellan, Brendan, 245n6
Draper, Don, 207
Duchamp, Marcel, 237n14
Durkheim, Emile, 98–100, 102, 103, 104, 143, 248nn3, 4
Durkheimian, 103, 263n18
Van Dyck, Antoon, 179–80, 192, 220, 221, 223, 260n8, 267n21

eccentricity, eccentric positionality, 11, 12, 17–19, 42, 47, 52, 73, 91–95, 146, 159, 227, 232

Elias, Norbert, 79, 102, 124–25, 139, 172, 189, 246n23, 250n17, 251n2, 257n1, 266n10
Ellison, Ralph, 151, 254n6
Enwezor, Okwui, 266n12
Escola, Marc, 244n4
Esposito, Elena, 240n11
Esprit, Jacques, 70
exhibition, 180–83, 207, 208, 212–14
exposure, 24–27, 89, 90, 209–15

Fabiani, Jean-Louis, 241n5
Fairbrother, Trevor, 266n12
Fairey, Shepard, 184
Falasca-Zamponi, Simonetta, 248n13
Faret, Nicolas, 125
Fellini, Federico, 63, 64
Feuerbach, Ludwig, 82, 85
Ferrara, Alessandro, 246n17
Ferreyrolles, Gérard, 262n2
figures (social images), 34–40
Fischer, Joachim, 237n18, 238nn20, 21, 240n16, 252n13
Fitzgerald, F. Scott, 64, 116
Fitzi, Gregor, 252n17
Flügel, John Carl, 23, 26, 239n9
Folkerts, Hendrik, 266n12
form and content, 31–33
Forster, Hal, 220, 267n20
Foster, George M., 254n5
Foucauldian, 209, 224
Foucault, Michel, 88, 225
Frank, Manfred, 253n30
Freedberg, David, 109, 262n9
freedom of the mask, 20–23, 232
Freud, Sigmund, xii, 169–70, 205, 237n11, 264n38
Frisby, David, 235n5
Fuchs, Thomas, 237n12
Fumaroli, Marc, 243n11, 265n3

Gadamer, Hans-Georg, 146, 254n34
Gaga, Lady, 268n33
Gallup, Gordon G., 237n15

Gatsby, Great, 125, 176
Gebauer, Gunter, 252n15, 264n24
Gehlen, Arnold, 241n5.1
Gernet, Louis, 251n1
Girard, René, 205, 217, 264n22, 265nn39, 40
glamour, 37, 62, 105, 185, 197, 201, 223, 226
glory, 44, 60, 64, 66, 75, 88–91, 101–3, 132, 156, 213, 221
Goethe, Johann Wolfgang, 116, 120–23, 124, 125, 250nn11, 12, 250nn14–16, 251n19
Goffman, Erving, xiii, 7, 22–23, 39, 95, 151, 236n7, 239n4, 239n7, 240n13, 252n21, 255n7, 265n3
Göle, Nilüfer, 261n28
Gombrich, Ernst, 67, 244n18, 261n29
Gottschalk, Simon, 252n22
Gracián, Baltasar, 69–70, 207, 244n3
Griffero, Tonino, 256n29
Gronow, Jukka, 258n6
Groys, Boris, 248n13, 260n14
Guazzo, Francesco Maria, 125
Guermantes family, members of, 108, 118, 177, 192, 204, 206; *The Guermantes Way*, 259n4
Gundle, Stephen, 268n26
Guyau, Jean-Marie, 143–44, 253n28

Haber, Stéphane, 241n5.1, 257n41
Habermas, 121, 146, 158, 250n13, 254n34
Hals, Frans, 184
Hamilton, Richard, 229
Han, Byung-Chul, 239n3, 265n1
Harcourt, Bernard E., 265n1
Haroche, Claudine, 241n2
Harrison, Simon, 251n8
Haug, Wolfgang Fritz, 109, 248n11
Hebdige, Dick, 260n18
Hegel, Georg Wilhelm Friedrich, xvii–xviii, 10, 11, 24, 42, 64, 79, 111, 173, 174, 236n7, 240n10, 244n13, 244n16, 251n4
Heidegger, Martin, 6, 11, 90, 92, 142, 163, 241–42n1, 249n1 253n27, 257n39

Heinich, Nathalie, 253n23, 255n13, 263n16
Herwitz, Daniel, 241n4.4
Hobbes, Thomas, 60–61, 64, 75, 173, 174, 243n5, 244n13, 245n16, 259n16
Hoffmann, E. T. A., 14
Hogrebe, Wolfram, 239n8
Homo aestheticus versus Homo economicus, 111–27
Honneth, Axel, 154, 158, 163, 173, 174, 242n7, 244n14, 254n6, 255nn12, 13, 257nn40, 41, 257n1
Horkheimer, Max, 88, 187, 261n23
Horrigan, Bill, 266n12
Howes, David, 252n22, 256n23
Hughes, Robert, 215
Huizinga, Johan, 244n17
Hume, David, 174
Hunt, Alan, 261n25
Husserl, Edmund, 58, 237n18, 240n2, 256n19

Ikegami, Eiko, 251n3
Illouz, Eva, 268n31

Jaeggi, Rahel, 241n1
Jappe, Anselm, 246n2
Jaquet, Chantal, 256n15
De Jaucourt, Chevalier, 186
Jenkins, Bruce, 266n12
John, Elton, 229
Jones, Robert, 261n21
Joseph, Branden, 266n12
Jourdain, Monsieur, 118

Kant, Immanuel, 102, 111, 114, 116, 140, 147, 155–56, 174, 212, 249n1, 250n5, 254nn34, 35, 255n9, 255n14, 256n17, 256n20, 259n11
Kantian, 99, 102, 152, 164, 211, 252n13, 255n14, 258n6; anti-Kantian, 174
Karpik, Lucien, 253n23
Karsenti, Bruno, 264n21
Keasbey, Lindley M., 259n5, 263n16
Keaton, Buster, 14–15

Kennedy, Jackie, 217, 225
Von Kleist, Heinrich, 9, 237n14
Kluth, Heinz, 263n16
Kojève, Alexandre, 64–66, 106, 132, 244n13, 244n16, 251n4
Kolnai, Aurel, 256n25
Konings, Martijn, 249n16
Koselleck, Reinhart, 139, 252n20
Kracauer, Siegfried, xv, xvi, 94, 127, 138, 141, 236n6, 247n16, 248n17, 251n21
Kreis, Guido, 242n2
Kruger, Barbara, 266n12, 268n32
Krüger, Hans-Peter, 237n18
Kubrick, Stanley, 12

Lacan, Jacques, 48–49, 242n16, 242n17, 267n20
Lafine, Florence, 255n8
Lanham, Richard, 259n1
Largey, Gale Peter, 256n23
Larmore, Charles, 237n14, 246n17
Latour, Bruno, 263n18
Lavenia, Vincenzo, 260n18
Laver, James, 26, 240n14
Lefort, Guy, 265n40
Léger, Fernand, 182, 260n13
Leopold, Lewis, 263n17
Lepenies, Wolf, 266n10
Levinas, Emmanuel, 241n2, 255n11
Ligon, Glenn, 266n12, 268n24
Lilti, Antoine, 241n5, 252n20, 269n1
Lipovetsky, Gilles, 248n11, 261n26, 266n11
Louis XIV, 206, 251n2, 265n42
Low, Kelvin, 256n23
Löwith, Karl, 46, 50, 242n12, 242n19
Löwy, Michael, 247n5, 247n6
Luhmann, Niklas, 140, 239n4, 241–42n1, 253n31
Lukács, György, xv, 83, 87, 92, 97, 250n16
luxury, 176–80, 187

Machiavelli, Niccolò, 69–70
Macho, Thomas, 36–37, 241n3

Madonna, 227
Maffesoli, Michel, 253n30, 266n9
Mailer, Norman, 227, 268n34
De Mandeville, Bernard, 61
Mann, Thomas, 116
Marcuse, Herbert, 97, 250n16
Marin, Louis, 240n2, 262n2
Marinetti, 105
Marx, Karl, 6, 81, 83, 98, 112, 148, 167, 193–94, 262n10
Marxian, 88, 194
Marxism, 67, 83, 84, 97
Marxist, 41–42, 81, 82, 98, 106, 187, 222, 246n2, 250n16; neo-Marxist, 57
masks, 19–24, 69–80
Mauss, Marcel, 177, 195, 239n34
Mayer, Arno J., 117, 250n7
McCracken, Grant, 252n18
McLuhan, Marshall, 236n2
Mead, George Herbert, 12
media, 51–53, 137–42 and passim
medial surfaces, 20–27
Meier, Christian, 251n1
Meister, Wilhelm, 120–23, 124, 126, 250n11, 250nn13, 14, 251n19
Mengoni, Angela, 267n20
Merleau-Ponty, Maurice, 8, 11, 71, 236n1, 236n9, 237n18, 238n21, 242n15, 258n4
metaphysics of two worlds, 57–64 and passim
metropolis, 137–42
Michaud, Eric, 248n13, 260n7, 260n14
Milne, Kirsty, 243n7
Minkowski, Eugène, 161, 257n34
mirror, 9, 14, 15, 16, 46–49, 53. *See also* reflexivity
Mitchell, W. J. T., 109, 262n8, 262n9
Mitterrand, François, 184, 261n20
Moholy-Nagy, László, 247n12
Monod, Jean-Claude, 262n5
Monroe, Marilyn, xvii, 217, 225, 226–30, 231–32, 268nn33, 34, 268n36

Montaigne, Michel, 60, 70, 71, 244n2, 244n5
Montesquieu, 113
Morin, Edgar, 241n4.4
moralists (modern moralists), 69–72
Moretti, Franco, 123, 250n16
Morris, Wiliam, 144
Moscarda, Vitangelo, 46–49, 51

Nagel, Thomas, 239n8
Nagy, Gregory, 251n1, 263n16
Naukkarinen, Ossi, 239n8
Navaud, Guillaume, 244n1
Neuhouser, Frederick, ix, 245n8
Newton, Isaac, 143, 253n33
Nietzsche, Friedrich, xiii, xv, 13, 18, 47, 58, 70, 104, 158, 169–70, 174, 235n3, 238n31, 245n6, 256n26
Nussbaum, Martha, 158, 243n2, 256n25
Nye, Joseph S., 264n28

Obama, Barack, 184
O'Neill, Paul, 260n15
Origgi, Gloria, 238n32, 242n7
Orwell, George, 157, 256n24
Oughourlian, Jean-Michel, 265n40
Ovenden, Mark, 261n21

Pacino, Al, 25
Packard, Vance, 264n37
Pascal, Blaise 60, 61, 66, 71, 77, 94, 102, 171, 190–92, 205, 243n6, 246n18, 248n7, 261n1, 262n2
Pasolini, Pier Paolo, 221, 228, 268n36
Pastoureau, Michel, 261n25
Pater, Walter, 96
pathology and physiology of the social, 131–36
Paulicelli, Eugenia, 265n3
Petronius, 176
Pinotti, Andrea, 235n5, 247n12, 252n12, 257n40, 260n17, 261n19
Pippin, Robert B., 245n6

Pirandello, Luigi, 9, 23, 46–49, 50, 51, 52, 53, 242n10, 242nn11–15, 242n18, 242n20
Pizzorno, Alessandro, x, 239n1
Plato, 30, 58, 59, 84, 91, 93, 95, 141–42, 205, 206, 256n19
Platonic 18, 31, 58, 59, 64, 71, 77, 81, 83, 112, 131, 141, 171, 181, 204, 219, 232
play-acting (anthropology of the actor), 16–19
Plessner, Helmuth, xiii, 11, 12, 15, 16, 17, 18, 27, 42, 46–47, 73, 79–80, 121, 136, 142, 145–46, 236n1, 237nn18, 19, 238nn20, 21, 238nn26–29, 238n33, 240n16, 240n1, 241n1, 242n12, 245n15, 246n24, 252n13, 253n29, 258n4
Portman, Adolf, 7, 8, 236nn8, 9
Postrel, Virginia, 261n20, 268n26
power of images, 190–93
Presley, Elvis, 217
prestige, 65, 66, 190–205 and passim
Proust, Marcel, 15, 43, 63, 64, 70, 108, 116, 117, 151, 157, 160, 161, 176–77, 192, 204, 206, 215–17, 243n12, 244n4, 250n8, 254n6, 256n21, 256n28, 259n4, 264n35, 267n15
publicity, 41–44, 143, 213, 214, and passim

Rancière, Jacques, 92–93, 98, 147–48, 158, 245n13, 247n13, 248nn1, 2, 253n30, 254n36
Rebentisch, Juliane, 245n15, 248n12
Reckwitz, Andreas, 250n10, 253n23, 262n6
Reed, Lou, 222, 253n26, 266n14, 268n23, 268n25
reflexivity, 9–19, 46–49, 73–75
Reichel, Peter, 249n13
representation, 29–33 and passim
Ricoeur, Paul, 85, 154, 247n3, 255n12
Riefenstahl, Leni, 132
Rimbaud, Arthur, 108
Ripa, Cesare, 37
Robson, Ruthann, 261n28
Rocca, Giancarlo, 260n18

Rochat, Philippe, 237n13, 242n15
La Rochefoucauld, 60, 70, 77, 215, 244n5, 246n19
Romano, Claude, 246n17
romantic anticapitalism, 81–95 and passim
Rosa, Hartmut, 140
Rossellini, Roberto, 18, 206, 265n42
Rosenquist, James, 229
Rousseau, Jean-Jacques, xvii, 5, 10, 15, 23, 29, 38, 45, 47, 58, 61, 71, 72–80, 84–85, 91, 94, 95, 107, 113, 134, 141–42, 144, 145, 150, 171, 172, 174, 212, 214, 226, 227, 229, 231–32, 236n3, 242n8, 244n5, 245nn8–13, 245nn15, 16, 246n17, 246n20–22, 254n1, 259n13, 269n1

Saito, Yuriko, 251n6
Sanchez, Michael, 266n12
Sander, August, 184
Santayana, George, 239n1
Sarraute, Nathalie, 267n15
Sartre, Jean-Paul, 150, 238n28, 242n9, 254n2
Sayre, Robert, 247n5
Schaeffer, Jean-Marie, 237n16, 249n1
Schlemihl, Peter, 14
Schlesinger, John, 253n26
Schnapp, Jeffrey T., 248n13
Schneider, Alan, 14–15
Schoeck, Helmuth, 254n5
Schopenhauer, Arthur, 11, 47
Scull, Ethel, 220, 224
Searle, John, 262n7
Seel, Martin, 235n2, 256n29
Séguéla, Jacques, 261n20
self-display, self-presentation, 5–9 and passim
the senses, 3–5, 150–65
sensible logic, 68, 115, 134, 137, 154, 162, 192–95, 203
Serpico, 25
Serres, Michel, 236n1
Serroy, Jean, 248n11
Shapiro, Roberta, 253n23

Sharp, Becky, 62
Shusterman, Richard, 237n18
Shūzō, Kuki, 133, 251n5
Simanowski, Roberto, 243n12, 266n14
Simmel, Georg, v, xiii, xv, 16, 23, 36, 40, 53, 60, 66–67, 71, 100, 104, 135–38, 140–41, 150, 152–53, 155–57, 159–60, 161, 162, 164, 166–68, 169–72, 173, 174, 176, 177, 180–82, 184, 189, 194, 198, 199, 201–2, 211, 213, 235n5, 236n1, 239n6, 240n11, 240n14, 241n4, 241n2, 243n4, 246n21, 249n16, 252nn1013, 252n16, 252n17, 254n3, 255n9, 255n10, 256n18, 256n22, 256n27, 257n31–32, 257n42, 257n1, 258n2, 258n4, 258n7, 258nn9, 10, 259n11, 259n14–16, 259n2, 260nn9, 10, 261n19, 264n22, 264nn26, 27, 265n3, 266n5, 266n8
Sloterdijk, Peter, xii, 160, 235n1, 241n1, 256n27, 256n29, 257n30, 263n18
smell (see also nasal social sensibility), 152–59
Smith, Adam, 10, 112, 113, 164, 174
Smith, Barry C., 255n14, 256n16, 257n36
snobbery, 117, 118, 123, 132, 202, 211, 213, 215, 217
sociability, and *Geselligkeit*, 4–8, 79, 121, 169, 170–72, 200, 209–12
social arts, 205
social disease, 214–17
social immaterialism (*esse est percipi aut percipere*), 217–20, 225
social libido, 168–174
social romanticism, 69–80, 228–30
social sensibility, 150–65
social sensorium, 142–46
social taste, 165–74
Somaini, Antonio, 247n12
Sombart, Werner, 139, 172, 252n18
spectacle, 3–19, 81–95
Spitzer, Leo, 256n28
Stahlhut, Marco, 238n28
Staging, 14–19. See also anthropology of the actor; play-acting

278 Index

staging value, 106–7
Starobinski, Jean, x, 77, 244n5, 246n19, 246n22
Strathern, Marilyn, 251n8
suggestion (magnetism, influence), 198–205
sumptuary laws, 187–88
style, 183–89, 223
Strauss, Leo, 243n5, 244n13, 245n16
Svevo, Italo, 9
sympathy (antipathy-sympathy), 154, 161–65 and passim
Synnott, Anthony, 252n22, 256n23

Taine, Hippolyte, 118, 125, 250n9, 251n18
Tanizaki, Jun'ichirō, 133, 251n5
Tarde, Gabriel, 198–201, 203, 205, 263n18–20, 264n21, 264n23, 265n39
Taylor, Charles, 239n6
Taylor, Liz, 217
Tellenbach, Hubertus, 161, 257nn35, 36
Tertullian, 245n16
Thackeray, William Makepeace, 62, 63, 118, 202, 243n7, 243nn9, 10
Theophrastus, 70
Tillman, Lynne, 266n12
Toews, David, 263n18
Tönnies, Gustav, 253n29
Trichet, Louis, 260n18
Trilling, Lionel, 239n6
Trimalcione, 176
Türke, Christoph, 265n2

Ullrich, Wolfgang, 268n32

Vanity, 60–68 and passim
Vannini, Phillip, 252n22

Veblen, Thorstein, 102, 108, 125, 176, 177, 189, 198, 259n16
Velvet Underground & Nico, 219, 266n14
Vico, Giambattista, 146
Visconti, Luchino, 116, 233.
Viveiros de Castro, Eduardo, 251n8
Voltaire, 38, 210, 265n3, 266n4

Wagner, Richard, 144, 185
Warburg, Aby M., 109, 192, 242n5, 262n9
Warhol, Andy, xvii, 64, 133, 179, 208, 209–30, 232, 253n26, 266nn12–14, 267n16, 267n18, 267nn20, 21, 268n22–25, 268n28, 268n30, 268n32, 268n36
Warholian, 211, 217, 218, 220, 267n18, 268n33
Waskul, Dennis, 252n22
Watson, David Rodney, 256n23
Weber, Max, 189, 191, 197, 198, 257n1, 262n5
Wegener, Bernd, 263n16
Weihe, Richard, 239n1, 244n5
Welsch, Wolfgang, 249n1
Wiesing, Lambert, 236n2, 236n6
Wilde, Oscar, v, 96
Wilson, Elizabeth, 261n26
Wittgenstein, Ludwig, 71
Woolf, Virginia, 211, 266n7
Worldliness, 63–64, 79, 171, 209–13
Wulf, Christoph, 252n15, 264n24

Zahavi, Dan, 242n15
Zanker, Paul, 267n19
Zaoui, Pierre, 269n2
Žižek, Slavoj, 98, 248n2

Columbia Themes in Philosophy, Social Criticism, and the Arts

Lydia Goehr and Gregg M. Horowitz, Editors

Lydia Goehr and Daniel Herwitz, eds., *The Don Giovanni Moment: Essays on the Legacy of an Opera*

Robert Hullot-Kentor, *Things Beyond Resemblance: Collected Essays on Theodor W. Adorno*

Gianni Vattimo, *Art's Claim to Truth*, edited by Santiago Zabala, translated by Luca D'Isanto

John T. Hamilton, *Music, Madness, and the Unworking of Language*

Stefan Jonsson, *A Brief History of the Masses: Three Revolutions*

Richard Eldridge, *Life, Literature, and Modernity*

Janet Wolff, *The Aesthetics of Uncertainty*

Lydia Goehr, *Elective Affinities: Musical Essays on the History of Aesthetic Theory*

Christoph Menke, *Tragic Play: Irony and Theater from Sophocles to Beckett*, translated by James Phillips

György Lukács, *Soul and Form*, translated by Anna Bostock and edited by John T. Sanders and Katie Terezakis with an introduction by Judith Butler

Joseph Margolis, *The Cultural Space of the Arts and the Infelicities of Reductionism*

Herbert Molderings, *Art as Experiment: Duchamp and the Aesthetics of Chance, Creativity, and Convention*

Whitney Davis, *Queer Beauty: Sexuality and Aesthetics from Winckelmann to Freud and Beyond*

Gail Day, *Dialectical Passions: Negation in Postwar Art Theory*

Ewa Płonowska Ziarek, *Feminist Aesthetics and the Politics of Modernism*

Gerhard Richter, *Afterness: Figures of Following in Modern Thought and Aesthetics*

Boris Groys, *Under Suspicion: A Phenomenology of the Media*, translated by Carsten Strathausen

Michael Kelly, *A Hunger for Aesthetics: Enacting the Demands of Art*

Stefan Jonsson, *Crowds and Democracy: The Idea and Image of the Masses from Revolution to Fascism*

Elaine P. Miller, *Head Cases: Julia Kristeva on Philosophy and Art in Depressed Times*

Lutz Koepnick, *On Slowness: Toward an Aesthetic of Radical Contemporaneity*

John Roberts, *Photography and Its Violations*

Hermann Kappelhoff, *The Politics and Poetics of Cinematic Realism*

Cecilia Sjöholm, *Doing Aesthetics with Arendt: How to See Things*

Owen Hulatt, *Adorno's Theory of Philosophical and Aesthetic Truth: Texture and Performance*

James A. Steintrager, *The Autonomy of Pleasure: Libertines, License, and Sexual Revolution*

Paolo D'Angelo, *Sprezzatura: Concealing the Effort of Art from Aristotle to Duchamp*

Fred Evans, *Public Art and the Fragility of Democracy: An Essay in Political Aesthetics*

Maurizio Lazzarato, *Videophilosophy: The Perception of Time in Post-Fordism,* translated by Jay Hetrick

Monique Roelofs, *Arts of Address: Being Alive to Language and the World*

GPSR Authorized Representative: Easy Access System Europe, Mustamäe tee 50, 10621 Tallinn, Estonia, gpsr.requests@easproject.com

www.ingramcontent.com/pod-product-compliance
Lightning Source LLC
Chambersburg PA
CBHW021937290426
44108CB00012B/871